Organisational problems in European manufacture

Volume 2: Part 2. Production in the functional system
Part 3. Production in the human resources system

Organisational problems in European manufacture

Volume 2: Part 2. Production in the functional
                 system
             Part 3. Production in the human
                 resources system

Theodore D. Weinshall
Brian C. Twiss

Longman

LONGMAN GROUP LIMITED
London

Associated companies, branches and representatives
throughout the world

© Longman Group Limited 1973

First published 1973

SBN 582 45013 6

Printed in Great Britain by
William Clowes & Sons Limited
London, Colchester and Beccles

Contents

Part III: Production in the human resources system

List of Cases

British

French

German

Israeli

Spanish

List of figures

Acknowledgements

We are grateful to the following for permission to reproduce copyright material:

Fortune for an extract from 'At St. Gobain the First 300 Years Were the Easiest. Reprinted from the October, 1965 issue of *Fortune Magazine* by special permission. (c) 1965 TIME Inc; *Harvard Business Review* and authors for an extract from 'Production Under Pressure' by Wickham Skinner and an extract from 'Myth of the Well-Educated Manager' by J. Sterling Livingstone; Sawell Publications Limited for Fig. 3.6 adapted from Fig. in *Mass Production* Feb, 1968 and John Wiley & Sons Limited for Fig. 3.8 adapted from Fig. in *Demand Analysis* by H. Wold & L. Jureen.

Case list 1

Alphabetical list of case studies and their main subjects*

Case number and title	1 Prod. and Organis.	2 Prod. and Gen. Man-agement	3 Prod. and Market.	4 Prod. and Finance	5 Prod. and Personnel	6 Prod. and Trade Union	7 Preparing Production Managers
Chapter number and title							
8 Adir Electronics Ltd	+						
17 Art et Cuisine			+				
12 Atlas European		+	+	+			
13A Break Glass Push (A)		+	+	+			
13B Break Glass Push (B)			+				
13C Break Glass Push (C)		+	+				
13D Break Glass Push (D)		+	+				
21 Brit. Aircraft Corporation					+	+	
30 Conflict on the frigate *Samson*					+		
26 Dupont-Maynard					+		
14 Evershine Products Ltd				+			
32A Filfort S.A. (A)					+		
32B Filfort S.A. (B)					+		
32C Filfort S.A. (C)					+		
10 Frithof Ring Starts in A/S Sirus	+						
24 Geohrstahlwerke					+		
18 Gumish Tyre and Rubber Co			+	+			
19 Hadar (A)			+				
9 Hadar (B)	+						
1A John Hall Boilers (A)	+						
1B John Hall Boilers (B)	+						
31 Kavkav Shoe Factory					+		
4 'La Mediterranee'	+						
15 Midland Hosiery Mfg Co., Ltd				+			
16 Nocrode				+			
27 Pompadour Steel Mills					+		
5 Reinollier et Cie	+						
2A Robert Swallow (A)		+					+
2B Robert Swallow (B)		+					+
22 Sonning Mead Boilers Ltd							+
6A Sopalin S.A. (A)		+					
6B Sopalin S.A. (B)		+					
28 Technikon Larue S.A.							+
23 Tetley Tea Co., Ltd		+			+		
24 Thamesport						+	
20 Tiferet			+				
11 United Factories	+						
7 Volkswagenwerk A.G.	+						
25 Water-Tube Boilermakers' Assoc.					+	+	
3 D. Wickham & Co., Ltd			+				

*While the division of the cases by country and industrial area, which appears on the next page, is clear cut, the classification of the cases into main subjects (divided according to the chapters of the book) was arbitrarily established. Many cases could, as has been indicated in the introduction, be taught under other headings.
Cases 1-11 appear in 'Organisational Problems in European Manufacturing', Vol. 1.

Case list 2

Distribution of Case Studies into Country and Industrial Area

Area	Britain	France	Germany	Israel	Norway	Spain
Aircraft	British Aircraft Corp.					
Boiler manu-facturing and erection	John Hall Boilers (A) and (B); Sonning Mead Boilers Ltd; Water-Tube Boilermakers' Association					
Building Materials		'La Mediterranee'				
Canning (Vegetables and Fruits)				Hadar Prod. (A) and (B)		
Chemical	Evershine Noccode Thamesport	Technikon-Larue S.A.				
Electrical/ Electronics		Societé Reinollier Dupont-Maynard		Adir Electronics		
Food Products	Tetley Tea Co.			Tiferet		
Furniture		Art et Cuisine				
Mechanical Engineering	D. Wickham and Co. Ltd		Goehrstahl-werken			
Motor manufacture			Volkswagen-werk A.G.			
Paper Products		Sopalin S.A. (A) and (B)				
Safety equipment	Break Glass Push (A),(B), (C) and (D)					
Ship repair				Conflict on the frigate Samson		
Shoes				Kav-Kav Shoe Factory		
Steel Mills		Pompadour Steel Mills				
Textiles	Robert Swallow (A) and (B); Midland Hosiery					Filfort S.A. (A), (B) and (C)
Tyres				Gumish Tyre and Rubber Co.	Frithof Ring Starts	
Not specified	Atlas European				United Factories	

Part 2
Production in the functional system

3

Production management and marketing

3.1 The growth of a market orientation in European manufacturing companies

The need for effective marketing assumed an increasingly important role during the 1960s as business became more competitive. When Europe was starved of goods in the immediate post-war period the prime objective for most businesses was the achievement of a high production volume coupled with low manufacturing costs in order to satisfy demand.

During the 1950s a pronounced shift of power away from the manufacturer in favour of the customer began to occur. This was accompanied by a shift of emphasis and influence within the company. No longer was the production department always pre-eminent. Marketing departments grew in both size and status. New ideas were imported from the USA where these influences had developed many years earlier than in Europe. Amongst these the 'marketing concept' had the most profound effect; it focussed management's thinking out of the company towards the customer rather than inwards towards its products. The purpose of the company was seen as the identification and satisfaction of the customer's needs. The product itself ceased to be all important. This was a significant development for those whose thinking had been focussed on the manufacture of a product to be sold to a customer who may have had little alternative but to accept what he was offered. Many companies are still finding it difficult to adapt to this changed orientation. For the effects upon a company's organisation are profound e.g. sales departments are replaced by marketing departments; product changes arise from new market needs rather than novel technological capabilities; prices are related to what the market can bear rather than to production costs with a margin added for overheads and profit.

The traditional attitude of many European manufacturing organisations is illustrated by the attitude of the French glass manufacturer St. Gobain in the early 1960s (R. A. Smith, 1965):

> Some indication of how far the company would have to go in creating an effective sales organization may be learned from Saint Gobain men themselves. 'The company has never emphasized sales; production has always been king,' declared a top executive.
>
> 'The salesmen are just production people who've been thrown out of the plants for blowing the fuses. The sales service manager at all our plate plants is

called *le chef de magasin*, the head of the warehouse! The *production* manager is really in charge of sales; it's he who decides how much glass the customer is going to get and when, or if he's to get any at all. In the US, as you know, the service manager at a plant is under the service chief in the head office. He's not even responsible to the plant manager. I know an American plant that changed its product run six times in one hour, or once every ten minutes. But at Saint Gobain changes take weeks or months. Changes are too much trouble for the production manager. We haven't been selling glass, we've been distributing it.'

An important consequence of the increased role of marketing has been a status change within the company. Whereas previously the salesman was given the products and told to sell them, now it is the marketing man who takes the initiative by defining the customer's needs for the design and production staff and who largely determines what they are required to manufacture. This gain in the status of the marketing department is reflected in the widening gap between the salaries paid to marketing and production managers. It is thus not surprising that there is frequent inter-departmental conflict. Some of this conflict is possibly inevitable, but often it arises from a clash of interests provoked by the organisation's own policies.

It must be emphasised that a major objective of all functions must be the maximisation of overall profitability within the company's corporate strategy. This strategy may well involve considerations other than simple profit maximisation. These considerations could usually be regarded as constraints set by the prime objective of the organisation, its survival. In this respect all departments have a common objective. However, they are all elements within an integrated business system and it is not possible to contain the effects of a decision solely within the department taking it. Consequently, circumstances arise whereby a decision taken within one department, say to improve its own profit contribution may adversely affect the contribution made by another department. Thus conflict arises. This situation can easily be exacerbated where formal departmental objectives are established and where managers regard the achievement of these as their main concern irrespective of the effect their decisions may have upon other parts of the organisation. One of the major criticisms which can be levelled against formal techniques such as Management by Objectives is that gains in departmental effectiveness may be achieved at the expense of the development of an inter-departmental team approach to problems.

We shall now examine the main areas where production and marketing interact, highlighting where company organisation and policies can stimulate conflict between departments and lead to decisions not in the company's best business interest.

3.2 Production rate and sales volume

We have seen that a major objective for the production department is often unit cost reduction because of the importance of the manufacturing costs. Similarly the success of the marketing department is often correlated with sales volume. Closer examination of these two objectives reveals that under certain circumstances they may well be incompatible. This is not immediately apparent since the economies of scale which undoubtedly exist in most companies should lead to falling unit costs as sales volume increases and one would expect no conflict to occur. This relationship, is, however, only valid in the long term and we shall see that it is possible for considerable distortions to arise when only short-term fluctuations are considered. Because of the immediacy of pressing short-term problems they are more likely to lead to conflict where a difference of interest does exist.

This effect can be seen from an examination of a break-even chart which shows costs and sales income plotted against volume. The relationships are usually drawn in the form shown in Fig. 3.1. *OB* represents the sales income and is a straight line through the origin if we assume that the selling price is maintained constant irrespective of the volume. Because production costs are partly fixed and partly variable the cost/volume line *FA* does not pass through the origin since there will be a residual cost *OF* at zero volume. Total costs will then rise from point *F* in a linear fashion but with a lower slope than the line for sales income. The two lines cross at the break-even point *X*. At volumes greater than break-even a profit is earned represented by the difference between the two lines. Figure 3.1 is the classical break-even chart which appears in the textbooks. It supports the argument for economies of scale since the unit production cost falls with volume due to the spreading of the fixed cost element over a larger number of items.

Fig. 3.1 Break-even chart

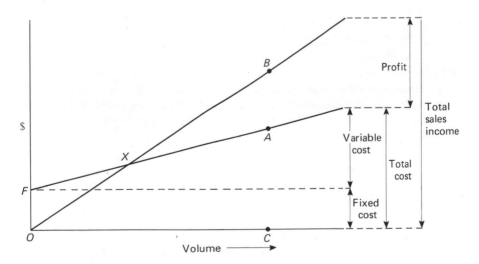

If, however, we consider what usually happens in practise, for short term fluctuations about a given state, we find irregular relationships such as those shown in Fig. 3.2. This figure represents an enlargement of a small part of the break-even chart. At the point *AB* production and sales are in balance with a profit *P* being earned. When production volume is increased by a small amount the total

Fig. 3.2 Possible production cost variations for small volume changes

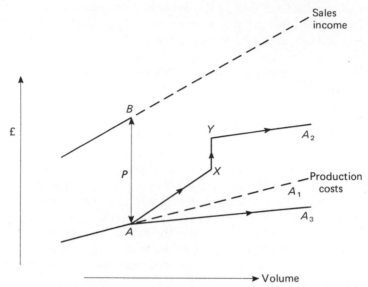

production costs may change in a variety of ways. Three possibilities are represented by the lines AA_1, AA_2, and AA_3:

AA_1 is what would be expected from the break-even chart of Fig. 3.1. However, a pre-condition for this is that the increased volume of production is achievable:

  a. with existing fixed assets;

  b. by employing additional resources which generate variable costs at the same rate as previously.

AA_2 is one example of a family of possible alternatives. Along the line AX production volume can be increased with existing physical resources but the higher rate necessitates overtime working. This is reflected in higher variable costs represented by the slope of the line AX which is greater than that of AA_1. Beyond this point production cannot be sustained without additional capital expenditure, perhaps a new machine or a factory extension. This results in an increment of fixed cost (XY) and a corresponding rise in unit product costs. Thereafter it is probable that the new equipment will introduce operational savings, for example through a greater degree of automation, with a consequent lowering of the slope of the line YA_2.

AA_3 occurs when capacity is under-utilised. Volume can be increased with existing physical resources and direct labour can be regarded as a fixed cost for small volume changes. The only cost increases incurred would thus be very small, represented mainly by materials.

Although in the long term these changes would all approximate to the smooth line of Fig. 3.1 it is important to realise that it is impossible to predict cost/volume behaviour for small changes without investigating closely what would happen to each element of cost in the actual conditions applying at the time.

In general the decision to change a production rate will be based upon sales forecasts. As with all forecasts there is no certainty that the actual sales will achieve the predicted level. Thus when making a decision to expand production it is by no means certain that the additional sales income and its associated profit contribution will be earned.

From a viewpoint of immediate profitability the probability of achieving a forecast sales volume needs to be weighed against the certainty that the production costs necessary to meet the forecasted demand will be incurred. In some cases, however, it has been seen that expansion may well involve an increase in unit production costs beyond the control of the production manager. Unless these essential additional costs are recognised and isolated the production manager is likely to be held accountable for costs which were unavoidable and outside his control. Alternatively he may either consciously or subconciously frustrate the efforts of the marketing department by failing to achieve the production levels they require because of his awareness of their impact on unit costs. In either case conflict between the two departments may ensue. This conflict arises solely because the performance by which the departmental managers are judged, unit cost or sales volume, is dependent partly upon factors arising outside their own departments.

Long-term business objectives must also be considered. The maximisation of immediate profitability may need to be sacrificed in the interest of long-term growth. For example, a company may decide to launch a new product at a low price in order to establish itself in a new market thereby postponing profits for one or more years until sales volume has grown to a significant size. The alternative might be a high initial price, low sales volume but immediate profits.

Examination of the apparently simple matter of establishing production rates in relation to sales forecasts has revealed a number of issues which were not immediately evident. These have arisen from the difficulties experienced in setting precise and easily understood departmental objectives where decisions cross departmental boundaries or where there is a time dimension in their effect.

How can these problems be resolved? Although there are no panaceas we suggest that consideration given to the three areas noted below will usually remove the major causes of conflict and lead to an improvement in the quality of decision making:

Firstly—identify and eliminate areas where the organisation's policies, for example in the setting of objectives, artificially stimulate conflict.

Secondly—ensure that the company's information system produces good quantitative information relevant to the decisions which have to be made so that these decisions can be taken more objectively.

Thirdly—develop within departmental managers a general management approach to problem solving and decision making so that, when considering matters of mutual interest, the production and marketing managers can examine the problems from an overall business viewpoint. This implies that the production manager must regard himself as being as much a member of the general management team as a departmental head.

3.3   Product variety

Definition of product range

A single product is the ideal product policy from the manufacturing manager's viewpoint. This enables him to adopt standard production processes and procedures, such as flow-line production, which might be un-economical with a greater range of products. Long production runs make it possible to utilise specialised equipment efficiently thereby reducing unit costs. Inventory costs will also be lower since he will need a lower aggregate of buffer stocks to meet a specified service level. Consequently, he can be expected to resist the introduction of additional products to the range and will particularly resent short run low volume products which interrupt the smooth flow of work through his factory.

Conversely, the marketing manager will often wish to offer the customer a wider choice of product. He may argue that in these days of increasing competition it is necessary to cater for a broad range of consumer tastes if a significant share of the market is to be retained. Some products will inevitably sell better than others but he may consider that customers will be lost if the company cannot satisfy all their requirements even at the expense of low profitability from some of the products. The benefits derived from the ability to offer a wide range of products are hard if not impossible to quantify. It is also often difficult to allocate manufacturing costs precisely between products. Furthermore the additional costs involved in the disruption of production lines for a short run product are virtually impossible to isolate. But there is little doubt that they are considerable.

Product policy decisions are too vital to be resolved by either production or marketing managers. However, together they should be able to establish most of the factors which must be taken into account although they may not necessarily agree on the relative importance of these factors. There are also a number of corporate considerations which must be taken into account in addition to those arising solely within the manufacturing or marketing departments. But since the outcome is of considerable importance to the production manager he must be prepared to express a view on the production implications of alternative policies including cost estimates and timing recommendations.

The justification for the retention of a particular product must rest primarily upon its ability to contribute to company profitability in the near and more distant future. Once again we face the type of problem discussed when considering the break-even chart. It may be difficult to establish the cost associated with a particular product at any given time. But the contribution it makes to the company's profitability will be a function of time and the circumstances facing the company at that time. The reasoning is similar to that underlying a decision of whether to engage in an incremental change in production volume. Thus at a period of under-utilised capacity any product which can generate a sales income greater than its variable costs will make a positive contribution to the company's overall profitability, for it can be assumed that if there were alternative ways of generating a greater profit the unfilled capacity would have been utilised for that purpose already. This assumes, of course, that factory space is the critical factor which determines capacity. In practice it may be some factor other than floor space which sets the limit of productive capacity, such as the extent to which different products use a particular machine.

A simple example is illustrated in Fig. 3.3. In Case (*a*) we have a factory manufacturing two products. It has empty capacity that cannot be filled. One of these products, A, is not very profitable. It makes a contribution of $5,000 towards overhead costs and profits but this changes to a deficit of $6,111 if the factory costs of $100,000 are allocated on a basis of the ratio (1:8) in which the products use factory space. Nevertheless we see that under these circumstances Product A should be retained since the company is better off with it than without it. In Case (*b*) we have the same factory and the same products but at a different time. Nothing has changed except demand for Product B which has increased; the empty floor space has been brought into use and production of Product B could be expanded further to fill the whole factory but for the capacity utilised by Product A. In this case we see that although Product A has not changed in any way, i.e. the same sales volume and variable costs, it is now the right decision to discontinue its manufacture.

Similar considerations apply when deciding the product-mix, that is the relative proportions of the products comprising the company's product line.

In all these cases we see that timing is of importance particularly in relation to factory utilisation and costs. New production methods, equipment or material will also affect the situation since they will change the relative variable costs between products. Decisions relating to new product introduction and the abandonment of existing products are decisions for the future. Consequently they need to take account of forecasts of future factory utilisation and projected trends in production costs rather than the situation existing at the time the decision is made. It is thus clear that if the optimum use is to be made of manufacturing facilities the production manager should be closely involved not only in product-range decisions but also in the selection of the optimum timing for changes in the range.

The traditional resistance of the manufacturing manager to a wide product variety is, however, undergoing a transformation under the impact of recent developments:

(*a*) Modular production which enables a wide range of end products to be assembled from a limited number of components.

(*b*) Techniques which enable the economic scheduling of small batches—group technology, computer scheduling.

(*c*) Numerical controlled machine tools which considerably reduce machine set-up times.

Because of this new found capability for satisfying the demands of the market it is likely that the main centre of concern will shift away from the problems of manufacturing variety to those of storage and distribution of what could become in theory an almost infinite product range.

Fig. 3.3(a) Profit contribution from an under-utilised factory with no possibility of achieving increased sales volume

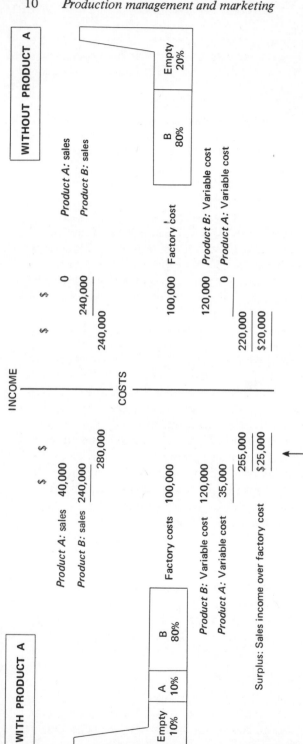

WITH PRODUCT A

Empty 10%	A 10%	B 80%

WITHOUT PRODUCT A

B 80%	Empty 20%

INCOME

	$	$
Product A: sales	40,000	
Product B: sales	240,000	
		280,000

COSTS

	$	
Factory costs	100,000	
Product B: Variable cost	120,000	
Product A: Variable cost	35,000	
		255,000
		$25,000

Surplus: Sales income over factory cost ←

WITHOUT PRODUCT A

	$	$
Product A: sales		0
Product B: sales		240,000
		240,000

	$	
Factory cost	100,000	
Product B: Variable cost	120,000	
Product A: Variable cost	0	
		220,000
		$20,000

[**Note:** 1. Total surplus *with* product A retained *$5,000 greater.*

2. However if factory costs were allocated on basis of floorspace utilisation :

Costs	Product A	$		Product B	$
	variable	35,000		variable	120,000
	Allocated factory			Allocated factory	
	cost $\dfrac{\$100,000}{9} = 11,111$			cost	88,889
	Total cost	46,111		Total cost	208,889
c.f.	Sales income	40,000	c.f.	Sales income	240,000]

'Notional' loss on product A $6,111

3. Contribution to profit and overhead must be the criterion *not* the production cost including allocated overheads.

Fig. 3.3(b) Profit contribution from a fully utilised factory. Sales expansion of profitable product restricted by lack of production capacity.

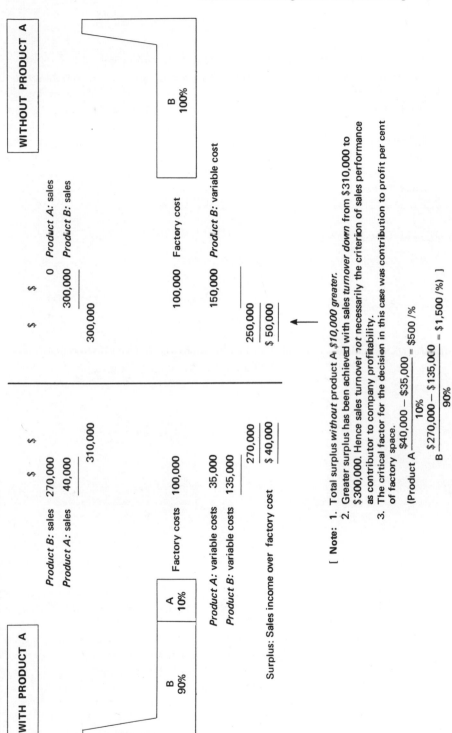

WITH PRODUCT A		

	$	$
Product B: sales	270,000	
Product A: sales	40,000	
		310,000
Factory costs	100,000	
Product A: variable costs	35,000	
Product B: variable costs	135,000	
		270,000
Surplus: Sales income over factory cost		$ 40,000

WITHOUT PRODUCT A		

	$	$
Product A: sales		0
Product B: sales	300,000	
		300,000
Factory cost	100,000	
Product B: variable cost	150,000	
		250,000
		$ 50,000

[Note: 1. Total surplus *without* product A *$10,000 greater.*

2. Greater surplus has been achieved with sales *turnover down* from $310,000 to $300,000. Hence sales turnover *not* necessarily the criterion of sales performance as contributor to company profitability.

3. The critical factor for the decision in this case was contribution to profit per cent of factory space.

(Product A $\dfrac{\$40,000 - \$35,000}{10\%} = \$500\ /\%$

B $\dfrac{\$270,000 - \$135,000}{90\%} = \$1,500\ /\%$)]

Modular production

'Modular production' is a term coined by Martin K. Starr (Starr, 1965) to describe the capacity to design and manufacture parts which can be combined in numerous ways to produce a range of products which satisfies a great variety of consumer needs and tastes. The concept is illustrated in Fig. 3.4. In this example we have a range of five products each of which contains six components. With traditional design and production methods the company would probably be manufacturing a total of 5 x 6 = 30 components each of which would be incorporated in only one product. By suitably modifying the design of products and components it may be possible to satisfy the same customer needs with five products assembled from different combinations of twelve standard components.

Fig. 3.4 Modular production

Consumer needs satisfied by **products** assembled from **standard components**

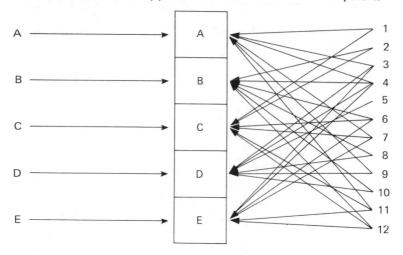

Standardisation of parts is not a new concept. Modular production however differs from standardisation in that it adopts a systems approach to the process of: consumer satisfaction→product design→manufacture. In contrast, conventional standardisation tends to take existing products and introduces inter-changeability by modification of product or component so as to minimise the number of different parts employed.

Modular production has been widely used in the electronics industry where a large range of end products can be assembled mostly from standard integrated circuits with a minimum number of special-to-product components. The motor industry is also moving in this direction where body shells are now being offered with a selection of different engines or seating arrangements. One of the largest lorry manufacturer's in the United Kingdom claims that it need produce no two identical vehicles in an annual production of many thousands.

There are, however, certain penalties as well as benefits which arise with the modular concept. Although component manufacture is simplified and component stocks reduced the scheduling of final assembly is made more complex by the wider product variety which usually follows its adoption. Frequently it is necessary to hold finished stocks as parts and to assemble them in response to customer's product specifications since it would be impracticable to hold the complete range of final products in store. This may lead to longer delivery delays since distributors also are unable to hold stocks of more than a small proportion of the varieties available. Many new car purchasers are already finding that, although they have a wider range of choice, it is not unusual to have to wait several months for the delivery of a car of the required specification.

Modular production is likely to be introduced by an increasing number of companies as they strive to satisfy markets which are demanding greater individuality in product design. But because it is a systems approach it will not function effectively unless there is a much closer integration of planning between the marketing, design and manufacturing departments than has been usual in the past. Each will find it necessary to compromise to a greater extent. For example, the marketing department will find it necessary to accept constraints in design imposed by the limitations of standard components.

Group technology

Group Technology is a recently developed planning technique which enables the more economic manufacture of small batches of components.

It is similar in concept to modular production and it reduces the financial penalty of batch production compared with mass or flow line production. Since one of the production manager's main objections to product variety is the high cost of manufacturing small batches due to their scheduling complexities and high set-up times, it is clear that any technique which improves the economics of batch production will at the same time reduce the relative advantages of mass producing a standard article.

The principle of Group Technology consists of grouping together a family of components which require nearly identical manufacturing processes. Thus, although a batch may contain a number of different parts they will have common features which enable them to be grouped into a large batch for a particular manufacturing operation. Figure 3.5 shows how this can be arranged. Process 1 may be a shaft turning operation which is required on components A, D, F and H for which purpose they will be grouped together as a single batch. But for process 2, say a drilling operation, component A will be grouped with B, E, F and G.

Production scheduling and real-time machine-loading by computer

Production scheduling for large numbers of different components, each requiring several manufacturing processes, is highly complex particularly when much of the information on which schedules are based is uncertain or inaccurate. Re-scheduling

Fig. 3.5. The principle of group technology

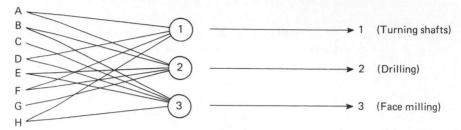

Components collected into families of components related to common processes

after a disruption through an un-programmed event such as machine breakdown is not easy. This leads to poor machine utilization. The problem also becomes more complex as the number of components rises. On the other hand flow-line production, where batch sizes are virtually infinite, largely eleminates scheduling problems since output is determined by the design and operating speed of the production line.

Much of the penalty associated with batch production would be eliminated if it were possible quickly to re-schedule production after a disruption and also to ensure that a machine was allocated new work immediately upon completion of a batch of parts.

Although the use of the computer for production scheduling is now not uncommon, only a few companies are experimenting with real-time machine loading for batch processing. One such company is C.A.V. which manufactures diesel fuel injection and electrical equipment. The complexity of their problem is evident from their 5,000 item product range comprising 100,000 components and 400,000 machine operations. In addition to a complete computer-based scheduling system, shopfloor activities will be planned and controlled through a 'Telecontrol' monitoring equipment which will link machine tools directly to the computer and will enable job sequences to be organised if they are not going to plan and will also anticipate the effect of delays on later operations.

Although a great deal of development is required before real-time applications of the computer become widespread it can be expected that they will become much more common during the next decade. They will not only greatly ease the production manager's task but will also enable him to respond far more quickly to changes in demand as well as to accommodate small batches economically.

Numerically controlled machine tools

The major economy introduced by the use of numerically controlled machine tools stems from their automatic programming which eliminates the time-wasting and costly process of manual setting-up. When numerically controlled machines can be easily programmed for a range of operations, either manually or by computer, considerable savings can be achieved.

An extension of this system is to group a number of standard or specially designed NC machine tools together, as in the Cincinnati Variable Mission system or Molins System 24. The very considerable savings achievable from these NC multi-station systems are shown in Fig. 3.6 from which it can be seen that unit-costs for batches as small as ten items are comparable with mass production flow lines using transfer machines. This is a first step towards the automatic factory

Fig. 3.6 Cost comparison of batch manufacturing processes. Source: Mass Production Feb. 1968.

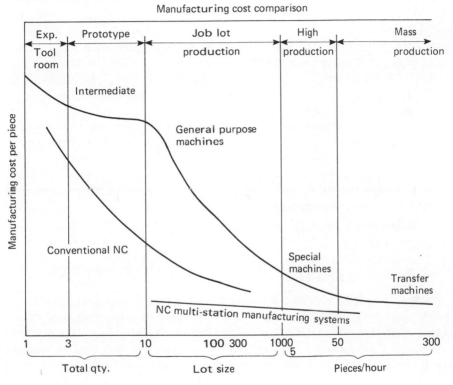

Manufacturing cost comparison

of the future. It should be noted, however, that the savings claimed for these systems depend upon them being used efficiently. Since they are capital rather than labour intensive their full economies can only be achieved by multi-shift working. For this reason few NC machine installations have yet to meet the claims made for them by the manufacturers. There are some indications that the main impetus for their adoption will come not so much from financial considerations but from the shortage of skilled workers.

These developments in production technology and planning techniques are demanding a new relationship between production and marketing managers. The problem is changing. In the future the production advantages of a restricted product range will for many types of product, be considerably diminished. The problem will become one of selection, marketing and distribution of the wide variety of alternatives which can be manufactured economically. The resultant changes in the flow of information and materials in the production-marketing system will probably take the form as shown in Fig. 3.7.

3.4 Quality

Marketing, design and production are all concerned with product quality. But the very word 'quality' can take on a variety of meanings for different people. The unsophisticated consumer may instinctively equate 'high quality' with high price, particularly if the performance of a product is difficult for him to assess; there are, for example few motorists who are able to evaluate the quality of a lubricating oil. A performance engineer is apt to equate quality with reliability, the ability of the product to operate for long periods at a specified performance without failure. A design engineer may add an aesthetic or emotional value to an aspect he alone may consider connotates quality; he may for example regard a machined surface as of higher quality than a rough cast finish irrespective of the function of the part or whether it is visible to sight or touch. Finally the factory inspector will see quality primarily in numerical terms, as a proportion of the items submitted to him which fall within a specified tolerance of performance or dimension. These differences occur because there is no agreement amongst them of:

the product characteristics which determine quality and their relative importance;
the standards to be used in assessing a particular characteristic;
the assessment of a product in relation to a standard.

In order to resolve this problem and create a coherent systematic approach to quality throughout the company we need to turn to the marketing concept as a starting point. We see from this that the product is not an end in itself; it is merely a vehicle for satisfying a customer's need. Thus we must first start by defining which customers we wish to satisfy. Tornqvist's demand functions (Fig. 3.8) shows how the utility of a particular type of product varies with income. Four broad categories of product are postulated—luxuries, relative luxuries, necessities and inferior goods. In practice each of these categories will sub-divide further. A matrix of the type in Fig. 3.9 can be derived and quantified so far as possible, which will enable the characteristic of a market segment to be assessed.

The broad definition of the target market segment is normally a matter of company policy. But this policy will have a continuity based upon the company 'image', traditions and expertise. Changes are often extremely difficult to achieve. Where it is desired to appeal to a market segment 'higher' up the scale the company's identification with a 'lower' segment in the eyes of the customer makes it difficult to obtain acceptance of the product irrespective of its inherent quality. Conversely, attempts to move down the scale are often frustrated by the inability of the production department to work to the different, and in their estimation

Fig. 3.7 Flow of information and material between marketing and production

A. TODAY

B. FUTURE

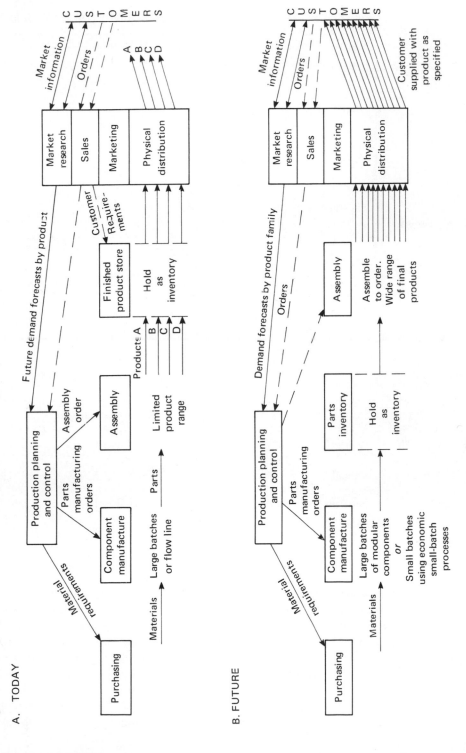

Fig. 3.8 Tornqvist's demand functions. Source: Demand Analysis by H. Wold & L. Jureen, John Wiley & Sons Inc.

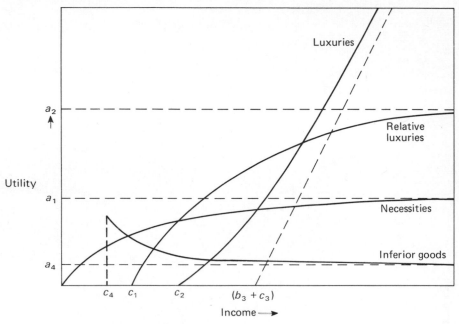

Fig. 3.9 Market segment characteristics

				Proportion of income devoted to		
Income group		Size of group	Inferior goods	Necessities	Relative luxuries	Luxuries
High	A	Small	Nil	Low	High	Very high
	B	Medium	Very low	Low	Fairly high	High
	C	Very large	Fairly high	High	Low	Very low
Low	D	Large	High	High	Low	Nil

inferior, standards necessary to meet the lower cost of higher volume production. This problem has been experienced by a number of aerospace companies, acustomed to working to fine tolerances and high reliability almost irrespective of cost, when they have attempted to manufacture products for a commercial market.

Once the market segment within which the company operates is defined, market research should reveal the needs of potential customers in the chosen category together with some evaluation of the utility to the individual of a particular need being satisfied. It is then necessary to select a combination of needs which it is desired to satisfy, formulate alternative product configurations, select the most suitable and then specify it's properties in detail. This over-simplification of a complex process is shown diagrammatically in Fig. 3.10. It can be seen, however, that when one starts with the customer's needs it is possible to relate to them by means of the product specification all those aspects which are variously called 'quality'.

Fig. 3.10 Product specifications related to identified needs of a group of potential customers

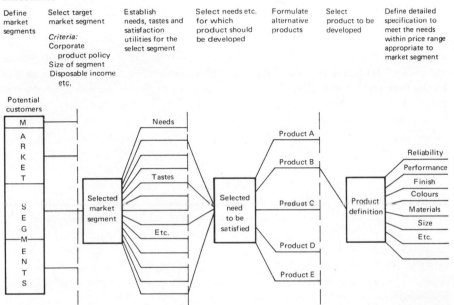

Many features of the final product quality can be quantified by the marketing department, but they must then be translated into technical terms by the design or manufacturing departments. This is not always easy to accomplish if there is imperfect understanding across the departmental interface. Although precise specifications are essential where possible, they often fail to give a complete picture and it still remains possible for misinterpretations to occur through ambiguities. Furthermore, many aspects are not quantifiable.

The process shown in Fig. 3.10 is, however, mechanistic in that it over-simplifies what should be an interlocking system embracing marketing, design and manufacturing. Since a considerable period often elapses between the initial definition of a product requirement and the time it first reaches the market, we are concerned with a dynamic process which must take account of any changes which may occur in the considerations which led to the formulation of the original specification. The sales forecasts, for example, may prove to be either pessimistic or, what is more often the case, optimistic in the light of later knowledge. But the choice of the most economic manufacturing process and consequently the design, depends upon the production volume. The prompt notification of changes in the anticipated sales volume from marketing to design and production is thus of great importance if appropriate modifications are to be incorporated in the design and manufacturing processes. Similarly, technological advances may be made which enable additional customer needs to be satisfied at little cost. Continuous feedback between the three departments and a flexible attitude to changed requirements are therefore essential, although a time will come when design must be 'frozen' if serious delays in the commercial introduction of the new product are to be avoided.

The implications of the marketing concept are slowly permeating into design and production departments although old attitudes are slow to die particularly amongst traditional engineering companies. Systematic attempts to bridge the gap have resulted in the development of techniques such as ergonomics and value engineering. Ergonomics achieves this by considering the machine and its human user as an inter-acting system. Value engineering and value analysis focus attention of the function to be performed and the most economic method of satisfying that function.

The term 'industrial design' is now used to embrace a wide range of inter-related activities. Until recently the engineering design of most products has been concerned solely with meeting the performance and reliability criteria of quality. At a later stage the design may undergo the cosmetic treatment of 'applied art' or 'styling' to give it the aesthetic appeal required by the customer. This two stage process has serious drawbacks. Sometimes the packaging detracts from the function, as in some cars where the rear passengers sit in considerable discomfort because of a low roof resulting from the shapes emanating from the styling department. Sometimes high production costs are incurred through the use of complex shapes or double curvatures which are expensive to manufacture. The industrial design concept, on the other hand, integrates all aspects of quality from the outset—engineering, marketing and sometimes also the projection of a corporate image.

The 'over-design' of products is also commonplace. This occurs when products are designed to produce a higher performance, a greater reliability or a longer service life than the user requires or wishes to pay for. There are a number of reasons why this happens:

imprecise specifications or an imperfect understanding of what the customer really requires from the product he is buying;

the designer's or manufacturer's professional desire to achieve a high degree of technical excellence;

anticipation of possible future requirements which could be satisfied by a 'stretched' version of the product;

lack of appreciation by the design engineers of the manufacturing cost penalties caused by excessively close tolerances.

Almost invariably over-design means increased cost and should be avoided without good reason. We may conclude, therefore, that the quality standard should be set at the lowest level acceptable to the majority of customers even though this may result in dissatisfaction of a small minority. It may, of course, be a wise policy to incorporate the facility to enhance the performance of the product at a later stage. If this is so it should be a product planning decision taken by the marketing and technical departments together after due consideration of all the factors involved. But all too often it is a unilateral decision built in as an additional safety factor by the design engineers which detracts from the profitability of the product through unnecessary cost penalties as well as frequently increasing the user's operating costs.

The aspect of quality which is the constant concern of the production manager is quality control or quality assurance whereby he ensures that the products he delivers are of the required 'quality' as defined by the manufacturing specifications for performance, reliability and dimensional accuracy. This topic will not be discussed further since the many techniques commonly used are covered in depth in standard textbooks on production management. But vital though quality control undoubtedly is, the production manager must not forget that this is only one aspect of the wider implications of quality with which he should be involved.

3.5 Service

The customer's needs which require satisfaction relate not only to the type of product but also to the ready availability of the product itself and of any spare parts which may be required. If a certain level of satisfaction of his need is not reached the customer will usually go elsewhere for his purchase this time if the product is not available, or next time if spare parts are not available. It follows that there must be a relationship between delivery delay and sales volume. Other things being equal maximum sales are achieved when the goods are on the shelf ready for immediate delivery. This then is the marketing ideal.

But the reverse relationship is also true, since the greater the sales demand the less likely is the item to be in stock and the greater will be the delivery delay. Indeed industries whose products are generally made to order, such as ships and power stations, suffer severe cyclical fluctuations ranging from capacity working and lengthening delivery delays at one extreme to severe unemployment of resources at other times when work can start immediately an order is placed.

The problem arises from a cyclical pattern of sales in most industries which is superimposed upon long-term demand pattern changes, the future trends of which can only be forecast. Industry cannot adjust its manufacturing capacity to short term cyclical fluctuations and its sales forecasts will frequently contain significant errors. Consequently, the only way to satisfy the marketing ideal would be to have excessive manufacturing capacity which would adjust its production volume to meet all expected demands or, alternatively, to build up large inventories of finished goods. Both those are expensive solutions. The cost of excessive capacity or inventory holdings can be quantified. But the loss of sales through delivery delays remains largely a matter of opinion and cannot be accurately quantified.

Obviously there must be an optimum for each of three variables: manufacturing capacity, inventory levels and delivery delays. The difficulty is that there is no objective method for establishing what it is. It is also clear that the interests of the manufacturing department, namely minimum factory overhead and inventory costs, run counter to those of the marketing department. A compromise must be made, but it is unlikely to approach the optimum solution unless both departments are prepared to examine it as a common problem.

The alternative payoffs are illustrated in Fig. 3.11 where the forecast demand for a product follows an irregular pattern leading to the cumulative demand shown as

Fig. 3.11 Cumulative demand and production volume v. time

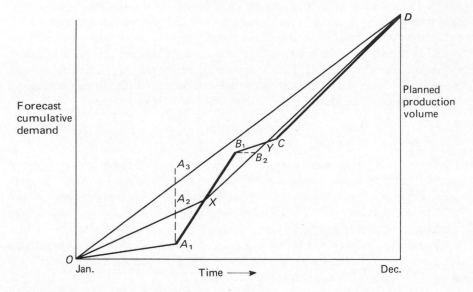

OA_1B_1CD. We can examine the implications of three alternative production programmes:

1. Uniform rate throughout the year
This is represented by the line OD from which we note:

(*a*) The cumulative production is always in excess of demand, hence NO delivery delays

(*b*) Required production capacity represented by the slope of the link OA is a minimum

(*c*) Inventory = cumulative production—cumulative demand, is represented by the vertical difference between the two lines. Required storage capacity is the maximum difference $A_1 A_3$ and is high

(*d*) Inventory costs are proportional to the average inventory, i.e. proportional to area between the two curves—in this case high.

2. Production rate adjusted to match demand
In this case the planned production volume will follow OA_1B_1CD from which we note:

(a) No delivery delay

(b) Maximum production capacity proportional to slope of $A_1 B_1$ very high

(c) No inventory storage space or costs involved.

3. A compromise consisting of two rates of production

The line $OA_2 XB_2 YD$ represents one of a family of compromise alternatives from which we note:

(a) Between X and Y demand exceeds production. The maximum delivery delay is represented by the horizontal difference $B_1 B_2$ between the two lines

(b) Production capacity represented by XD is greater than case 1, but considerably lower than case 2.

(c) Maximum storage capacity represented by $A_1 A_2$ is again between the two extremes as is the cost of holding inventory.

A compromise will almost invariably lead to the best solution. All possible alternatives need to be examined seriously. For example, many production planners might be reluctant to plan for the delivery delays represented by $B_1 B_2$ and yet these delays may be of little significance particularly when the marketing department can be shown that they will only be temporary.

Spares policy involves two separate issues. The first of those involves considerations similar to finished goods inventory policy. The problem is of how large an inventory should be held to ensure a satisfactory service level at minimum cost. The second consideration concerns the time for which spares for a given model should be supplied. All too often spare parts gather dust in stores for many years after the last new product has been delivered.

3.6 Summary

We have seen that the relationship between production and marketing managers is continuously changing. The one constant factor is the growing need for closer linking of their activities into what is a continuous system embracing all stages from the evaluation of customers' needs and the forecast demands for their satisfaction to the delivery of the finished product. Because companies are increasingly operating in a dynamic business world there must be constant feedback of marketing information so that product design and manufacturing can respond rapidly to changes in the market.

Two major obstacles to effective management in this area have been identified:

slow management response to change;

organisational barriers

Many companies are still experiencing difficulty in adapting to the implications of the marketing concept. It is all too frequently that troubles are encountered through a reluctance to abandon the production orientation which may have been appropriate in the 1950s but is sadly out of tune with the conditions of the 1970s. While the marketing concept is slowly being digested, new developments in production technology and customers' needs introduce fresh challenges which will profoundly affect both the relationship between the two departments and the organisation of manufacturing operations in the coming decade. The companies which will succeed as businesses in the future will be those which can respond to these challenges.

It has also been noted that the conflicts of interest which often occur between the two departments can be amplified by a concentration on departmental objectives. There is consequently a need for the development of company policies and organisations to reflect the need for a closer working relationship between marketing and manufacturing activities.

4

Production and finance

4.1 The production manager and accounting information

The purpose of a business has been defined in a variety of ways but in Western Europe both survival and profit are regarded as essential elements of this purpose. Other social aims such as security of employment must be regarded as secondary in so far as they cannot be sustained unless the company survives and generates sufficient profits for its continued existence and support of the secondary aims. From this it follows that a manufacturing company is in business to produce both a product to retain the goodwill of its customers and a profit generated by the sale of its products to satisfy its owners and bankers. Similarly the purpose of the production function is to contribute to the profitability of the company by using efficiently the resources entrusted to it. These resources are essentially financial although they are transformed, by a process which is only partially reversible, into material resources by investment and capital expenditure. No production manager would deny his financial responsibilities when they are presented in this way. Nevertheless in his daily decision making he is more likely to adopt a product than a profit orientation. Although not disregarding cost factors his training and motivation will inevitably give an emphasis to the technical rather than to the financial factors, albeit often subconsciously.

If the production manager[1] is to be regarded as a custodian of financial resources it follows that he needs to be trained not only to understand the elements of accountancy and financial management but also to be able to select and interpret financial data relevant to decisions he has to take. Few production managers have received this training and consequently frequent and serious errors are made in the financial assessments and cost calculations which form an important part of many decisions.

Since the figures upon which the production manager bases his decisions are almost invariably provided by the company's accountant it is important that each understands the other's problems. For the accountants are concerned in using financial data for two purposes. Firstly they require to collect the information necessary to compile the company accounts. Secondly, and of increasing importance, is the part they play in the company's information system by providing the data necessary for management control and decision making. The presentation of figures for these two requirements differs considerably. Accounting conventions

1. The term production manager is used in this and other chapters in its general meaning i.e. referring to all managers in production from the foreman to the head of the manufacturing function.

25

and company law frequently lead to a different interpretation of the figures from that required in reaching a management decision. Consequently, when the production manager asks for information the accountant should ascertain from him what he wants the information for so that he can select the relevant figures. This should not offend the production manager if he appreciates that the accountant is trying to ensure that he receives the appropriate figures; but if there is a poor understanding between them he may easily form the impression that the accountant is being secretive or trying to interfere in his affairs. Similarly when he is referring to published information he must find out the purpose for which it was prepared so that he can determine its relevance to his own situation.

4.2   Profit maximisation rather than cost minimisation

Manufacturing costs are usually the largest single element in the cost of a product. Since profit margins may be relatively small compared with manufacturing costs, a small reduction of cost can have a highly geared effect upon profit. For example, if costs under the control of the production manager represent 40 per cent of a product's selling price, on which the profit margin is 10 per cent, it follows that a 1 per cent reduction in production costs (i.e. from 40 per cent to 39·6 per cent of selling price) results in a profit margin increase of 4 per cent (i.e. from 10 per cent to 10·4 per cent of selling price). Because of the significance of production costs rigorous systems for controlling unit cost and cost reduction programmes receive a great deal of attention. While not disputing the importance of the cost factor one must guard against efforts to reduce cost becoming an obsession. Expenditure as such is not an evil in itself provided it results in added value to the company. This can be illustrated by examining the following equations:

Total company profit = Total sales income − Total costs
(*P*   =   *S*   −   *C*   )
Total sales income   = Unit selling price   × Number of units sold
(*S*   =   *U*   ×   *N*   )
Total costs   = Unit production costs × No. of units sold
(*C*   =   *Cp*   ×   *N*   )
                            + Non production variable costs × No. of units sold
(+   *Cn*   ×   *N*   )
                            + Total fixed costs
(+   *F*)

Combining these equations we get:

$$P = N(U - Cp - Cn) - F.$$

The condition that *P* is maximised is thus only satisfied through the minimisation of unit production costs if *Cp* is not a function of either sales volume (*N*) or selling price (*U*). But this is rarely the case. For example, the additional profits generated by higher sales volume when demand is strong may justify the higher unit costs associated with overtime working, the use of less efficient machinery or the use of more expensive raw materials. Or, improved product quality at some cost penalty may increase customer appeal such that the profit from increased sales more than offsets the reduced margins. In the longer term, costs which improve the product may enable an increase in selling price.

These relationships are complex and cross-functional. But the interests of a company are ill-served by an undue emphasis on unit cost reductions which react against the prime purpose of maximising overall company profits.

It is beyond the scope of this book to examine in detail all aspects of management accountancy and financial management which have an impact on production management. These topics are covered fully in several excellent textbooks published in recent years. (Anthony, 1970; Batty, 1963; Hartley, 1965; Sizer, 1970). Nevertheless they tend to understress some of the pitfalls which the production manager is likely to encounter. Consequently, in this chapter some of those problems which production managers have been found to have difficulty in appreciating will be highlighted.

Difficulties often arise from the inability of the accountant and the technologist to communicate effectively. This often stems from the fact that, although they both use the same figures they are using them for different purposes. The accountant is primarily concerned with the recording of expenditures and information for control purposes—this function is largely historical and a great emphasis is placed on accuracy. But the production manager requires to use much the same figures as the basis for decision making affecting the future, sometimes for control purposes and sometimes for investment decisions—here absolute accuracy is less important then timeliness and the use of the figures appropriate to the purpose.

4.3 Investment decisions

Evaluating a new investment

Both technical and financial factors are involved when considering the purchase of new equipment. In some cases a purchase may be essential to meet changed product specifications or a new product; there is a firm requirement but the choice will lie between alternative machines. On the other hand the purchase might be justifiable solely on the grounds of cost savings. Many of the technical factors to be considered cannot be quantified in financial terms and their importance must be weighed carefully against the costs involved. But it must not be thought that judgement is not required in calculating the economics of the purchase. Though the final outcome is expressed in numbers their quantification can hide a variety of judgemental decisions, both in selecting the criteria to be applied and in the choice of the data to be used.

It can be assumed that the capital cost of the equipment is known accurately although the installation costs which must be added to the capital cost to obtain a figure for the total investment may need to be estimated. This investment is to be justified in terms of cost savings. What are these savings, and how should their adequacy be assessed?

The cost savings may be thought to be obtained simply by calculating the costs with the present equipment and those that will be incurred with the new installation. Cost data for the current operations should be available from accounting records and the manufacturer will provide data for the new piece of equipment. At first sight it would appear that the answer is obtained by subtracting one from the other. But it is unlikely, however, that the present system will be operating at 100 per cent efficiency and the manufacturer's claimed performance for the new equipment may be doubtful of achievement under the anticipated conditions. If an actual performance is being compared with a promised performance, like is not being compared with like. Failure to appreciate this point is responsible for many a disappointment. At this stage it may be necessary to examine the use of the present equipment to establish whether its performance can be improved and also to amend the manufacturer's claim to decide what costs are thought likely to be achieved in practice. The production manager's judgement becomes a factor in the decision for the first time.

Costs are divided into two classes—fixed or variable. Fixed costs are those which do not vary with the production rate except in the long term. Some of these will arise outside the department—administration, catering, transport. Others will arise within the department—supervision, heating. In many companies the majority of fixed costs are not directly attributable to a particular operation or product; there are, however, exceptions such as specialised machines, tools or jigs which cannot be used other than for the sole purpose for which they were designed. Variable costs are those which vary with and are directly attributable to the volume of production. Practical difficulties may be experienced in categorising some costs as either fixed or variable and an arbitrary decision may often have to be made in the light of their nature and the decision to be taken. In a standard cost system the fixed cost will be allocated as an overhead cost; this may be done as an hourly rate for machines or floor space or directly applied as a percentage to direct labour. This overhead rate is arbitrarily fixed by the accounting department and the control of these costs when arising outside the production department is beyond the production manager's influence.

It is now possible to decide the cost savings associated with the purchase of a new machine. This can best be done by considering an example. The proposal is to purchase a new machine costing $20,000 which will produce the same output and occupy the same floor space as two existing machines originally costing $3,000 each. The maintenance of the new machine, because of its advanced design and complexity, is estimated to be $400 p.a. compared with $100 p.a. for each machine of the old type. Labour costs are $1,500 per machine p.a. for both types of machine and the allocated overhead rate is 100 per cent of direct labour. Other differences such as reject rates, power, are not estimated to be significant. The calculation of the unit costs for these two situations would be as follows:

	New machine ($)	Old machines ($)
Depreciation over 10 years (straight line)	2,000	600
Maintenance	400	200
Direct labour	1,500	3,000
Overheads	1,500	3,000
Total cost	5,400	6,800
Annual production	500 units	500 units
Cost/unit	$10·8	$13·6

The conclusion seems clear. By purchasing the new machine an annual saving of $1,400 will be achieved and unit costs will fall from $13·6 to $10·8.

It must be noted, however, that $1,500 of the saving is derived from the reduction in the overhead allocated costs. We must ask what has been saved in real terms which reduces the fixed costs of the company's operation? The answer is virtually nothing. There is no saving in floor space and the only reduction may be some slight administrative cost savings because one machine operator fewer is employed. If there is no real saving in the actual fixed costs for the company, the inclusion of the overhead charge in the calculation leads to the erroneous conclusion that there is an annual saving of $1,400 by the purchase of the new machines whereas in fact the company will be $100 a year worse off. This difference arises solely because of the arbitrary allocation of an overhead rate resulting from the accounting system adopted by the company. In this case it could have led to the decision to purchase the new machine on the basis of a fictitious saving of $1,400.

It is also important not to neglect the effect which the introduction of a new piece of equipment will have on the total production system. Inevitably skilled operatives and management time will be diverted to it, causing some decrease in the operating efficiency elsewhere in the factory.

Management accountants are divided amongst themselves in their attitude to cost systems. Many nowadays hold the view that managers should only be accountable for those costs over which they have control and that the contribution made to overhead costs and profit is what is important and relevant. Most companies, however, still accept the traditional view that the fixed costs are of such significance for control purposes that they ought to be allocated and the basis for the allocation must necessarily be arbitrary. But an increasing number are realising the need not to allocate for decision making.

Production managers find this aspect of the problem hard to appreciate and often have great difficulty in accepting that the overhead costs are usually irrelevant in the context of an equipment purchase decision. Indeed from a departmental viewpoint they may often be right since a decision to purchase, as in the example quoted, will reduce the total costs allocated to their department as defined by the accounting system. This is, of course, highly undesirable since it results in a decision which eventually reduces the company profit by $100 p.a. in the example given. It should be noted that this is an example where company policies may encourage decisions being taken which are not in the best interests of the business.

Another respect in which accountancy practise may give rise to misunderstanding is the treatment of depreciation. When a machine is purchased its useful economic life is estimated and the book value of the asset reduced each year by a pre-determined amount, the size of which depends upon the method of depreciation adopted by the accountants. For example a machine costing $10,000 with an estimated ten year life and no scrap value will have its book value reduced by $1,000 p.a. if straight line depreciation is used. But it is possible that after two years an improved model may make it obsolete and reduce its market value to little, although the book value has only been reduced to $8,000; alternatively it may be found to have a re-sale value of $3,000 when the ten years have expired. It is not practicable to revalue equipment annually because of the expense and complexity of the calculations. But it must be remembered that the current book value is only the result of a depreciation decision made some years previously and may bear little relationship to the real market value of the asset.

The size of a new investment is the cost of the new equipment less the value of what it is replacing. In considering the investment it is not the depreciated book value but the actual scrap or re-sale value of the replaced equipment which is relevant. When these are different, as they usually are, the accountant must make a book adjustment in relation to the disposal price. But in evaluating the project the production manager must ignore the book value and estimate what the equipment is actually worth, rather than what the accountant some years previously assumed it would now be worth.

Once the size of the investment and the anticipated savings have been estimated it is necessary to decide whether the savings justify the expenditure. If the economical life of the project is uncertain due to possible machine obsolescence in a rapidly changing technology or doubts about the product life, a simple payback formula will normally be used. The payback period is calculated as the time it will take until the investment is recovered from the estimated savings, i.e. net investment divided by annual savings. This period may be as low as two years but it can be chosen in relation to the uncertainties surrounding the life of the investment.

Most commonly investments are for longer-term benefits for which the finance department will have an established criterion, e.g. Return on Investment Rate, D.C.F. rate of return or net present value. If the proposal meets this criterion the investment would be justified if the finance is available and provided there are no more attractive proposals for the use of limited resources.

Throughout this analysis it is evident that the production manager needs to exercise his judgement over a variety of factors. Furthermore there are a number of pitfalls which he is unlikely to avoid unless he possesses sufficient accounting knowledge firstly to appreciate them and secondly to enable him to communicate effectively with the company accountants.

Sunk costs

Once a decision has been made and an irrevocable action taken the situation has changed and none of the figures on which the decision was based may have any future relevance. This has already been seen in the discussion of depreciated v. resale value of existing equipment when considering a new purchase. Nevertheless many managers find it difficult to accept that this is so. But circumstances are continually changed either through a new situation or new information.

The problem is perhaps largely psychological in nature. A decision is made and because an individual has been deeply involved in it he feels that it is an admission of failure to accept that it was a wrong decision although it seemed right at the time. It can be seen in personal investment decisions, for example in the purchase of a new car costing say $3,000. Immediately the car is driven out of the showroom the resale value drops to $2,400. After four weeks the purchase is regretted perhaps because the performance and reliability does not live up to the promise, perhaps because a new improved model has been introduced. How many people can erase from their memory the $3,000 spent and concentrate their thinking on whether they should invest another $900 to buy the improved model costing $3,300? Very few, because there is a tendency to regard such a decision as an admission of failure in the first decision. But it may have been right at the time it was taken.

Once an investment has been made the purchase price is a 'sunk cost'. It is no longer of any relevance since it is past history. Consequently it should have no further interest to anyone except the company historian—the accountant who needs to make book adjustments. What is relevant is the future and which is the better of the alternative futures offered by a choice of either a change or living with the results of a past decision which is now seen to be wrong.

It must be admitted that most people suffer from a sunk cost mentality, for although it is not difficult to appreciate intellectually that the past is history, it is still difficult to behave accordingly. However, business success is dependent solely upon the decisions we take about the future. Consequently the production manager must focus upon future opportunities and not allow past expenditure to cloud his judgement either sub-consciously or through the use of historical cost rather than the current market value when carrying out economic analyses.

Rates of return

The desirability of an investment in equipment or in inventory, the two areas where the production manager often has a considerable freedom of choice, will depend upon the company's financial position and financial policy. This can be illustrated using as an example a rate of return defined as the annual return divided by the average investment. This can be expressed as a required rate of x. The value of x is determined by the finance department but will have a profound effect upon many of the production manager's decisions. It will also vary from time to time with the general economic climate and with changes in company financial policy. It may be based upon a number of factors such as:

Current rate of return on Government securities
The company may be in a strong cash position, either because of a conservative financial policy or because it has a temporary surplus which is earmarked for a future major investment. This surplus may be invested in government securities or elsewhere where it is readily accessible at short notice but at a low rate of interest.

The rate currently being earned would be quite inadequate for a capital investment due to the business risks involved. However, it may be possible to invest this money more profitably in inventories on a short term basis. Because of the low rate the likelihood of this being an appropriate figure to take is not high but there may occasionally be exceptional circumstances which would make it desirable. It would of course be necessary for the production manager to accept the temporary nature of the situation and understand the reasons for it.

Current borrowing rate
The interest rate which the company has to pay on an increase to its debt will vary with the economic situation and will be higher than the lending rate. The ability to borrow also depends upon the extent to which the company is able to raise new debt finance and the policy of the top management towards risk and the level of debt they consider desirable. This again would be an inappropriate rate to use for long term investment but may be appropriate for financing inventories if it can be shown that the increase in inventories enables an increase in earnings at a rate higher than the borrowing rate.

Current return on investment or target return on investment
The current return earned on investment is an average resulting from some operations with above and others below the average return. Companies will usually wish to raise their R.O.I. and also ensure that capital investment is not undertaken unless it stands a good chance of earning above the current average. Consequently it is customary to set a target rate which is a few percent higher than that currently being earned. This is the basis most commonly adopted. Since, however, investment in inventory will usually be less risky than capital expenditure and more readily re-converted into cash it may well be appropriate to require a slightly lower rate for inventories than for capital expenditure.

Opportunity cost
In a period of rapid growth the financial resources of the company may be inadequate to support the expansion necessary to exploit all potential opportunities some of which may offer very high rates of return. Consequently any resources unnecessarily locked up in investments not yielding this rate of return to the company need to be examined critically. This may involve the discontinuation of products which although profitable do not yield a high return, buying components

more expensively outside or pruning inventories so as to release financial resources for the more profitable new opportunity.

The production manager is not expected to be a master of financial intricacies and the appropriate rate to be used would be established by the financial director. Nevertheless it is important that he should have some understanding of what determines the rate. Lack of understanding can lead to serious differences of opinion between the two departments and may lead to production management decisions being taken which run counter to the needs of the company.

Inventory levels may be taken as an example to illustrate how this can occur. When the business is expanding rapidly and sales demand for existing products is high, the production manager will wish to increase batch sizes and work in progress in order to satisfy the demands of the marketing department without production delays. But the existing product may have a lower profit margin than a new product which could be introduced but for a shortage of finance. The appropriate cost of the capital tied up in inventories could then be the opportunity cost for the new investment (perhaps 25-30 per cent) rather than a normal target rate of return (perhaps 15 per cent). In the interests of overall profitability inventories including work-in-progress (and consequently batch sizes) should be reduced to free cash for the alternative investment. This is a situation likely to cause considerable conflict and misunderstanding between marketing, finance and production management unless the reasons for it are fully understood, since it may result in a decision to reduce inventories at the very time when all non-financial considerations point to an increase in their size.

Conversely, consider the case of a cyclical industry such as machine tools, with an established product the design of which is unlikely to change for several years. The company is in a strong financial position and has surplus finances when the cyclical downturn in demand is experienced. At first sight it might seem logical to run down inventories as demand falls, but it may well be more profitable in the long term to reinvest the cash available in finished goods so that when demand again rises it can be satisfied quickly.

There would, of course, be business risks involved since the length of the recession and the post—recession level of demand cannot be accurately forecast. On the other hand there may be considerable long term and unquantifiable benefits to be derived from employee loyalty through security of employment, saving of redundancy payments, and recruitment and retraining costs. Here again we see a potential source of conflict, for this is essentially a financial investment decision taken in the business interest of the company which adds costs in an area for which the production manager is normally held responsible.

4.4 Make or buy decision

Frequently, the production manager will be faced with the problem of whether to make or buy a particular component. His decision will depend upon the relative costs of the two alternatives. In addition, however, he must satisfy himself of the supplier's ability to meet the technical specification and delivery requirements at a stable price.

The economic analysis must cover all relevant costs. Many of the associated costs may be difficult to derive or be easily overlooked. Reliance on an outside supplier involves the surrender of much of the control, the production manager has when manufacturing for himself. Where the component is vital for the operation of a continuous line, as in motor manufacture, the company is exposed to the risk of a major disruption due to a labour dispute at the component manufacturer. This may be partly alleviated by holding higher inventories but at a cost. Alternatively two sources of supply may be used but with some penalty in the reduction of volume discounts. If such factors are not taken into account when making the initial analysis the cost advantages can be quickly eroded.

Once again relevance of the costs is central to the analysis and those relevant at one point of time may not be relevant later. This is particularly true when considering whether overhead costs should be included in the analysis. If there is spare capacity in the factory the costs associated with the machine tools, supervision and factory space will still have to be carried when the component is bought in. But if there is no spare capacity and the alternative is to build a factory extension the savings can be appreciable. The time factor too must not be ignored. Many make-or-buy decisions are not easily reversible in the short term so it may not be immediate savings which are necessarily the appropriate ones to take into account. It may, for example, be better to initiate one's own manufacturing programme at the cost of overtime working if spare capacity in the near future is anticipated.

4.5   Direct labour—fixed or variable cost?

Accountants traditionally treat labour as a variable cost since it is associated directly with a production operation. This pre-supposes, however that total labour costs rise and fall with the volume of production; this would only be true if it were possible to adjust the labour force to match all variations in production rate. This is becoming increasingly more difficult for a variety of reasons—redundancy payments, shortage of skilled labour etc. In recent years trade unions have been agitating for guaranteed minimum earnings and the British motor industry is moving towards a situation of making payments to workers laid-off due to labour disputes in other factories. Thus the direct labour pay roll has ceased to be a variable cost in many industries, although it is not truly a fixed cost since there is some, though not proportionate, reduction with a fall in production volume.

The distinction between fixed and variable costs is not absolute. In the long term all costs are variable since the most fixed of all assets such as land, property, or factory can be disposed of in response to a major set back in production. In the short term almost every cost is fixed. A particular cost can thus be regarded as either fixed or variable according to the time scale of the situation being studied.

This may well result in the production manager deciding that for the economic analysis of a problem he is considering it is appropriate to regard a cost as fixed whereas the accountant classifies it as variable. Direct labour is the situation where this is most likely to occur and can be best illustrated by a simple example.

During a temporary reduction in sales demand the production manager is faced with the alternative of reducing his production rate or continuing to manufacture for inventory. The breakdown of unit cost is as follows:

		$
Direct materials		10
Direct labour		30
Overhead as 50% of direct labour		15
		$55

He estimates that the additional average inventory involved would be 1,000 units for a period of three months which could be stored in an existing warehouse. For stock valuation purposes the accountant may value the inventory as either (*a*) direct materials + direct labour or (*b*) direct materials + direct labour + overheads according to the accounting convention adopted. Accordingly the increased book value of inventory in this case would be either (*a*) $40,000 or (*b*) $55,000. Inventory holding costs are currently estimated at 20 per cent p.a.; thus the cost of holding the additional inventory would be (*a*) $2,000 or (*b*) $2,750. If, however, no employees would be laid-off anyway, either because of the difficulty of building up the labour force again or because of the combined cost of redundancy and retaining, then the actual additional investment would only be in material, i.e. $10,000 at a holding cost of $500.

4.6   Summary

A number of situations have been examined where misinterpretation of accounting information often leads to poor decision making in the production area. Frequently this is because the decision taker is unable to see the reality behind the figures.

The accountant is primarily concerned with presenting a true and fair account of the company's operations which will enable a meaningful comparison to be made between different periods of time. Thus certain costs such as equipment purchases are spread over the estimated useful life of the equipment by means of depreciation allowances which at best are only estimates. He must also be consistent in deciding whether costs should be regarded as fixed or variable although we have seen that the time factor is important since in the short term most costs are fixed and in the long term they are variable. Without adopting conventions and standardised procedures which are constant over a long period his task would be impossible if he is present a consistent picture of his company's performance from one period to another.

The production manager's requirements are different. He is mainly concerned with taking decisions. Some of these decisions may have only a short-term effect where he needs to be concerned only with the current situation which may bear little relationship to 'normal'. Other decisions will have a long-term impact and he must take a view of the operating circumstances over the duration of the influence of the decision. But, to him the past has gone and its only value is in the interpretation he can place on past events as a guide to the future. He is bound not by the demands of consistency but by the need for realism. If, for example, he is unable to dismiss or move his labour to other work this year, then he must regard his direct labour cost as fixed, although next year when alternative work is available he may judge it more appropriate to regard it as a variable cost. Thus in order to be successful his attitude to the use of accounting information must be flexible, selective, and dictated by the circumstances of the situation.

Furthermore quantitative data is only part of the information upon which the manufacturing manager bases his actions. We have seen that he must exercise his judgement upon a host of other considerations many of which cannot be expressed in precise numerical terms, but which may easily lead to a different conclusion from that arising from his economic analyses. Unlike the accountant who is recording facts, many of the figures he uses are based upon judgement and upon imperfect or uncertain data. Failure to appreciate these essential differences give cause to much of the misunderstanding and poor communication which exist between accountants and production managers.

List of cases

Atlas Europe Ltd.

The Problem

When Alex Beaumont, the sixty-two year old Managing Director of Atlas Europe Ltd., began his annual review of company and management performance late in 1964, he concentrated on two important problem areas:

1. During 1964, the company failed to reverse a declining profit trend, at least partially because expectations for the introduction of a new product failed to materialise as planned. After a preliminary review, Beaumont was unsure with whom the fault lay.
2. Because Beaumont could not assess responsibility for failures of the past year (and of previous years) he was uncertain what action he should take in training his subordinates, and which, if any, of his senior subordinates he should recommend to replace him on his retirement in three years.

Atlas Europe history

Located in the kingdom of Atlantis, Atlas Europe Ltd. was the wholly-owned subsidiary of Atlas International, which had world-wide interests in many consumer goods and industrial products manufacturers. Except for some financial direction from the parent company (mostly on major investments and dividend policy), Atlas Europe independently developed, manufactured, and marketed its line of industrial products.

Founded by Atlas International in 1920, Atlas Europe grew rapidly through the twenties, declined slightly in the early thirties, grew rapidly again during the late 'thirties and war years (when it produced several important military equipments for the government) and continued to expand after the war. From 1946 to 1960, Atlas' profitability was enhanced by the sale of industrial equipment developed originally for military use, most notably Product X-12, which in 1960 accounted for about twenty-five percent of Atlas Europe's sales and almost thirty per cent of its profits. By 1960, the company had 3,300 employees and almost $15 million in sales.

Throughout the late 'fifties and early 'sixties competition increased rapidly both because informal market-sharing agreements with customers and competitors expired and were not renewed, and because new domestic and foreign competitors entered the market with products that imitated (and in some cases improved upon) those sold by Atlas. By 1961-1962, volume and prices on most Atlas products had begun a steady decline, while unit costs rose as Atlas attempted to add attractive 'customised' characteristics to its existing products, and because company overheads were spread over a declining volume.

Early in 1961, a major competitor introduced the 'Lambast' as a direct challenge to Atlas' X-12. The Lambast was both cheaper and more effective than the X-12, and X-12 sales declined rapidly. For some years Atlas had been working on replacements for the X-12; several of these, which were based on new technical concepts, were relatively far advanced in design, but as yet were untested.

The appointment of Beaumont

In January, 1963, Atlas Europe's Managing Director died. Alex Beaumont, a member of Atlas Europe's Board of Directors and a prominent international banker, was asked to take his place. Beaumont had little knowledge of the complex technical aspects of design and manufacturing involved in Atlas' products. His instructions from Atlas International were to reverse the declining profit trends as rapidly as possible; to effect a major refinancing of Atlas Europe's debts—both to reduce interest charges and to simplify the debt structure; and finally to select and train someone to replace himself by 1967.

Soon after assuming control of Atlas Europe, Beaumont began a series of joint conferences with his key subordinates (see Exhibit 1 for a partial organisation chart of the company) to isolate major problems and to decide on responsive tactics. At the first of these conferences, Beaumont confessed that his lack of training in engineering, manufacturing, and sales would prevent him from determining exactly what steps were needed to improve the company's performance. His role, he pointed out, would be to set the overall policies for the company; to help formulate and approve objectives and strategy for individual departments; to review and approve capital commitments, plans and budgets; and to appraise the performance of the company as a whole, the departments, and the individual managers; and to handle top-level public relations, especially with the government. He added that the company was badly in need of refinancing, and that since this was the field in which he felt most competent, he would spend much of his attention on it. Beaumont concluded that although he would be available as needed to help coordinate tactics or resolve differences between the departments, he expected the managers to use their experience in working closely together to solve mutual problems as they arose.

Beaumont's first assessment

By February, Beaumont had also completed his preliminary assessment of his key subordinates. Excerpts from his notes on these men follow:

Marketing manager—Tom Drake—forty-seven years old

Received technical college degree in engineering; spent six years as design engineer, three years as sales engineer with major competitor; came with Atlas Europe as sales engineer in 1946, became District Sales Manager in 1956, Marketing Manager in 1960 on retirement of former Sales Manager. Great physical energy and drive; ambitious. Drives subordinates hard by setting quotas which he expects everyone to make. Impatient with excuses or less than maximum effort. Appears to be feared by subordinates because of his temper, but apparently liked by many customers who have said they find him very charming. At conferences is usually first to present his ideas which are typically imaginative, but often not worked through. Often impatient and interrupts others who talk more slowly than he.

Manufacturing manager—Harry Saul—fifty-eight years old

Received some technical training in engineering and joined company immediately afterwards as foreman; rose to production supervisor in 1932; factory superintendant in 1940; Manufacturing Manager in 1951. Apparently very capable in manufacturing, but not especially imaginative. Slow moving and slow talking, but always armed with facts and figures to support his arguments. In recent years has instituted several new manufacturing processes, apparently helped extensively by his new factory superintendent (Charles leBon, thirty-one, bright, aggressive, university-trained engineer). Saul apparently knows personally an amazing number of people working in the factory, calls many by first names. At conferences usually doesn't present ideas unless asked specifically, and then typically takes manufacturing point of view only.

Engineering manager—Dick Rapon—forty-one years old

Has Doctorate in Engineering from major university; joined company in 1948 as engineer; became senior engineer in 1952; head of Development Engineering Group in 1955; Engineering Manager in 1957. Apparently highly intelligent and inventive; holds several basic patents. Tends to be quite non-directive with subordinates, who appear to admire him personally, and respect him professionally. Sets no goals for subordinates as far as I can see, and lets subordinates perform as well as they are able. Lets subordinates come to him for help when they want it. In conference with other department heads, tends to have amused, relaxed air; teases Drake regularly and is fond of picking holes in his arguments. Appears to know something about both sales activity and manufacturing processes, more study than experience.

Personnel manager—Michael Singer—thirty years old

Has degree in psychology; joined company in 1958 as Assistant to the Personnel Manager, became Personnel Manager in 1962 upon retirement of predecessor. Appears willing to be helpful, and both intelligent and able, but little knowledge of engineering, manufacturing, sales, or finance. Tends to play passive role in conferences.

Finance manager-controller—Kingman Abel—sixty-two years old

Has training in accounting; joined company in 1920 as bookkeeper, became chief accountant in 1935; controller and Financial Manager in 1942. Knows accounting practice well, but has limited understanding of finance. Useful mostly as controller rather than in financial transactions. At conferences tends to take restrictive role with narrow interpretation of budgets. Neither admired nor respected by other department managers, who see him as a restriction on their activity rather than as an aid.

By the early spring of 1963, Beaumont and his department heads reviewed the development history of several new products whose introduction as a replacement for the X-12 might reverse Atlas' declining fortunes. Together they agreed that one of these, the Y-1, showed the greatest potential acceptance by Atlas' customers. Based on new technological concepts, the Y-1 was far advanced in design, but still untested.

As a result of their talks, Beaumont and the department heads agreed on two major tactical objectives for 1963:

1. The Y-1 development would get top priority while other developments would be retarded slightly; and
2. The marketing department would attempt to maintain high sales volume with the present product line so that manufacturing and other fixed overheads could be spread as widely as possible.

By the end of 1963, it was apparent that this combination of tactics had unfortunate results. In the face of increased competition from several new products, the Marketing department was able to maintain volume only by promising customers 'customised' variations on Atlas' standard products. Because engineers were in short supply throughout Atlantis, these customised variations could be accomplished on time only if some Atlas engineers were shifted away from development projects into customer engineering.

In December, 1963, Beaumont realised that although the decline in Atlas's volume appeared to be halted, profits had continued to fall, both because average prices had fallen during the year, and because the shorter production runs of customised products meant a rise in manufacturing costs, (see Exhibit 2 for sales and profit history of Atlas Europe, 1946-1963). Perhaps more important, development work on the Y-1 had been retarded because several development engineers had been shifted to customer engineering work.

Preparing for 1964

Late in 1963, Atlas International Headquarters required all subsidiary companies to introduce a system for appraising performance of individual managers. The system called for performance targets for individual managers, and comparison of actual results against the targets, (see Exhibit 3 for excerpts from a description of the system which was given to all managers in Atlas International companies). When Beaumont reviewed the system, he recognised that it might help him appraise individual performance at the same time as it provided a stronger hold on the operations of the several departments and the company as a whole.

Throughout January, 1964, Beaumont met regularly with the department managers to review 1963 performance and to draw guidelines for setting 1964 targets. At these meetings, the Marketing Manager argued that unless the Y-1 were introduced early in 1964 he could not be responsible for regaining the company's rapidly declining market shares. Atlas was getting the reputation, he said, of selling obsolete products; once that reputation became established, it would affect sales adversely for many years. The Engineering Manager pointed out that a prototype of the Y-1 was almost complete and testing could begin shortly. Beaumont then decreed that the marketing of the Y-1 should be a primary consideration in Atlas's 1964 targets. He asked each department head to suggest what targets would be appropriate for his own department, and to assure that the Y-1 played a prominent role. He added that he would review each manager's targets, and negotiate any changes that appeared necessary before final approval.

After several additional conferences with his department heads, Beaumont approved the following individual targets, relating to the development, production and sale of the Y-1:

Marketing manager

Launch marketing campaign to introduce Y-1.

Obtain sales of 55,000 units of the Y-1 if product effectively available for sale, June 1964.

Obtain average net selling price sufficient to provide average gross profit of forty per cent on Y-1.

Manufacturing manager

Introduce production line for the Y-1 in an efficient manner so as to be able to produce 55,000 during 1964 and at an annual rate of 100,000.

Engineering manager

Complete testing and any necessary redesign of Y-1 before 30 April 1964 so as to prepare for first production in June. Assure that the Y-1 is fully competitive with comparable products now on market.

When approving their final targets, Beaumont told his managers that he expected to operate on the theory of 'management by exception'. 'I do not expect to spend time,' he said, 'reviewing performance that meets expectations. I want to concentrate on areas where we are running into problems. Unless I hear otherwise, I will expect that we are meeting our targets. If we are not meeting them I want to hear from you.'

Performance in 1964

Beaumont held his first quarterly review with his department heads at the end of March. Each department head said he expected to meet his Y-1 objectives as planned in the following weeks. Beaumont was largely occupied with the financial problems on which he had concentrated in 1963. Because of them, he visited Atlas International for four weeks from mid-May to mid-June. When he returned, and called a meeting of key subordinates, he discovered that it was extremely unlikely that any of the Y-1 objectives would be met. Beaumont immediately asked each manager to review his Y-1 Targets, to estimate the extent to which each would be met, and to explain any discrepancies between the targets and present estimates of performance. Excerpts from the replies of the senior managers follow.

Marketing manager

The Y-1 is coming off the production line at approximately 25% higher cost than we anticipated at the beginning of the year. With these costs, we must charge $45 per unit to make a gross profit of forty per cent. At these prices, annual sales of 100,000 units (representing about forty per cent of the available market) are out of the question. The Lambast is now selling at $41 per unit, and indications are that Lambast prices will decline. In addition, the first Y-1's off the production line have been performing below agreed-on specifications. Apparently, testing at the end of the production phase is not being controlled properly. Without the manufacturing department's meeting its targets, I do not see how I can be held accountable for sales performance.

Manufacturing manager

The manufacturing department probably can produce 55,000 units before the end of 1964, but this cannot be done efficiently because of the large number of design changes. Although the Y-1 original drawings were released on schedule by Engineering, there have been 120 engineering change orders (design changes originated by engineering after production drawings had been released and requiring a change in design and/or production process), nearly one-quarter of which required changes in the production line. Many have increased production costs above our preliminary expectations and the changes in the line have meant that efficient processing has been impossible.

Engineering manager

Release of production drawings for Y-1 completed on schedule by 30 April 1964 in spite of heavy pressures from other work, and despite considerable delay in agreeing basic specifications for product with the Marketing Department. Unanticipated problems discovered late in the test phase necessitated several changes in design. If we had had full specifications from the Marketing Department two years ago, we could have completed the Y-1 without the costly delays and changes that always accompany crash projects.

When Beaumont reviewed these replies, he doubted whether he could decide just where responsibility for the company's failure to meet Y-1 targets lay. He wondered about the extent to which he, as Managing Director, was responsible for the problems:

Was he right to allow the managers to set their own targets, or should he have drawn the targets for them?

Were the original targets at fault in that they were either too broad or did not allow fixing of responsibility for performance?

Was the organisation structure at fault because it forced each manager to depend on each of the others to achieve targeted performance? Was there any way of dealing with this problem?

Were there any ways of collecting information which might reveal which manager was primarily responsible for the failure to meet the targets, and if so, how should this be done?

Should he forget past performance entirely, and instead concentrate on improving future performance? and if so, just what steps should he take?

Exhibit 1. Partial organisation chart

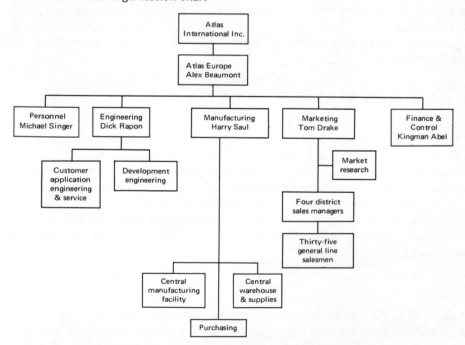

Exhibit 2. Sales and profits = 1948–1963

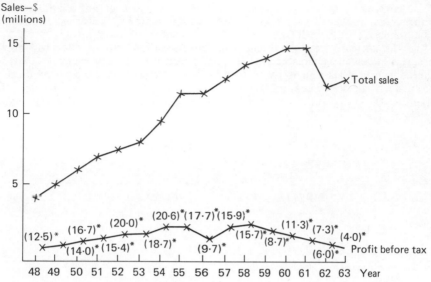

Sales—$
(millions)

* Profit before tax divided by sales times 100.

Exhibit 3. Excerpts from the Atlas International performance appraisal system

Purpose of system
● to establish a method of appraising individual managers by reviewing the performance of activities for which they are responsible.

Methods
● establishing specific key results (or targets) expected of individual managers;

● recording actual results attained and comparing these with results expected;

● determining areas of strength and weakness by analysing why actual results varied from targets;

● developing an action programme of work experience and training through which the individual can strengthen his performance.

The first step is to determine the key results expected of various individuals, that is, those major accomplishments which are required of him as a manager if the organisational component for which he is responsible is to make its proper contribution to the overall company profitability. Key result targeting must be done concurrently with long and short-range planning, and the final targets must be directly tied into the overall budget of the company. The result targets must:

1. be specific as to exactly what is to be accomplished and by when;
2. state expected results in positive, measurable terms;
3. list the results to be accomplished, not just the activities leading to them (indicate what, not how); and
4. establish definite, forward-looking goals in each major area of the manager's responsibility.

Accurate records of accomplishments against targets should be maintained, in most cases, as normal control reports. Where these reports do not provide required information, it shall be the responsibility of the manager concerned to maintain such simple records as will accurately reflect his accomplishment.

In the normal course of business the individual and his superior will discuss progress in achieving targeted results quite frequently. In any event, a discussion should be held at least quarterly on each target operative during the period. In these discussions, the supervisor and the individual should consider any problems that stand in the way of full accomplishment of targets and decide on necessary action.

The Break Glass Push (A)

This case can be used where the class has been divided into groups each of which has studied the development of the Break Glass Push from the viewpoint of either the Manager of Sales or the Manager of R & D or the Manager of Manufacturing. For this purpose all groups should study Part A and only one of Parts B, C or D, which should follow immediately Part A in the same bound case study.

The following assignment may be given to all study groups:

A meeting has been called for 14 October 1965 to establish targets for the Break Glass Push.
You should evaluate the implications of limiting the target to 3,000 units per year and weigh them against the implications of higher targets. These alternatives are summarised in Exhibit 8. Make a decision and be prepared to defend the plan you have chosen.

Note: For ease of calculation all financial data has been converted to British decimal currency.

On 14 October 1965 Mr Revans, General Manager of the Communication Equipment Division (CED) of Orbis England Ltd., held a meeting with his department managers to set targets for the Break Glass Push (BGP), a new product being added to the Fire Alarm Systems product line. Although originally considered as one element in an alarm system installation, the new design of the Break Glass Push appeared to endow it with considerable sales potential as an independent product. It was necessary to decide whether to set volume targets of about 3,000 units for 1966 as an 'in-house' product for traditional customers of CED systems, or to set targets of 30,000 units. Under the latter alternative, it would be necessary to make sales to electrical contractors as well as private brand contracts with outside companies to dispose of most of the units. Mr Revans supposed that each functional department would have its own reasons for preferring one alternative to the other, and therefore called to the meeting Mr Fowler, Manufacturing Manager, Mr Kean, Chief Engineer, and Mr Gibson, Marketing Manager.

The communication equipment division

The Communication Equipment Division of Orbis England Ltd. (OEL) (see Organisation Chart, Exhibit 1) was engaged in the design, manufacture and installation of communication equipment systems on a sale or rental basis. Sales of £1,742,000 in 1964 were divided into major types of equipment for purposes of business planning. The following table shows the actual breakdown of sales and market shares in 1964 as well as corresponding 1970 targets:

	1964		1970	
	£ 000	market share %	£ 000	market share %
PABX[1]	874	29	1,450	26
PAX[1]	311	13	630	14
Fire alarm	56	9	740	22
Installation	257	16	380	17
Maintenance	179	11	140	9
Other	65	4	320	11
	1,742		3,660	

In the search for expansion opportunities required for achieving the five year objective of doubling sales and profits, CED management began investigating the feasibility of expanding into the fire alarm field by adding new products to the existing line. CED had manufactured municipal fire alarm systems for many years and in the United Kingdom much of this market was captive to CED. Other CED fire alarm products included specially designed 'one off' manual and automatic systems as well as systems associated directly with telephone installations (PABX and PAX). Sales of CED fire alarm equipment had been running at approximately £40,000 for the previous three years.

The fire alarm system market

Information obtained in a market survey carried out in 1964 will be summarised below:

There were two basic types of fire alarm equipment: systems for fire protection and prevention and systems for fire extinguishing.

Protection and Prevention systems

Protection and prevention systems consisted of four parts: an alarm initiation device; an indicator board; signals such as bells, horns, sirens; and batteries and chargers which made it independent of the main power supply. An alarm could be initiated simply by breaking the glass of a wall-mounted box. This box, called a 'Break Glass Push' contained a switch which was connected to the signal by a control relay. In a small system the relay was used only for switching off the alarm signal and for periodic tests of the **Break Glass Push** units in the circuit. In larger systems it might be necessary to identify the zone from which the alarm came. For this purpose more complex relays were developed, mounted in zone indicator boards. In place of the Break Glass Push or to supplement the manual system, automatic devices could be used to initiate alarms either at a certain fixed temperature, or to respond to rapidly rising temperature, or to detect smoke.

Special systems were designed for large industrial sites and municipalities. They provided for central recording of the origin of the alarm on punched tape.

Fire extinguishing systems

Extinguishing systems used CO_2, foam, powder or water. They could consist of simple manually operated devices or be part of an automatic system. The most effective kind of installation was the sprinkler system which normally used automatic detection devices. In operation, sprinklers caused damage to goods and equipment and therefore had to be carefully controlled.

Size of the Market

The fire alarm equipment market in the UK was estimated to amount to about £16 to £18 million in 1965, increasing at a rate of approximately 7% per annum.

By major type of equipment the market estimate was broken down into:

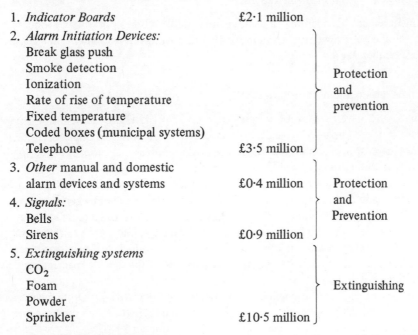

1. *Indicator Boards*   £2·1 million
2. *Alarm Initiation Devices:*
   Break glass push
   Smoke detection
   Ionization   } Protection and prevention
   Rate of rise of temperature
   Fixed temperature
   Coded boxes (municipal systems)
   Telephone   £3·5 million
3. *Other* manual and domestic
   alarm devices and systems   £0·4 million   } Protection and Prevention
4. *Signals:*
   Bells
   Sirens   £0·9 million
5. *Extinguishing systems*
   CO_2
   Foam   } Extinguishing
   Powder
   Sprinkler   £10·5 million

Fire damage in Great Britain had risen from £40 million in 1961 to £66 million in 1963. During 1964, fire insurance companies increasingly favoured the installation of automatic detection and extinguishing systems by granting up to 70% discount on premium for the most effective automatic extinguishing system and about 10 to 15% for automatic detection systems. No discounts were granted for the manual alarm system.

Conclusions from the market survey

Mr Revans believed that CED had to be very selective about adding new products. A major competitor was known to be in financial difficulties because of its excessive range of products.

Although the market for fire extinguishers and in particular sprinkler systems showed the most rapid growth rate, entry to this market was not considered promising for CED, because the field installation required plumbers rather than the electricians who constituted CED's own installer crews.

The market survey also included information on competitors (summarised in Exhibit 2) engaged in the fire alarm field. It revealed a few products for which competition was relatively weak. The market research group therefore recommended development of the following fire protection equipment:

(a) Break Glass Push
(b) Open and closed circuit indicator boards
(c) Automatic detection devices
(d) 'Domestic' systems for small premises

Top management decided to undertake feasibility studies for these products immediately and to review progress in monthly 'Fire Alarm Development Meetings' starting September 1964.

New product development procedure at CED

Initiation of the development of a new product at CED could come from any department in the company. Typically it was either the Marketing Department, as the result of customer enquiries or competitive moves, or the Engineering Department, as the result of design improvement or new product ideas.

The first step, a feasibility study, was taken after a management decision that typically was made during one of the Product Review Meetings held weekly among Product Line Managers, Production Control Manager and Chief Engineer. Quarterly Product Review Meetings included the Marketing Manager and representatives of other functions. The weekly meetings covered each product at least once per quarter, while the quarterly meetings reviewed progress of the weekly meetings and special problem areas.

Feasibility Studies involved engineering studies of competitive products, market research into potential volume, price, and product characteristics, and clearance of other Orbis Europe companies to check out similar products.

After the issue of a Marketing Requirement Specification to the Engineering Department, rough drawings, development cost estimates and unit cost estimates were prepared. Simultaneously the Production Control Department solicited suppliers' quotations for the volume estimated by Market Research.

On the basis of the Feasibility Study the decision was taken as to whether the product should be bought out or whether an internal development study should be authorised. This decision was the responsibility of the New Product Development Meeting, held monthly by the General Manager together with all department managers.

If the decision was 'make', the Engineering Department started a Development Project. When the first prototypes were available, they were forwarded to the Manufacturing Department together with drawings and schedules. The accompanying letter was called Three Part Letter. Its purpose was to summarise Engineering and Manufacturing information as a basis for Marketing approval to proceed with the project.

The Manufacturing Department, together with Production Control and Methods, prepared a Cost Estimate (unit and tooling) as well as a Time Estimate from reception of complete drawings to stock availability. With these data the Three Part Letter was forwarded to the Marketing Department. The Marketing Manager either approved or disapproved further development and forwarded the Three Part Letter to the Engineering Department. At this stage, target dates for Engineering, Manufacturing, Production Control (for bought-out parts and tools) and Marketing were decided. Progress was then reviewed in the monthly New Product Development Meetings. This case is confined to the development of the Break Glass Push as part of the new fire alarm product line.

The Break Glass Push

A BGP was basically a switch, manually operated in the case of fire, and serving to initiate an alarm. Most designs consisted of a small round or rectangular box mounted on the wall, coloured red for quick visibility, and containing a switch that was held in an 'Off' position by the glass front of the box. When the glass was broken, the switch was automatically turned on and either opened or closed a circuit to ring the alarm (Exhibit 3).

The individual BGP was connected to the signals via an indicator board, normally grouping zones with a number of BGPs in each. The indicator board provided for central identification of the origin of the alarm, cancellation of the alarm, and testing of the circuit.

The installation of BGP's was required by law as a minimum fire precaution in all premises housing more than twenty employees. Its exterior appearance and technical operation were regulated by a British standard.

CED's interest in the BGP was mainly motivated by the fact that it was a necessary part of any type of manual fire alarm system and was frequently used to supplement automatic systems. Although the sales value represented by all BGP units in an installed system was not high in itself, the ability to supply BGP's was considered useful in selling the more important equipment items in a system such as indicator boards, automatic detection devices, batteries, battery chargers and signals. Another argument advanced for adding BGPs to the product line was that they provided a publicity medium, prominently mounted and displaying the company's name.

The first step taken at CED had been to look for a usable BGP in other Orbis Europe system houses. A unit was found in the product line of an Orbis Europe subsidiary in a Common Market country. However this unit was designed to meet legal and industrial specifications which were more stringent than those of the UK. The delivered price to CED would be £2·70. Since most BGPs on the British market sold at £2·50 retail price, the unit would permit no profit (see Exhibit 4 for breakdown of CED sales, cost and profits).

The next step had been the analysis and evaluation of competing BGP's on the British Market, carried out by the Engineering Department. The study revealed that competing units showed only minor differences in metals used, sizes, mechanical and electrical features.

While the study of competitive BGP's was proceeding in 1964, the Production Control Department contacted some makers of BGP's to ask for quotations. The only quotation that was basically acceptable, providing for the CED trademark and a price 25p below the industry-wide wholesale price of £2·12½, was obtained from Brent & Co. However, the shortest delivery promise Brent could make was twenty-six weeks.

A twenty-six week delivery delay meant that an order would have to be placed immediately in the autumn of 1964 if the BGP's were to be available in April 1965, when other fire alarm equipment, such as indicator boards, were scheduled for release. The commitment to buy out a certain volume and model of BGP from a single supplier was considered undesirable. It was therefore decided in the Fire Alarm Development Meeting of September 1964 to start a development project for CED's own Break Glass Push.

Exhibit 1. Organisation Chart, as of 10 October 1965

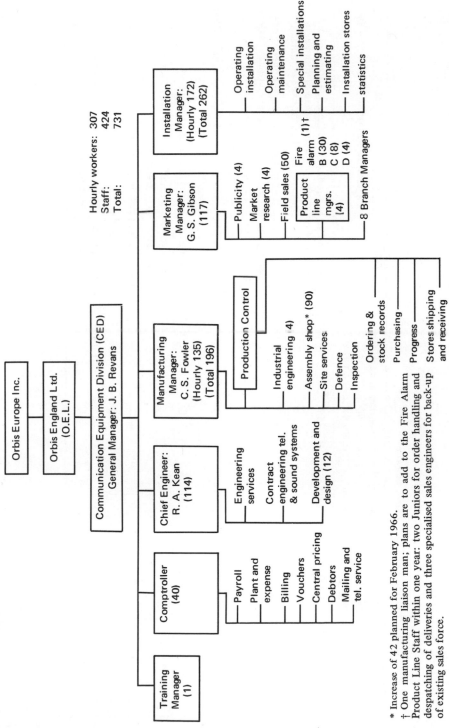

Hourly workers: 307
Staff: 424
Total: 731

* Increase of 42 planned for February 1966.
† One manufacturing liaison man; plans are to add to the Fire Alarm Product Line Staff within one year: two Juniors for order handling and despatching of deliveries and three specialised sales engineers for back-up of existing sales force.

Exhibit 2. Major competitors in fire alarm market

Company	Number of employees	Sales of fire alarm equipment in 1963 (£ 000)			Other information
		Manual	Automatic	Extinguishing	
1. Company A	1,150	1,200	750	400	Widest range of products of all competitors; group consists of over 30 companies, some of them very small; active sales and excellent service organization.
2. Magna Ltd.	over 600	–	3,000	240	Markets unique ionisation detector; supplies extinguishing equipment imported from Germany; associated with other fire alarm manufacturers.
3. Brent & Co. Ltd.	550	740	320	–	Specialises in component manufacture; supply other fire alarm companies.
4. Company B	2,500	280	140	N/A	Concentrates largely on extinguishing equipment.
5. Company C	100	200	–	–	Concentrates on small alarm systems; active in Lancashire and North England.
6. Company D	200	–	410	–	Specialises in automatic detection systems.
7. Company E	120	170	65	–	
8. Company F	3,500	–	–	1,140	Concentrates on fire appliances, fire engines, hoses, etc. and sprinkler systems.

Exhibit 3. The Break Glass Push

Exhibit 4. CED income statements in percent of sales

	64(Actual)	65(Forecast)	66(Plan)
Sales	100·0	100·0	100·0
Cost of sales	75·1	73·0	74·0
Gross margin	24·9	27·0	26·0
Marketing expense*	13·5	14·2	14·7
A & G and other expense	2·9	3·1	2·8
Net profit before tax	8·5	9·7	8·5
Tax	4·2	4·8	4·3
Net profit after tax	4·3	4·9	4·2

* The breakdown of this item in 1964 was: 39% Direct Selling, 6% Adv. Promotion, 37% Stores, Shipping, 18% Administration.

Case 13B
The Break Glass Push (B)

In September 1964, after the Fire Alarm Development Meeting, Mr Gibson, Manager of Marketing, met with Mr Coley, one of three product managers of the communication equipment lines to discuss the preparation of a Marketing Requirement Specification for the BGP to be issued to the Engineering Department. Mr Gibson pointed out that they might consider the BGP as a possible source of profits and not only as an ancillary product. There was, for instance, the possibility of selling to other fire alarm manufacturers in large quantities, as discussed with Mr Revans. Therefore the specification would have to establish a low unit cost limit.

Before writing up the Marketing Requirement Specification, Mr Coley tried to derive a sales forecast from existing market research information. His best estimate was annual sales of 2500 indoor and 500 outdoor BGP's, to existing customers of CED.

Mr Coley then discussed the findings of the Engineering study of competitive products with Mr Kean, the Chief Engineer, and learnt that competitors' shop cost was probably above £1·25 and that it would be difficult to go below this cost if CED wanted to make the BGP in metal with similar mechanical features. Mr Kean therefore recommended consideration of a plastic housing. After having gathered other information on dimensions and operating voltage ranges Mr Coley drafted the Marketing Requirement Specification, (Exhibit 5). Before issuing this document, he checked and made sure there were no objections from any official body to the use of plastic material.

Late in October 1964, the target dates for the fire alarm development programme were reviewed. The best delivery promise Manufacturing could give for the BGP was July 1965 (Exhibit 6).

Two months later, engineering completed rough drafts of three basic design possibilities of BGP. One was a simplification of the normal BGP on the market. This design was too expensive to meet the new £1·0 cost limit which marketing had set after checking price data on volume contracts currently granted by other fire alarm equipment manufacturers. Another design eliminated the glass entirely, using a plastic twist-off knob. Although the idea seemed ingenious, cheap, and even patentable, Mr Gibson and Mr Coley agreed that it was too unconventional for CED which had yet to build a reputation in the fire alarm field. The third design used a plastic case but was otherwise similar to BGPs on the market. It could probably be produced at about half of competitors' unit costs once the moulding dies had been amortized.

In January 1965, results of the BGP feasibility study were discussed in a Fire Alarm Development Meeting. The decision was then taken to proceed rapidly with development of the third design so that manufacturing drawings would be completed at the same time as the new indicator board drawings, in February 1965. Mr Gibson had the impression that, although plastic was accepted by the engineers as the only feasible material because of cost reasons, they had little experience with this material and were concerned about design problems.

At the February 1965 fire alarm meeting, Mr Kean described a new design made possible by using a flexible plastic material, polypropylene. The entire BGP case, both cover and base, would consist of a one-piece plastic housing with an integral hinge. This design would allow substantial savings in tooling costs. Although pleased with this solution, Mr Gibson expressed concern about widening time lag between the BGP and the indicator boards, which were on time and being prepared for production. It was clear now that completion of final BGP drawings had to be rescheduled to April 1965.

On 8 March 1965, Mr Gibson received the Three Part Letter (Exhibit 7) with estimated unit cost of 60p. The unit cost was below the limit allowed by the Marketing Requirement Specification and Mr Gibson gave Engineering clearance to proceed. The delivery quotation given by Manufacturing in the Three Part Letter, as four to five months after completion of drawings, forced Marketing to delay launching the BGP until late 1965.

In May 1965, information sheets were made out on the basis of photographs of two wooden models of the BGP and distributed to CED's eight branch offices and forty-four agencies. The agencies handled mainly low price items like simple intercom sets rather than complete systems as did the branches. There were thirty-eight salesmen attached to the branch offices and eight area salesmanagers who were also actively selling when necessary. Agencies typically had no salesmen or very few. The information passed out to the sales organisation indicated that the BGP would be available for delivery by September 1965.

Thereafter, in July 1965, the wooden models were again used at the International Fire Exhibition where CED showed its whole line of fire alarm products. The results of this exhibition were negative because the visiting public consisted mainly of members of the Fire Brigade and their families rather than contractors or architects. A subsequent advertising campaign consisting of two runs of a 'Fire-prevention-is important' message in three national daily newspapers was equally unrewarding. A colour advertisement in a monthly architectural review for the whole new fire alarm line resulted only in two enquiries about the BGP. The total cost of these sales promotion activities amounted to £3,200.

Engineering reported in the July Fire Alarm Development Meeting that changes in the drawings had been decided upon with Preston Mouldings. Difficulties were being encountered in the moulding process.

In the autumn of 1965 Marketing was informed that tests of prototypes, the first with plastic housings, had revealed some structural difficulties. It had also been found that the colour of the BGP faded rapidly when exposed to sunlight. Until this problem could be overcome in cooperation with the colour supplier, the BGP would not be feasible for outdoor installation. A glass breakage test indicated that changes in the moulding die would be necessary.

Mr Coley requested the current estimates of total tooling cost and found that it was more than double the original £750. Mr Gibson and Mr Coley decided to review their sales forecasts so as to consider an alternate marketing policy which would allow for higher volume to amortise the investment.

(a) The system market

The system market for which the BGP was originally intended seemed hardly able to be increased over 2,500 units representing sales of £6,250 for 1966.

The sales forecast for all fire alarm products was (in thousands of pounds):

	1965	1966	1967	1968	1970
Old products	60	70	90	120 ⎫	740
New products	–	150	250	350 ⎭	

The figures for 'new products' represented sales of complete fire alarm systems, both manual and automatic. Systems using BGPs were expected to represent about one sixth or £25,000 in 1966. The average price of a manual system could be broken down into:

	£
indicator board	56
battery and charger	60
bells and sirens	34
BGPs (25 indoor, 5 outdoor)	75
	225

As the market for automatic systems was expanding more rapidly than that for manual systems, only £50,000 out of the £350,000 in 1968 were expected to be manual systems. Even assuming that the plastic BGP would by then be adapted for outdoor installation, sales to traditional customers would not exceed 8,000 units or £20,000 by 1968.

All fire alarm equipment including BGP's would be handled by the existing sales force of thirty-eight representatives attached to eight branch offices. Mr Gibson considered the high technical know-how of CED salesmen in their traditional communication equipment field as a major reason for CED's success. Therefore, a short training course would be held to give the salesmen sound product knowledge in the new fire alarm line. A change in the bonus system to interest salesmen in the new line would also be studied. A salesman would be able to realise £50 out of a possible annual bonus of £600 by achieving his fire alarm budget. Inasmuch as achievement of the much higher budget in the PAX line would provide the same £50, this plan was expected to provide a strong incentive for fire alarm sales.

(b) Electrical contractors

One particular volume market had not been considered originally because it was captive to two major competitors. This was the electrical contractor trade, comprising about 3,000 potential customers. Their interest in changing to a CED product would depend on the discount offered. Typically they were granted 25% off the £2.50 price. Mr Coley estimated that a 25% plus 15% introductory offer would secure sales of 15,000 to 20,000 units per year to this market because competitors were most probably unable to meet such an offer. The electrical contractor market could initially be approached by direct mail campaigns. The goal for three mail campaigns would be to obtain orders from about one quarter of all contractors. The rest would have to be contacted by company salesmen. In addition to the change in the bonus system mentioned above, Mr Gibson thought that new targets for the number of daily calls should be set for salesmen in order to cover this market. A CED salesman currently made an average of four calls per day to top management level of large and medium sized corporations and to architects and building consultants. Visits to electrical contractors would certainly be less time consuming and twelve calls per day seemed possible, thus increasing the overall average to eight calls per salesman per day.

(c) Private brand contracts

High volume could also be obtained from sales to other fire alarm equipment manufacturers presently either making their own BGP's or buying them from other sources. The attraction would be a low contract price. In September 1965 one of these manufacturers, Magna Ltd., had been contacted. Magna was planning to develop its own BGP. The company was also negotiating a contract to supply its patented automatic detectors to CED. Mr Gibson considered the chances for a contract for 5,000 to 10,000 BGP's with Magna to be very high if the price could be brought down to £1 per unit and if delivery could be promised by February 1966.

Before entering the Fire Alarm Development Meeting, on 14 October Mr Gibson and Mr Coley wondered which of their alternative plans (summarised in Exhibit 8) was preferable. In view of the low cost of the BGP it seemed probable that large volume could be achieved soon. However, before fixing a target they wished to consider what the implications would be to their marketing strategy and what the effect would be on their product image, distribution, and other marketing factors.

Exhibit 5. Marketing requirement specification for Break Glass Push

Issued to: Mr Kean
Issued by: Mr Gibson
Issued on: Oct. 15, 1964

Summary of Requirements: One basic type is required and this should be suitable for:

1. Open or closed circuit operation
2. Surface or flush mounting
3. Indoor or outdoor use

It will be necessary to provide an additional plate for the flush mounting version or alternatively a completely different case may be required.

Dimensions:
Rectangular or Circular $3\frac{1}{2}''$ x $4\frac{1}{2}''$ x $2''$ deep, $4''$ diameter x $2''$ deep.

Material:
Case should be constructed in robust plastic material.

Appearance:
Case in red to British Standards No. 381C with front aperture approximately $2''$ square or $2\frac{1}{2}''$ diameter, with hinged lid.

Operating voltage:
From 24 volts d.c. to 350 volts d.c. at 3 amperes.

It is necessary for the break glass push to operate at mains voltages, as in certain circumstances mains powered bells, buzzers or hooters will be operated direct.

Facilities:
1. When the glass in the front aperture is broken, the contact should operate.
2. Under normal conditions the glass should hold the contact in the non-operated position by means of a button or similar device impinging on the glass when the box is closed.
3. Test button arranged to override the normal contact so that the box may be opened for test purposes without sounding the alarm.
4. Facilities for conduit entry.
5. The legend 'In case of Fire—Break Glass' should be clearly inscribed, either on the case or on the plate behind the glass cover.
6. The case and any parts exposed to a person ringing the alarm must be insulated from the electrical supply.

Regulations: The break glass unit should conform to the relevant British Standard—a copy of which is already held in the Development Section.

Economics: Shop cost—£1·25
Costing should be estimated on the basis of anticipated annual quantities of 2,000.

Exhibit 6. Product development Programme fire alarm systems

	Complete drawings	Stock available
1. Break glass push		
(*a*) Closed circuit indoor and outdoor versions	January 65	July 65
(*b*) Open circuit indoor and outdoor versions		
Surface and flush mounting		
2. Automatic detectors		
(*a*) Rate of rise thermal detector	March 65	July 65
(*b*) Ionisation detector with facilities for adding thermal detector to form 'Dual Detector'		

3. Indicator boards
  (a) 10 line radial open circuit system   26/10/64   February 65
  (b) 20 line radial open circuit system   End Sept.
  (c) 10 line radial loop system   V.A. 3/10   March 65
  (d) 10 line frequency loop system   March 65   July 65
  (e) 20 line frequency loop system   —   —
  (f) Modernised and redesigned municipal
      type board. 2–4 loops   26/10/64   May 65

4. Manual fire alarm system

5. Domestic fire alarm system

Exhibit 7. Three-part letter: Costing of new development

Eng. code	Description	Sales code	Forecast Sales this year/next year
P.236	Fire Alarm Break Glass Push		2,000 2,000

Mr C. S. Fowler   Date: 10th February 1965

Will you please let Mr Gibson have a cost estimate for the above new product. Price required at this stage to enable Marketing to assess whether it is economic to proceed further with the development.

The list of information or models which are available to assist in this costing is as follows:

8 prints of drawing P.238, and rough notes, herewith Drawing Sheet 2 of 2

The development engineer to be contacted for any further information is Mr Simpson.

(R. A. Kean)

Mr G. S. Gibson   Date: 8th March 1965

Our estimate of the cost of the above:

	Cost each	Total tool costs
Material	45p.	£750
Loaded Labour	15p.	

Delivery could commence in 4/5 months after receipt of complete manufacturing information.

(C. S. Fowler)

Mr R. A. Kean   Date: 15th March 1965

On the basis of the cost given by Mr Fowler, we consider that the development above will/will not be an economic proposition and should/should not proceed.

(G. S. Gibson)

Exhibit 8. Alternative marketing plans for Break Glass Push

Alternative (1):

	1966	1967	1968*	1969*	1970*
Volume Objective:					
Units	3,000	5,000	8,000	10,000	11,000
Sales (£)	7,500	12,500	20,000	25,000	27,500
Gross Margin (£)	5,850	9,750	15,600	20,000	22,000

Market: Traditional and new system customers

Distribution: Existing 8 branch offices with 38 sales engineers in connection with other fire alarm products as indicator boards, automatic detectors (system installation). Change in bonus system.

Alternative (2):

	1966	1967	1968
Volume objective:			
as in Alternative (1)			
Units	3,000	5,000	8,000
plus additional:			
Units	20,000†	30,000	50,000
Sales (£)	28,000†	43,100	67,500
Gross			
Margin (£)	18,600†	28,100	42,500

Market: Traditional and potential system customers; Office-buildings, factories, etc., new and modernisation, and other fire alarm manufacturers, telephone companies, etc.

Distribution: Through independent electrical contractors (3000 in UK) and factory direct for large contacts. Sales force required to increase calls per day to eight, change in bonus system.

* Assuming an outdoor unit will be available at the same cost.

† Assuming introductory special discount of 25% plus 15% for 15,000 units and secured Magna contract of 5,000 units at £1.

Case 13 C
The Break Glass Push (C)

After this meeting Mr Kean, Chief Engineer, sent a request for Marketing Requirement Specification on the BGP to Mr Coley, one of the product managers. In subsequent discussions Mr Coley and he agreed that the possibility should be explored of using a plastic material for the box, as suggested by the engineer in charge of the feasibility study.

When the Marketing Requirement Specification (Exhibit 9) arrived in October, Mr Kean reviewed target dates for the whole of the fire alarm development programme. Although Engineering expected to supply complete drawings for the BGP by January 1965, it was noted that Manufacturing would not be able to deliver until July 1965, which was some months after most models of the new fire alarm indicator boards would be available in stock.

In November 1964 Mr Kean heard from the project engineer that the Marketing Department was considering contract sales of the BGP to other manufacturers. This alternative would require a cost limit per unit of £1·00. In view of this new cost target, Mr Kean instructed his project engineer to study the possibilities of simplification of competitive designs in metal, and also to prepare some rough drawings based on plastic. In December, three alternative designs were finished and discussed in the Fire Alarm Development Meeting.

The first alternative was a conservative metal box consisting of two parts fitting together with a hinge but containing only one switch, though all existing BGP's on the market had two. The second switch was only used for testing the circuit. By equipping the indicator board with a buzzer signal which would be switched on for testing, it was possible to use the single switch. This modification, however, was not expected to bring the cost down to £1·00.

The second alternative was a new design concept. The alarm would be activated by breaking or twisting off a plastic knob, thus turning the switch on. The box was also designed for plastic material which would permit low unit cost.

The third alternative was again plastic, with one switch but an otherwise conventional glass front design.

Marketing rejected the twist-off plastic version though CED submitted a patent application for the design. However, the main development efforts from this point on were directed to the glass front-plastic housing. As CED had no experience with plastics, the BGP engineer consulted his colleagues at the Preston Mouldings Division and with them developed a grid of feasibility of various plastics for criteria applicable to the BGP (Exhibit 10).

In discussions with Preston Mouldings engineers, the idea emerged of using Polypropylene to obtain the advantage of an integral hinge and therefore a one-piece plastic moulding. Polypropylene was a plastic material with very high flexibility. This made it possible to mould parts in one piece that would otherwise be connected by a mechanical hinge. The integral hinge was simply the connection strip between the two box halves, normally thinner than the rest of the material in order to take best advantage of the flexibility factor. Tests showed that integral Polypropylene hinges could last more than a million bendings.

Another idea was to design the polypropylene housing so as to fit into ordinary plastic electrical conduit boxes which could be either surface or flush mounted. Such boxes were standard items easily available at low price.

Because of a shortage of draughtsmen, the new designs could not be finished before February 1965. In the meantime some mechanical and supply problems were solved by using a cheap, standard microswitch which CED engineers knew to be as reliable as competitors' mechanical switches.

In March 1965, when the plastic-housing drawings were finished, a quotation was obtained from Preston Mouldings stating that the price per 100 BGP-housings would be £14·63 in lots of 2,000; £7·95 in lots of 5,000; or £5·07$\frac{1}{2}$ in lots of 10,000. Tooling cost was budgeted at £750. On this basis Manufacturing worked out a cost estimate which allowed Marketing to authorise further development (Exhibit 11, Three-Part Letter).

The order with Preston was placed in May 1965, after the drawings for the moulding die had been revised, and after Marketing had agreed to authorise 10,000 mouldings in order to achieve the economy of scale proposed by Preston.

The major concern of the engineers was the impossibility of testing the operation of the BGP as designed before the expense of the moulding tooling was incurred and plastic samples available. The flexibility and resistance of the wooden model could not provide reliable indications of the mechanical stresses that would be found in plastic housing. Before Preston Mouldings actually made the die, dimensional changes were necessary in the drawings, and it was only in late June 1965 that they moulded the first prototypes.

The moulding operation encountered difficulties with the integral hinge. It was found necessary to use two injection points rather than one because the plastic flow through the hinge was constricted. The colour of the prototypes was found to be a lighter red than required by British Standards. Upon enquiry, the colour suppliers confirmed that fading occurred frequently with red during moulding operations and that a darker shade should be used. They also pointed out that all red would fade into pink rapidly when exposed to sunlight. Exposure to ultra-violet radiation would also reduce the flexibility of Polypropylene. This indicated that the BGP would not be feasible for outdoor use.

In September, 1965, when the first plastic samples with standard colour arrived, several changes had to be made:

> Since the spring key was too strong, the housing bent so that the glass broke under the stress. The pre-stressing of the spring had to be altered, therefore, and additional ribs and pillars material around the key were required.

> The plastic screws used for attaching the unit to the standard conduit box did not work and had to be replaced by metal screws.

Actual testing by glass breakage showed that the alarm did not always go off because glass pieces sometimes stuck to the housing.

Mr Kean knew that Marketing was very anxious to have the BGP available soon because of a proposal from Magna Ltd., a fire alarm manufacturer, for delivery of a large quantity in February 1966. But in the light of all the difficulties in the development up to now and the still insufficient testing, he wondered whether it would be wise to support the idea of a commitment to deliver so soon. First this would mean that they had only two months left until the completion of all drawings and tests and that Manufacturing would have to be tooled up and assemble in the remaining month before delivery. Even with an optimistic view of further complications he would have to assign several more engineers and draughtsmen to the BGP, thus delaying other projects. There were currently about seventy-five major and twenty to thirty minor projects going on. The reliability of the BGP was another problem: the limited experience with plastic material showed the need for close tolerances to achieve proper operation of the device.

Up to now they had made almost twenty modifications in the die and each one had been time consuming. If further tests should show that a major change was necessary, such as different dimensions of the material around the glass front, a completely new die would have to be ordered.

Mr Kean was particularly concerned about the reliability testing of the BGP. Reliability meant that the alarm had to activate every time the glass was broken. However, it was difficult to foresee the way in which the glass would be broken. A preliminary test of this kind had been carried out with CED personnel: a group of twenty people, men and women, chosen at random from the plant had been suddenly asked to smash the glass. The result was astonishing. Some people used their elbows, others keys, slide rules, high heeled shoes, pencils, pens and the like. While the sample of breakages was not representative, still the alarm did not go off four times and this established the need for further such tests. Under time pressure from the Magna contract there would hardly be time for extensive testing and consequent improvement.

The problem of colour fading and material deterioration, including loss of flexibility in the hinge under exposure to weather in outdoor installation was completely out of their control. Mr Kean had not been able to obtain a satisfactory solution from the large plastic materials suppliers. Therefore he could not make any promise for development of an outdoor BGP to Marketing. If CED wanted an outdoor unit to complete the system, they might be obliged to develop a metal one for that purpose.

Finally, as the design and the die stood now, it would probably necessitate a number of awkward operations in assembly. Given the original forecast of sales around 2,000 to 3,000 a year, this had seemed to be of minor importance, but in view of possible volume of 30,000 or 50,000 changes would be justified even if a new die had to be ordered. (See alternative plans for completion of the BGP development, Exhibit 12.)

Exhibit 9. Marketing requirement specification for Break Glass Push

Issued to: Mr Kean
Issued by: Mr Gibson
Issued on: Oct. 15, 1964.

Summary of Requirements: One basic type is required and this should be suitable for:

1. Open or closed circuit operation
2. Surface or flush mounting
3. Indoor or outdoor use

It will be necessary to provide an additional plate for the flush mounting version or alternatively a completely different case may be required.

Dimensions:
Rectangular or Circular $3\frac{1}{2}''$ x $4\frac{1}{2}''$ x $2''$ deep, $4''$ diameter x $2''$ deep.

Material:
Case should be constructed in robust plastic material.

Appearance:
Case in red to British Standards No. 381C with front aperture approximately $2''$ square or $2\frac{1}{2}''$ diameter, with hinged lid.

Operating Voltage:
From 24 volts d.c. to 350 volts d.c. at 3 amperes.

It is necessary for the break glass push to operate at mains voltages, as in certain circumstances mains powered bells, buzzers or hooters will be operated direct.

Facilities:
1. When the glass in the front aperature is broken, the contact should operate.
2. Under normal conditions the glass should hold the contact in the non-operated position by means of a button or similar device impinging on the glass when the box is closed.
3. Test button arranged to override the normal contact so that the box may be opened for test purposes without sounding the alarm.
4. Facilities for conduit entry.
5. The legend 'In case of Fire—Break Glass' should be clearly inscribed, either on the case or on the plate behind the glass cover.
6. The case and any parts exposed to a person ringing the alarm must be insulated from the electrical supply.

Regulations: The break glass unit should conform to the relevant British Standard—a copy of which is already held in the Development Section.

Economics: Shop cost—£1·25.
Costing should be estimated on the basis of anticipated annual quantities of 2,000.

Exhibit 10. Plastic material feasibility for Break Glass Push

Colour must match British Standard No. 381c, Signal Red

Material to be:	*Polyvynil chloride*	*Nylon*	*Acetal*	*Polypropy- lene*	*Polyethy- lene*	*High Impact Polystyrene or Acetate- Butyrate- Styrene*
Shock resistant	good	good	good	good	good	good
Heat resistant	fair	good	good	good	poor	fair
Weather resistant (no colour fading)	fair	fair	fair	black only	poor	fair
Acid resistant	good	fair	poor	good	good	fair
Cost	medium	high	high	medium	low	low to medium

Not considered: Acrylic –shock resistance very poor
Polycarbonate – cost, weather and acid resistance fair
Cellulosics – heat, weather, acid resistance poor
Our 'best buy'– Nylon or High Impact Polystyrene

Exhibit 11. Three-part letter: costing of new development

Eng. Code	*Description*	*Sales code*	*Forecast sales this year/next year*
P.236	Fire Alarm Break Glass Push		2,000 2,000

Mr C. S. Fowler   Date: 10th February 1965

Will you please let Mr Gibson have a cost estimate for the above new product. Price required at this stage to enable Marketing to assess whether it is economic to proceed further with the development.

The list of information or models which are available to assist in this costing is as follows:

8 prints of drawing P.238, and rough notes, herewith Drawing Sheet 2 of 2

The development engineer to be contacted for any further information is Mr Simpson.

(R. A. Kean)

Mr G. S. Gibson   Date: 8th March 1965

Our estimate of the cost of the above:

	Cost each	*Total tool costs*
Material	45p	£750
Loaded Labour	15p	

Delivery could commence in 4/5 months after receipt of complete manufacturing information.

(C. S. Fowler)

Mr R. A. Kean   Date: 15th March 1965

On the basis of the cost given by Mr Fowler, we consider that the development above will/~~will not~~ be an economic proposition and should/~~should not~~ proceed.

(G. S. Gibson)

Exhibit 12. Alternative engineering plans for BGP

Status on 10 October, 1965:
  First 12 sample housings on hand
  First breakage tests completed

Development Cost to 10 October, 1965:

Study of Competitive Products	£201·50
Preproduction Drawings	£148·00
Preliminary Models	£151·00
Design Modifications, Tests	£304·50
Production Drawings to date	£201·25
	£1006·25

1. *Crash Completion of Development of Indoor BGP* (Dec. 10, 1965)

Drawing Modifications (4 Man-Weeks)	£201·20
Completion of Production Drawings (3 Man-Weeks)	£150·90
Testing (1 Man-Week)	£ 50·30
	£402·40

2. *Normal Completion of Indoor BGP* (Feb. 15, 1966)

(*a*) Minor additional Project effort (optimistic estimate)

Drawing Modifications	£100·60
Completion of Production Drawings	£150·30
Testing	£ 50·30
	£301·20

(*b*) Major additional project effort (pessimistic estimate)

Drawing Modifications	£251·30
Completion of Production Drawings	£301·80
New Tools	£425·50
Testing	£150·90
	£1129·50

Estimated Total Development Cost of BGP:

Development Cost to date	£1006·25	£1006·25
Additional effort (estimates)	£ 301·20 to	£1129·50
Adaption for Outdoor use (estimates)	£ 150·00 to	£ 600·00
TOTAL	£1457·45 to	£2735·75

Case 13D
The Break Glass Push (D)

Some weeks after this meeting Mr Fowler, Manager of Manufacturing, received from Engineering a Product Development Programme for Fire Alarm Systems with estimates of completion dates for drawings. He then discussed possible production schedules with Mr Trenton, Manager of Production Control. These schedules had to be decided for the Fire Alarm Development Meeting in October 1964.

CED's Manufacturing Department employed 105 people as direct labour, in addition to thirty indirect and a staff of sixty-one. The production task was similar to that of a job shop. Most production runs were short, 'one off' jobs were frequent. About 20% of direct labour were highly skilled operators capable of wiring directly from drawings. For complex wiring and cable forming tasks (relays selector panels) an operator would need an average of forty to fifty weeks to achieve 75% efficiency. Another 50% of labour had a lower grade of skill for simpler wiring tasks (such as intercom system assembly). 30% were semi-skilled. Female labour represented the majority in all grades of skill. The pay system consisted of an hourly rate based on grade of skill and supplemented by a merit scheme providing for bonuses for productivity, quality and time keeping.

Given the labour shortage, Mr Fowler thought it would be impossible to schedule stock availability of all new fire alarm products for April 1965 as had been requested by Marketing.

In particular for the BGP Mr Fowler was uncertain whether it would be made of metal or plastic nor did he know what delivery terms could be obtained from a plastic moulding company. Therefore he decided on a six months leadtime. This would still make the BGP available in July 1965 together with the automatic detectors. (See 'Product Development Programme' Exhibit 13.)

Mr Fowler had followed the BGP discussion during the last months with interest and had been involved in the cost analysis of competitors' products. It seemed to him that the device was not as simple as it appeared. The largest selling competitive unit consisted of a two part aluminium housing with fairly close tolerances. The two parts were held together by a hinge and were locked on one side. The lock was combined with a spring mechanism and had to be operated with a hexagonal key. The main alarm switch was heavy duty, and there was a smaller mechanical test switch. The main switch was held in the off-position by a round glass fitted into the hole in the front part of the housing. Although the wiring of the two switches was simple compared to CED's communication equipment, Mr Fowler could imagine that the mechanical problems of stress might be difficult with a plastic housing.

In the October 1964 Fire Alarm Development Meeting Mr Fowler expressed doubts about a plastic housing for the BGP. Although he was aware of the emphasis that Marketing put on low unit cost, he wondered if it was useful to acquire a completely new engineering and manufacturing know-how with a small item like the BGP. Even if unit costs were low, the tooling cost for a plastic moulding die was high. The anticipated annual volume was only about 3,000 units, which seemed low to profit from the investment in the die.

However, the development of plastic versions of the BGP was carried on in the Engineering Department, and in the December 1964 meeting, two of the three alternative BGP designs were in plastic. The aluminium version was rejected for cost reasons. One plastic version, an ingenious idea with 'twist-off-knob' rather than 'break-glass' activation was rejected as being too unconventional. The adopted version consisted of a two-part housing in plastic with a glass front. It was similar to existing designs, but with simplified switch and plastic housing. It was then decided that Engineering would provide a first set of drawings for the required plastic housing to Mr Trenton, Manager of Production Control, to obtain suppliers' quotations. The probable supplier for the plastic parts was Preston Mouldings, another division of OEL located in the same town. Since Mr Trenton reported to Mr Fowler, the Manufacturing Department kept in close touch with suppliers' schedules.

During the preparation of the housing drawings, CED engineers consulted Preston Mouldings and found that the use of Polypropylene, a flexible plastic material, would permit them to mould the entire housing in one piece, the front cover and base being held together by an integral hinge. Made of Polypropylene, the hinge could last for a million openings and closing of the BGP. The red housing would be assembled to a standard conduit box for either flush or surface mounting, easily available at low price.

Drawings for the new design were not ready before the end of February 1965. The quotation from Preston arrived in March and showed tooling cost of £750 and unit costs of £14·63 per hundred units in lots of 2,000 or £7·95 in lots of 5,000 and £5·07½ in lots of 10,000 units.

On the basis of the Marketing information that batches of 2,000 should be assembled, the cost estimate of Manufacturing was 60p per unit (Exhibit 14, Three-Part Letter; Exhibit 15, Parts Lists). Before the mouldings were ordered, however, Engineering made changes in the drawings. The actual order was placed in May 1965. At this time Preston offered a five-month delivery period. The Marketing Department insisted that lead time had to be reduced because a campaign for the complete fire alarm line was already under way. Mr Fowler was obliged to pay 25% premium to obtain a two-month delivery promise. In the meantime, Marketing had authorised a batch of 10,000 housings, encouraged in their sales forecasts by the fact that unit cost would be reduced to approximately 55p—by ordering the larger batches.

When Preston Mouldings started working on the die, they encountered dimensional problems in the housing drawing. These were eliminated by CED engineers by June 1965. It then required two months until Preston Mouldings had solved the problems that arose in the injection moulding process. They found that it was impossible to inject the Polypropylene at one single point because the plastic did not flow smoothly into the part of the mould beyond the integral hinge. They also encountered rapid colour fading under exposure to sunlight. Until this had been solved with the colour supplier, the BGP would not be feasible for outdoor use.

In September 1965 the first samples arrived and were tested. Several failures were encountered. Pieces of glass sometimes remained stuck in the housing, preventing the switch from activation. After modification, the next batch of samples was expected in October, 1965.

Mr Fowler estimated that, barring further complications, a batch of 10,000 housings might be available in late November and therefore planned to phase assembly of the first run of one thousand BGP's into manufacture during December. The methods study based on existing samples showed that the assembly operation was optimally performed in three steps plus inspection:

Operation No. 1	2 minutes
Operation No. 2	1·5 minutes
Operation No. 3	2·5 minutes
Inspection	2 minutes

These time estimates were based on 75% efficiency of a semi-skilled operator.

The method study also contained sketches of two holding fixtures and four jigs that would be needed for assembly. These fixtures were expected to be inexpensive and could be provided promptly. However, the methods engineer pointed out that he could not balance the cycle times of the operations better or reduce them further because of the nature of the design.

With this information in mind, Mr Fowler discussed with Mr Trenton the position the Manufacturing Department should take on the BGP in the forthcoming Fire Alarm Development Meeting of 14 October 1965. He had heard that Marketing was negotiating a high volume contract with Magna, another fire alarm manufacturer. Magna allegedly would start producing its own BGP if CED could not offer them delivery of a satisfactory unit in high quantities and at low price by February 1966. Mr Fowler was concerned about this new development: he had originally planned to make use of the BGP in the framework of the expansion programme which would start in March 1966. CED would then take over new space and employees of a neighbouring division and the BGP seemed useful for training some of the new unskilled labour. The wiring skills required for assembly of communication equipment would have to be developed by a training program for the new labour, and the BGP would be a good test for the basic digital skills of operators. In case they did not qualify in the BGP operation, they would not be admitted to the training programme. This would help keep the training cost down. With the original volume forecast of about 3,000 BGP's for the next year, Mr Fowler had expected to test about thirty to forty operators during the first three months of the expansion project, assuming that each operator would be put to BGP assembly for one week.

But with an almost immediate need for 10,000 BGP's and annual volumes of perhaps 30,000 or 50,000, the BGP would interfere with operations rather than help them. In order to produce 10,000 BGP's by February 1966, it would be necessary to set up four lines for assembly. It seemed hardly possible to predict which assembly line might be stopped and dismantled for the BGP operation but it was improbable that it would be one of the few lines employing low skilled labour. Therefore it would be necessary to use twelve operators and four inspectors qualified for complex wiring tasks on the low grade BGP assembly or else try to hire new manpower just for this job. After its completion Mr Fowler could see no way of keeping the additional labour, because forty new men would arrive in March from a neighbouring OEL division.

The equipment on the dismantled line would have to be set aside and separate space might be needed for packaging unless the dismantled area were sufficient for stocking finished units so as to permit packaging at the end of the line. Mr Trenton also pointed out that Production Control would have to reschedule all materials for the shop temporarily.

On the other hand a high volume of BGPs would be a good filler once all the new labour and space were available. It would also present an opportunity for trying out incentive payment schemes because long runs would be possible, though this would be somewhat true even if they worked in batches of 1,000 for annual volumes of less than 8,000. In order to clarify the alternatives for the meeting of 14 October 1965, Mr Fowler outlined the requirements of low volume, high volume, and high volume under a February 1966 deadline (see Exhibit 16).

Exhibit 13 Product development programme fire alarm systems

	Complete drawings	Stock available
1. Break glass push		
(a) Closed circuit indoor and outdoor versions	January 65	July 65
(b) Open circuit indoor and outdoor versions Surface and flush mounting		
2. Automatic detectors.		
(a) Rate of rise thermal detector	March 65	July 65
(b) Ionisation detector with facilities for adding thermal detector to form 'Dual Detector'		
3. Indicator boards		
(a) 10 line radial open circuit system	26/10/64	February 65
(b) 20 line radial open circuit system		

		End Sept.	
(c)	10 line radial loop system	V.A. 3/10	March 65
(d)	10 line frequency loop system	March 65	July 65
(e)	20 line frequency loop system		
(f)	Modernised and redesigned municipal type board. 2–4 loops	26/10/64	May 65

4. Manual fire alarm system

5. Domestic fire alarm system.

Exhibit 14 Three-part letter: Costing of new development

Eng. code	Description	Sales code	Forecast sales this year/next year
P.236	Fire Alarm Break Glass Push		2,000 2,000

Mr C. S. Fowler   Date: 10th February 1965

Will you please let Mr Gibson have a cost estimate for the above new product. Price required at this stage to enable Marketing to assess whether it is economic or proceed further with the development.

The list of information or models which are available to assist in this costing is as follows:

8 prints of drawing P.238, and rough notes, herewith Drawing Sheet 2 of 2.

The development engineer to be contacted for any further information is Mr Simpson.

(R. A. Kean)

Mr G. S. Gibson   Date: 8th March 1965

Our estimate of the cost of the above:

	Cost each	Total tool costs
Material	45p	£750
Loaded, Labour	15p	

Delivery could commence in 4/5 months after receipt of complete manufacturing information.

(C. S. Fowler)

Mr R. A. Kean   Date: 15th March 1965

On the basis of the cost given by Mr Fowler, we consider that the development above will/will not be an economic proposition and development should/should not proceed.

(G. S. Gibson)

Exhibit 15. Parts specification

Title: alarm, manual, fire, break glass

Model	C.S. Closed CCT Surface Mounting (Qty per Unit)	C.F. Closed CCT Flush Mounting (Qty per Unit)	O.S. Open CCT Surface Mounting (Qty per Unit)	O.F. Closed CCT Flush Mounting (Qty per Unit)	Description	Price	Stock of Order Qty	Available
1		1		1	Moulded Flush Box	3·3p each		
2	1		1		Moulded Surface Box	5·1p each		
3	1	1	1	1	Fastener & Spring	4·3p each		
4	1	1	1	1	Cover Moulding (see note 1)	5·5p each		
5	1	1	1	1	Glass	0·5p each		
6			1	1	MicroSwitch 'Open'	11·8p each		
7	1	1			MicroSwitch 'Closed'	11·8p each		
8	2	2	2	2	Terminal	2·5p each		
9	1	1	1	1	Designation Plate (C.E.D.)	1·95p each		
10	2	2	2	2	Screw Fin Nickel 6BA x 1⅛"CH	0·52p/per 100		
11	2	2	2	2	6BA x ⅛" CH (Fin 4003)	5·8p/100		
12	2	2	2	2	Shakeproof Washer (Fin 7133)	2·1p/100		
13	2	2	2	2	6 BA x ¼" CH Screw (Fin 4003)	5·8p/100		
14	2		2		No. 6 x ¾" LGC SK HD Woodscrew (Fin Cad Plate)	12·2p/100		
15		1		1	No. 6 x ¾" LG RD HD Woodscrew (Fin Cad Plate)	13·5p/100		
16	1	1	1	1	W.3 Hexagon Wrench (3/3 across Plate)	0·8p/100		
17	1	1	1	1	Spring & Spring Plate (see note 2)	1·0p/100		
18	1	1	1	1	Packing Carton			

Notes: 1. Assuming order of batches of 8,000 units.
2. Item 17 to be supplied as free issue to Manufacturer of Item 4.

Exhibit 16. Alternative manufacturing plans for break glass push as of 10 October 1965

Alternative (1)
Volume/Delivery requirements: approx. 3000 units in lots
of 1000; First lot   18 March '66
            Second lot   1 April '66
            Third lot   15 April '66

Action-Plan:	*Completion —*	*Date*
Order parts	Finish preparation:	
Method Study	all parts available by	4 March '66
Preparation of fixtures, jigs and tools		
Set up one assembly line for 3 operators		
assemble first lot of 1000 units		
test for dexterity 15 to 18 new operators	1000 units available for stock/delivery on	18 March '66
time study, revise times and methods		
assemble second lot of 1000 units	1000 units available for stock/delivery on	1 April '66
test 15 to 18 new operators		
assemble third lot of 1000 units	1000 units available for stock/delivery on	15 April '66
try out incentive scheme with 3 operators		
time study — evaluation incentive scheme		

Alternative (2)
Volume/Delivery requirements: 10,000 units on 25 January 1966, subsequently
monthly lots of 2,500 units.

Action Plan	*Completion —*	*Date*
rush-order parts		
method study		
preparation of fixtures, jigs and tools		
vacate space for four assembly lines (where?)	finish preparation, all	
hire 12 semi-skilled operators and four inspectors if possible (or take from INTERCOM assembly)	parts available on	27 December '65
assemble 10,000 units	10,000 units available on	
transfer new labour (where to?)		25 January '66

When new space and labour become available (mid February 1966):
Set up one assembly line with 3 operators	lots of 2500 units available monthly starting 11 March 1966.	
Test and train new operators as required.		

Evershine Products Ltd.

On 1 March 1969, the price of Evergloss was raised from $17\frac{1}{2}$p a bottle to $22\frac{1}{2}$p. During the following two years sales fell by nearly a quarter. At $17\frac{1}{2}$p Evergloss had been competitively priced but manufacturers of similar products had not followed the lead of Evergloss and had held their prices stable from 1967 to 1971. In February 1971, the Marketing Manager and the Chief Accountant of Evershine Products Ltd., the manufacturer of Evergloss, met to review the company's policy for the following year.

Evershine Products of King's Lynn, Norfolk, was an old established firm marketing a wide range of domestic cleaning materials. For many years the company had been the leader in the field for a wide range of products catering for the housewife. Prices were fixed once a year to take effect on 1st March before the annual 'Spring Cleaning' demand peak. Although Evershine has a number of competitors, the individual sales of each were small compared with those of Evershine.

Evergloss

Evergloss is a speciality product which in 1970 accounted for nearly 10% of the company's total sales. There are a number of competing products on the market comparable in most respects. However, because of special properties which seem to be unique to the product, Evergloss retains its lustre and shine even in high temperature and humid conditions when competing products rapidly deteriorate.

A highly toxic substance is used in the manufacture of Evergloss. At one time Evergloss was manufactured in the company's main factory building but in 1968 following a factory inspectors adverse comments on the danger to workers health, production was transferred to a new building away from the main plant. The layout of the Evergloss plant is such that it cannot be adapted for the manufacture of other Evershine products. In spite of the toxic nature of the materials used in the manufacturing process, Evergloss itself is harmless.

Shortly after the move to the new building, Mr Augustus John, the Chief Accountant, reviewed Evergloss's pricing policies. He took into account recent increases in the cost of raw materials and labour as well as the re-allocation of overhead costs due to the separation of the Evergloss production line from the company's other products. His calculations showed that the total cost was greater than the current selling price of $17\frac{1}{2}$p. Consequently at the 1969 annual pricing review the selling price was increased to $22\frac{1}{2}$p.

Total industry sales rose in 1969 and 1970 but Evergloss suffered a reduction not only in its market share but also in the volume of sales. (See Exhibit 1.)

Pricing review 1971

In February 1971 Mr John and Mr Gilbert Whiting, the Marketing Manager, met to discuss the pricing policy for the following year. Mr Whiting had been with the company since 1960 and had introduced a number of changes in the firm's marketing methods. A notable success had followed his decision in 1962 to replace wholesalers by a force of salaried company representatives selling the full product range direct to retailers.

Mr Whiting pressed for a return to the price of $17\frac{1}{2}$p a bottle for Evergloss; at this price he was confident the company could raise the Evergloss market share to 25%. He estimated that total industry sales would continue to increase in 1971 to about 1,200 thousand bottles. Because Evershine had a modern production facility and a manufacturing output greater than any rival company he was confident that production costs in the factory were the lowest in the industry. By reducing the price and 'squeezing' other firms he believed that before very long a number of competitors must be forced out of business.

At a price of $22\frac{1}{2}$p Mr Whiting was sure that sales would continue to fall. Nevertheless, he felt there would always be a market for Evergloss because of special properties it possessed and he believed that annual sales were not likely to fall below 125,000 bottles even at the present price.

Mr John replied that he was well aware of the problems being experienced by selling the higher priced product. Nevertheless at $22\frac{1}{2}$p the cost of Evergloss was covered even at the lowest volume of sales envisaged, whereas $17\frac{1}{2}$p was below the cost even if sales volume rose as high as 40,000 bottles. He produced detailed cost analyses to support his argument (see Exhibit 2). These figures, he stated, were based on actual data from past years; where data was not available he had based his calculations on what he regarded as realistic assumptions.

Question: What price would you suggest for Evergloss?

Exhibit 1. Evergloss–sales and prices* 1958-64

	1964	1965	1966	1967	1968	1969	1970
Total industry sales (thousands of bottles)	795	820	900	880	930	1,040	1,160
Evergloss sales (thousands of bottles)	208	222	243	251	261	235	200
Evergloss % of market	26	27	27	29	28	22·5	17·2
Evergloss price	15p	17p	17p	$17\frac{1}{2}$p	$17\frac{1}{2}$p	$22\frac{1}{2}$p	$22\frac{1}{2}$p
Competitors' prices	$14\frac{1}{2}$p– $15\frac{1}{2}$p	16p– 17p	16p– 17p	17p– $17\frac{1}{2}$p	17p– $17\frac{1}{2}$p	17p– $18\frac{1}{2}$p	17p– $18\frac{1}{2}$p

Exhibit 2. Estimated costs of Evergloss at varying volumes of production

Cost in pence/bottle	Annual production in thousand bottles						
	125	150	200	250	300	350	400
Direct labour	4·30	4·30	4·25	4·15	4·30	4·36	4·45
Material	2·10	2·10	2·10	2·10	2·10	2·10	2·10
Departmental overhead							
variable	2·20	2·20	2·15	2·10	2·10	2·10	2·10
fixed	3·35	2·77	2·08	1·68	1·39	1·19	1·04
Factory overhead at 25% of direct labour	1·08	1·10	1·06	1·04	1·08	1·09	1·12
Factory cost	13·03	12·47	11·64	11·07	10·99	10·84	10·81
Selling and administration cost at 70% of factory cost	9·12	8·63	8·15	7·75	7·68	7·59	7·56
Total cost	22·15	21·10	19·79	18·82	18·65	18·43	18·37

* Converted to British decimal currency equivalents for data pre-1971.

Case 15

The Midland Hosiery Manufacturing Company Ltd. (MHM)

In the Spring of 1964, Mr Albert Jay, the Chairman of the Albert Jay Group of Companies was examining the cost structure of stocking production at the Midland Hosiery Manufacturing Company, a knitwear and hosiery manufacturer and a member of the Albert Jay Group of Companies. He realised that the company must reduce costs for producing stockings if it were to remain in business in the face of severe Italian competition.

The Albert Jay Group consisted of a marketing organisation and eight manufacturing companies, and had grown from a small wholesaling firm into the present-day group of companies with an annual turnover of £3·5 million. Mr Albert Jay, although in his sixties, still took a lively interest in the management of the Group and was active in most policy decisions. The Chairman's attitude towards MHM was summed up by his statement: 'We are in the women's hosiery business to stay. We may not be making money in this business at present but some day the pendulum will swing the other way. The first function of a business is to survive. That is what we have to do now. The hosiery business is the only unprofitable section of the Group.'

Mr Jay described the United Kingdom hosiery industry as follows: 'There are seven large companies which produce advertised brands of stockings. Their products do not cost substantially more than ours to produce, but sell for two to three shillings (10-15p)[1] a pair more at the retail level. Then there are four other smaller companies of about our size which produce good middle-quality stockings. These companies have national distribution but do almost no advertising. Our company sells to chain stores and to small retailers through our own sales force, but we do not spend much on advertising our brand name. In addition to these companies there is a large number of small producers who sell primarily on price as opposed to brand-name or quality. It is manufacturers from this group that are at present going out of business due to the low price prevailing in the UK market.'

1. *Note*: For ease of computation all financial data has been converted to British decimal currency.

The MHM machinery

MHM began manufacturing hosiery in 1931 and was an early producer of seamless hosiery in Great Britain. The company purchased most of its hosiery knitting machinery before the Second World War. This machinery consisted almost entirely of seamless stocking equipment. A seamless stocking knitting machine was a small, rather complicated machine which automatically took yarn from spools and knitted a tube. The tube, which was eventually to become the stocking, was produced with a reinforced section for the heel and a finished end at the top. After the knitting machine, the tube was inspected and sent to a heat-treating machine where it was treated to prevent damage during handling. The toe was then closed up and the stocking sent to the dyers where it was coloured and shaped, and after another inspection, packaged (see Exhibit 1).

The knitting machines were arranged in banks in the plant. A bank consisted of a number of machines which one man (a knitter) would attend. The knitter was responsible for loading the yarn into the machines (each machine held enough yarn for about twenty-four hours of operation), for making minor repairs and adjustments to the machines, and for collecting and inspecting the stockings as they came out of the machines.

In the Spring of 1944, the plant had 187 single-feed and eighty-eight two-feed seamless machines, producing about 5,000 dozen stocking per week. The number of feeds indicates the number of spools of yarn feeding into the machine and, for similar types of machines, was roughly proportional to the output of the machine. The machine arrangements in the plant are shown in Exhibit 2. Normally the single feed machines were worked for only one shift whereas the two feed machines were operated round the clock for three shifts.

Development of the present competitive position

Following the Second World War, when the most popular style was fully-fashioned hosiery (hosiery with a seam in the back) MHM produced seamless stockings and added a false seam at the end of the knitting process in order to utilise its machinery to meet the demand for fully-fashioned hosiery. As demand grew, the company added some fully-fashioned knitting machines.

In 1958-59, however, there was a sudden change in the style of women's stockings. The seamless stocking became almost overnight the only style acceptable to women. With the sudden change in fashion MHM found itself in a good position to supply the market. It was one of the few companies with seamless hosiery producing equipment. The company's profits in the period immediately after the fashion shift were very high since competitors were unable to get immediate delivery of seamless producing machinery. Machine producers in the United Kingdom were at that time quoting delivery times of two years because their production was committed to the export markets where the fashion shift to seamless stockings had occurred earlier.

By 1962, however, British competitors had obtained new seamless equipment and the capacity of the industry had reached about double the demand, according to MHM's estimates. The competitors had purchased new machinery which was much faster and more economical to operate than MHM's older seamless equipment. However MHM was still able to sell all its output.

In the Autumn of 1962, during the ordering period for the Christmas rush. Italian-made stockings began to come into the country. The United Kingdom tariff on Italian stockings was 50p per dozen. By Autumn 1963, even after tariff payments, Italian stockings were being offered to the retailer at $117\frac{1}{2}$p per dozen to be sold at retail for $14\frac{1}{2}$p per pair. MHM estimated its total factory cost at 130p per dozen even for the cheapest grade of stocking. MHM executives, therefore, in concert with other stocking manufacturers considered that the Italians were 'dumping' their excess stockings at an uneconomic price and they could not continue for long to sell at this 'knock-down' price. (See Exhibit 3 for breakdown of price.) However, as a result of the over-capacity in the industry and the influx of Italian stockings the prices of stockings fell to the levels shown in Exhibit 3.

Mr Jay concluded that total overhead expenses could not be substantially reduced and that little could be done in the way of reducing raw material costs. Consequently he thought the only answer to be a reduction of direct labour costs through purchasing faster action machinery and at the same time persuading the unions to change their existing attitude to what was considered an acceptable work load.

Union negotiations

In the Summer of 1964, under the threat of lost jobs as a result of competition from cheap Italian imports, the labour union agreed to the new work rules shown in Exhibit 4. Company negotiators had secured an unofficial agreement to perform work loads as shown in this Exhibit. The Union, however, demanded a severance pay for any knitters laid off by modernisation or by increased work loads. The demands for severance pay were for one week's salary at the highest rate the worker had received during his employment with the company times his total number of years with the company. Mr Jay hoped that this demand could be reduced. If the worker were retained, he could be put on another job but must receive pay at the old rate if it were higher than the rate for the new job. The knitters, who were the workers who would be made redundant by the new machinery and new rules, were the highest paid workers in the plant (average wage £22 per week). Their average time with the company was twelve years.

Mr Sutton's investigation

Mr Jay thought that labour costs under these new work arrangements and with the availability of faster multi-feed machines, might be substantially reduced. He therefore assigned his assistant, Mr David Sutton, a student at a well-known

Midlands management school, the task of investigating the purchase of new machinery.

Mr Sutton found that possible choices were limited to the machines described in Exhibit 5. He discovered that the company was paying approximately 50% tax on profits. Divisions other than the stocking division were profitable and losses in one division could be written off against profits in another. The cash position of the Group was very good.

Capital allowances on new machinery (both of British and foreign manufacture) which could be set against taxes were as follows:

Investment allowance   30%
Initial allowance   10%
Annual allowances   15%

For internal calculations, the machinery would be depreciated by the straight-line method over five years. The equipment was considered to have a life of ten years, although new developments could make the machines obsolete much sooner, often within five years. An example of the taxation allowances on a new hosiery machine is shown in Exhibit 6.

Mr Sutton also found that a bank of machines could be manned in a variety of different ways:

1. By the existing method each machine dropped the finished stockings into a bucket underneath. The knitters would then collect the stockings and examine them.
2. An alternative would be to have an examiner-collector (average wage £20 per week) for each bank who would collect and examine the stocking output, thus relieving the knitter of these tasks.
3. A further variation would be to have a collector (£10 per week) collect the buckets for 300 machines and bring them to examiners (£18 per week), each of whom could examine the output of one bank.
4. Another method would be to install a 'downstream' type system. The machines would then feed directly into a vacuum system which moved the stockings to an examining point at the end of the bank. The system cost about £2,000 for each bank and would last about five years. An examiner (£18 per week) could examine the output of the bank.

Exhibit 4 gives the maximum number of machines a knitter was expected to operate under each system and his wages. There was sufficient space available in the existing plant for the installation of any of these arrangements, or for adding more machines.

Mr Jay was willing to assume, as a first approximation of costs and savings, that the overhead figure of £68,000 per year for the plant would not change, except for the added depreciation. Overheads consisted of:

Needles: Consumption would probably be slightly reduced with the new machines.
Power: No significant change expected.

Repairs and conversions: The number of mechanics could probably not be reduced, although their work load would be lighter with new machines.

Staff

Depreciation

Telephones, etc.

The old seamless machines could not be converted for other uses and had almost no scrap value. Their book value is shown in Exhibit 7.

Discussion with Mr Jay indicated that a return on new investments of 10% after taxes would meet the company's requirements for the use of capital.

Mr Sutton's recommendations

In a brief report Mr Sutton suggested that the company should purchase twenty four-feed Bentley Knitting Machines for £30,000, a down-stream system for £2,000, scrap all 187 single feed machines, and retain the eighty-eight two-feed machines.

His calculations are summarised in Exhibit 8 and indicated a potential labour cost reduction from $17\frac{1}{2}$p to 11p per dozen pairs of stockings. Mr Sutton accepted the majority opinion of MHM executives that the American S & W machine was unsuitable as it produced a patch heel.

Exhibit 1. Production flow for hosiery

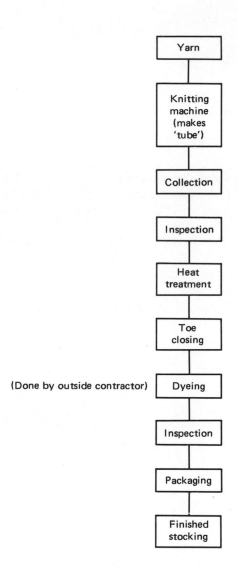

Exhibit 2. Hosiery plant arrangements—Spring 1964

Single-feed machines	*Total machines*
8 Banks of 16 Machines	128
3 Banks of 15 Machines	45
1 Bank of 14 Machines	14
Total machines	187

Knitting time	= 15 minutes per stocking
Maximum output per machine per week	= 20 dozen pairs (assuming 3 shifts)
	(= 3740 dozen pairs)
Normal output per week	= 1250 dozen (1 shift only)

Double-feed machines	
3 Banks of 16 Machines	48
1 Bank of 14 Machines	14
2 Banks of 13 Machines	26
Total Machines	88

Knitting time	= 8 minutes per stocking
Maximum output per machine per week	= 37 dozen pairs (assuming 3 shifts)
	(= 3,256 dozen pairs)
Normal output per week	= 3,256 dozen (3 shifts)

Summary

	Total machines	Maximum (three shifts)		Normal working (Single-1 shift) (Double-3 shifts)	
		Operators	Output/wk (dozen prs)	Operators	Output/wk (dozen prs)
Single feed	187	36	3,740	12	1,250
Two feed	88	18	3,256	18	3,256
	275	54	6,996	30	4,506

Exhibit 3. Prices and costs† of stocking–spring 1964

Type of stocking	*Retail price* *per pair*	*Price to retailer* *per doz. pairs*	*Price ex-factory (i.e. price to whole-salers)* *per doz. prs.*	*MHM's factory* **cost/* *doz. prs.*	*% of MHM's sales*
Advertised brands	34½p 29½p	£2·77½ £2·40	£2·25 £1·97½		
MHM's stockings	24½p 19½p 14½p	£1·37½ – £1·52½ £1·62½ £1·40	£1·47½ £1·40 £1·20	£1·42½ £1·37½ £1·30	40 50 10
Italian stockings	14½p	£1·17½	£1·10 (inc. import duty of 50p)		

* Mr Sutton estimated costs for the mix (at present volume and with previous labour arrangements) as follows:

Yarn	36p	42½p	47½p
Labour (toe closing and mending)	10p	11p	11p
	46p	53½p	58½p
Labour (knitting and examining	15½p	15½p	15½p
Finishing (sub-contracted)	41p	41p	41p
Overheads (based on 5000 doz. prs. per wk)	27½p	27½p	27½p
Total cost	£1·30	£1·37½	£1·42½

† Converted to decimal currency.

Exhibit 4. Union agreements on workloads and wages

Old agreement		New official agreement (Summer 1964)		New unofficial union agreement (Summer 1964)	
Number of feeds on machine	Number of machines allowed per operator	Number of feeds on machine	Number of machines allowed per operator	Number of feeds on machine	Number of machines allowed per operator
1	16	1	60	1	60
2	16	2	40	2	40
		4	30	4	40
		6	20	6	30
		8	20	8	20

Wages = £22 per week for a knitter who collects and examines.	Allowed only with 'down stream' collection system (cost = £2,000 for each bank). Wages = £27 per week for a knitting worker and £18 per week for an examiner for each bank (No collector)	Allowed with bucket collection, (a) by an unskilled examining collector, or (b) by a collector who brings the stockings to the examiner. Wages = £30 per week for knitter and (a) Wages £20 per week for an examiner-collector—one required for each bank of machines. or (b) Wages £18 for an examiner—one required for each bank. Wages £10 for a collector who collects for 300 machines.

Exhibit 5. New knitting machines available

Number of feeds	Machine makes	Price	Output-dozen of pairs per 24 hours per machine	Other factors
4	Zodiac (Italian)	£1,464	15	Six months delivery time; believed difficult to obtain spare parts; one machine tested and found to be not very reliable.
6	Maxima (Italian)	£1,500	25–30	Six months delivery time; no test machine available, but a machine in another Leicester plant was rumoured to be having considerable troubles. Sample stockings from Maxima machine showed defects, and in the opinion of MHM executives and store buyers were unsaleable.
4	Uniplet J4Dc34 (Czech)	No quote available	15	MHM could find nobody with experience of this machine.
4	Lonati (Italian)	£1,400	20	Output of 15 with conventional heel; not sure if could sell type of heel produced with higher output. Experience with Lonati twin-feed showed them to be unreliable.
6	Sawo (Italian)	£1,400	30	Test machine worked well. Requires more yarn, adding $1\frac{1}{4}$p per dozen to cost of stockings.
4	Bentley (English)	£1,500	20–22	Bentley factory one mile from MHM plant; service quickly available; delivery from five months. Test machine satisfactory.
8	S. & W. (USA)	£2,200	80	Produced a patch heel which executives thought could not be sold in UK.

Exhibit 6. Example of capital allowances (for taxation purposes) on new hosiery machines

			Cost	Taxation allowance
		£	£	£
Purchase cost			1,000	
Year I Investment allowance 30%		300		300
		—		
Initial allowance	10%	100		100
Annual allowance	15%	150	250	150
		—	—	—
			750	550 Year I
Year II Annual allowance	15%		112	112 Year II
			—	—
			638	
Year III Annual allowance	15%		96	96 Year III
			—	—
			542	
Year IV Annual allowance	15%		81	81 Year IV
			—	—
			461	
Year V Annual allowance	15%		69	69
			—	
			392	
Year V Balancing allowance if machine is scrapped			392	392
			—	—
			–	461 Year V
			—	—

Note			*Gross*	*Tax shield (@ 50%)*
1. Summary of allowances	Year I:		£550	£275
	Year II:		112	56
	Year III:		96	48
	Year IV:		81	40
	Year V:		461	231
			£1,300	£650

2. Under tax regulations the investment allowance is not deducted from the resulting balance. Company is therefore credited with a £1,300 allowance for a £1,000 investment.

Exhibit 7. Purchase price and book value of machines in use in spring 1964

Number of feeds	Machine makes	Number of machines	Total purchase price £	Total book value £
2	Bentley	32	31,334	26,239
2	Lonati	114	16,207	5,118
2	Lonati	14	16,587	11,635
2	Lonati	28	36,926	32,126
1	Brayson	2	NA*	40
1	S. & W.	6	NA*	203
1	S. & W.	4	NA	108
1	Various	175	NA	175
		275		£75,644

* NA = Not Available.

Exhibit 8. Summary of calculations in Mr Sutton's report of July 1964

1. Machines
Scrap the 187 single-feed machines and install 20 four-feed machines, keeping the 88 two-feed machines.

2. Arrangements
Arrange the machines as follows: (all on 3 shifts, 5 day week—assume working five × $7\frac{1}{2}$ hours shift).

> *Two-feed machines:*
> 2 banks of 40 machines
> Knitting time = 8 minutes per stocking
> Output   = 2,960 dozen per week

> *Four-feed machines:*
> 1 bank of 20 machines with a downstream collection system.
> Output at $3\frac{1}{4}$ minutes per stocking = 1,800 dozen per week.
> Total proposed output 1,800 + 2,960 = 4,760 per week.

3. Cost saving
Weekly labour cost of present machines   :
18 banks of machines, 18 knitters serving as knitters, collectors and examiners.

Cost of knitters: £22 × 30 knitters	= £660 per week
Output per week = 4506 dozen pairs	
Labour cost per dozen pairs for knitting, collection and inspection	= $14\frac{1}{2}$p

Weekly labour cost under proposed system
3 banks of machines, 9 knitters.

Cost 9 knitters at £27 per week	= £243
Cost 9 examiners at £18 per week	= £162
Cost 1 collector at £10 per week	= £ 10
Total cost of labour for knitting, collection and inspection	= £415
Output per week	= 4760 dozen pairs

Labour cost per dozen pairs for knitting,
collection and inspection $= 8\frac{1}{2}p$

Extra depreciation: calculated as straight line after first year's allowances of 55% times tax rate of $53\frac{1}{2}\%$ (i.e. standard rate of $38\frac{1}{2}\%$ plus excess profits tax of 15%).

$$\frac{20 \text{ machines} \times £1,060/\text{machine} + £1,410 \text{ (for downstream system)}}{5 \text{ years}}$$

$= 1\cdot8p/\text{dozen (assume 2p/dozen)}$

∴ Labour savings less depreciation $= 4p$

$=$ savings per dozen stockings.

Nocrode Limited

The Board of Directors of Nocrode Limited met in January 1965 to decide how the Company's planned expansion programme could best be financed. During the latter part of 1964 the company had received a number of large orders for equipment to be installed in new chemical plants. These orders had been placed by the main contractors, members of a consortium, which had recently won several large contracts in the face of severe competition for the construction of new chemical plants in the United Kindgom and Overseas. Delivery to a strict schedule was required in the period 1966-68 and severe penalty clauses would be invoked if the dates specified were not met. In view of this influx of new orders it was necessary to expand production capacity as a matter of urgency. This was to be achieved by the construction of a new factory, costing £2·5m. to build and equip, which would be available for occupation in February 1966.

Background

The company, under the name Steam Products Ltd., started life in 1876 as a small machine shop manufacturing precision components for steam engines. During the next seventy-years the company had steadily expanded and by the outbreak of the Second World War was making a wide range of pumps, glands, valves and other accessories used in steam engines and heating installations. Parts for steam locomotives accounted for 70% of production in 1938. During the war the firm was awarded a Defence Research Contract to develop a range of components for use in plants manufacturing nuclear materials. This activity proved highly successful, largely due to the efforts of a small team of research scientists engaged specially for the project. At the end of the war it was decided not to disband this team and the research facilities were expanded to concentrate on the development of a range of equipment with a high resistance to corrosion from chemicals. Manufacture and sales of the first designs began in 1948.

A short period of high demand immediately after the war was followed by a steady decline in the market for steam equipment as railways throughout the world converted to diesel or electrically powered locomotives. As early as 1950 it was becoming apparent that the traditional markets for Steam Products Ltd. were shrinking and that a new range of products would be needed if the company was to survive. Therefore, increasing attention was paid to the needs of the chemical industry and in particular for equipment required to operate in a corrosive environment. By 1950 this side of the business was already beginning to show a small profit and two years later the company decided to concentrate all future new activities in that field. In 1956 there was an extensive re-organisation of the company, the building of a new factory was authorised and the change of product emphasis recognised by changing the name to Nocrode Ltd.

The period 1956-64 was one of steady growth apart from a temporary setback in 1960-61 due largely to a reduction of new capital projects initiated during the recession of 1957-58. By 1964 the value of sales was almost three times the 1956 level, steam equipment sales had declined to almost nothing and Nocrode had established itself as a leading supplier of equipment to the chemical industry. In early 1965 there was every prospect that Nocrode sales would continue to rise at a high rate over the next few years, particularly now that the company had begun to obtain substantial orders from chemical plant construction companies. It was estimated that sales would exceed £6·5m. in 1965 and would probably be as high as £7m. in 1966.

Steam Products Ltd. had been a private company owned by the Bennett family until 1937. Mr Josiah Bennett, father of the present Chairman and Managing Director, and his family maintained a controlling interest until his death in 1956. In recent years the family had progressively sold its shareholdings and by 1965 the total Bennett interest amounted to only 15% of the shares, just over half of these belonging to Mr Algernon Bennett, the present Managing Director.

Financial policy

It had always been the policy of the company to finance expansion as far as possible from internally generated funds, supplemented on rare occasions by a bank overdraft when additional working capital was needed. Although dividends had been progressively increased over the last ten years as earnings grew (with the exception of 1959 and 1960 when profits fell) it was company policy to restrict them to a third of the net profit in order to retain sufficient earnings to finance expansion. An exception to the rule of self-financing was made in 1956 when capital was raised for the construction of the new factory; on that occasion the ordinary share capital was increased 50% by means of a 'rights' issue to ordinary shareholders. There had been considerable argument amongst the members of the Board of Directors at the time both as regards the terms of the rights issue and the timing, particularly since the main expenditure was not due to be paid until nearly eighteen months later. Mr Bennett, the Managing Director expressed the majority view in the following words, 'In the forty years I've been with this company we have always had the money in the bank to pay all its bills. I'm not going to sign a contract for this new factory unless I am sure we shall have enough money to pay for it'. The funds for all subsequent expansion had come from retained profits and depreciation allowances.

Early in 1964 a plan had been drawn up for a further phased increase in productive capacity to be financed from internally generated funds.

However, the unexpected increase in orders received in the second half of 1964, necessitated a reappraisal of these plans. It was then decided to reduce the scope of the extension to existing buildings and to build an entirely new factory. Nevertheless re-equipment costs in the existing factories were estimated at £700,000 in 1965 and £750,000 in 1966; these expenditures were expected to be spread evenly throughout the year. The cost of the new factory was estimated to be £2·5m. a sum of money which could not be raised without additional long term finance. It was a bad time for any firm seeking new capital. Following a year of economic uncertainty, a Labour Government had been elected for the first time in thirteen years in the General Election of October 1964. Shortly afterwards the Bank Rate was raised to 7% and there seemed every prospect of an extended 'credit squeeze'. Not only did the credit squeeze make it virtually impossible to obtain a bank loan, it also made the cost of obtaining long term capital very high.

Board of Directors meeting—15 January 1965

On 15th January, 1965, the Board of Directors met to discuss the financing of the expansion programme. Mr Towers, the Financial Director, was able to present the Preliminary Balance Sheet for the year ended 31 December, 1964 (Exhibit 1), to together with ten year statistical summaries for the Balance Sheet (Exhibit 2), Income and Dividends (Exhibit 3) and Share Price and Yield Data (Exhibit 4). These showed a continued upwards trend of both sales and profits. He did, however, sound a word of warning for the immediate future, for although orders were continuing to be received at an increasing rate, profit margins were falling as competition grew; this was particularly true of large orders for new chemical plants. In considering the provision of new long term capital Mr Towers told the Board that two questions need to be answered:

1. How much capital must be raised?
2. What is the cheapest way of raising it?

Turning to the first question he said he felt that the amount of money it was intended to raise should be kept to a minimum consistent with providing enough capital to meet the company's known commitments. He would also like to see the company's liquidity ratio improve from its present value of 0 . 9:1 to nearer 1:1. Retained earnings would, of course, continue to provide a source of funds for investment, though obviously inadequate for Nocrode's immediate needs. Mr Towers did not rule out the possibility of obtaining assistance from the bank. Past experience had shown him that after the first impact of a credit squeeze a slow relaxation took place about six months later. Mr Towers considered himself justified in assuming that some short term assistance would be forthcoming if the company was temporarily short of working capital in a year's time. He estimated that of the £2·5m. required, £0·5m. would be payable in the first half of 1965, £1m. in the second half of 1965 and the remainder during the first half of 1966.

At this point Mr Bennett interjected, 'We must be careful not to try to be too clever. We all know how Mr Towers likes to walk a financial tightrope. I'm against any proposal to finance any part of an expansion to which we are committed from profits we have not yet earned and bank loans we may not obtain. If we know we need £2·5m. then we should be sure the cash is available before we proceed with our plans. That's the way we have always run this business and we have never yet been in serious financial difficulties'. Mr Towers replied that they should not forget that the cost of raising new capital was high, particularly at the present time. It was most important that they should agree on a figure for the capital to be raised from outside sources since it had a direct bearing on the choice of the most economical way of raising capital. The anticipated level of profits must also be taken into account since this also influenced the choice as he would show later. He would now like to examine this aspect further.

Mr Towers explained that he had considered three alternative sources of long term capital; preference shares, debentures and ordinary shares. Preference shares he had rejected because of tax uncertainties; in addition, preliminary analysis of the proposed Corporation Tax the Governement was intending to introduce in the next Finance Bill indicated that payments on preference shares would bear both Corporation and Income Tax. On the other hand, debenture interest could be charged to profits before Corporation Tax was applied. He proposed, therefore, that they should confine the examination to the relative merits of a debenture or a 'rights' issue of ordinary shares. He had worked out some figures (Exhibit 5) showing the net profit available per ordinary share under a variety of circumstances. Current rates of taxation had been used in these calculations. He had also tried to assess the effect of Corporation Tax, but so far as he could see, it would have no significant influence on the relative merits of a debenture or a rights issue. He was pleased to note that because of the high proportion of profits which the company retained in the business, Nocrode's total tax bill was to be smaller than under the existing system of tax assessment.

At that time a debenture issue would bear an interest rate of at least 7%. Mr Towers knew that the price of a 'rights' issue would have to be fixed in relation to what the stock market would bear. A high price was desirable, but he realised that if it were too high the share offer would not be taken up by shareholders. Stock Market prices were declining as could be seen from the price movement of Nocrode shares over the last six months (Exhibit 6). No direct comparison could be made with firms making the same products, but compared with companies making similar products, the stock market rating of Nocrode Shares was good (Exhibit 7). Mr Towers concluded his statement to the Board by saying that conditions could well change before the date of announcement of the terms of an issue. The meeting should not, therefore, come to a definite decision on the terms, but should establish criteria to enable a rapid decision to be made immediately before they were to be made public.

Mr Bennett thanked Mr Towers for his remarks and helpful financial statements. 'They look very impressive, but I am opposed to a "rights" offer whatever you may say. I remember the discussion we had in 1955 before the last issue. This was, of course, before you joined the company, and we did not do all the calculations for ourselves then; we relied upon the advice of our Merchant Bankers. They recommended a rights issue at 5/- and within six months these shares were worth 6/3. That's an increase of £½m. in the share value and we didn't get a penny of it. I would much prefer to borrow the money rather than raise it through a sale of equity. If the banks won't let us have it then I suppose a debenture issue is the next best thing; at least we shall be paying back our borrowings over twenty years'.

'I don't agree with you', said Mr Simmons, the Marketing Director, 'what happens if our plans don't work out as well as we expect? We should have to pay our debenture interest in any case, so there may be little money left for ordinary dividends. On the other hand if we increase the equity our dividends might be cut but at least we wouldn't be saddled with the necessity for meeting debt payments. A stockbroker friend told me recently that there is a certain share price for every level of earnings below which the cost of equity becomes more than the cost of the debt. I feel that if the Board can agree on this figure the alternatives of an equity or a debenture issue could easily be decided upon right up to the moment when the offer is made. I was also told that it was necessary to make a "rights" issue at a discount on the current market price in order to attract support. I see in this morning's newspapers that the Zeta Company has announced a rights issue at 17/6 for its ordinary shares which were quoted at 19/2 on the Stock Exchange yesterday. This is another factor we shall have to take into account when making our decision'.

Exhibit 1. Preliminary balance sheet—as at 31 December 1964

			£
Capital employed			
Owners equity:			
Ordinary shares (5/-)	authorised	20,000,000 shares	
	issued	16,000,000 shares	
			4,000,000
Capital reserve			250,000
Revenue reserve			3,261,223
Future taxation			620,000
			8,131,223
Employment of capital			
Fixed assets:			
Property — at cost			585,231
Plant and equipment—at cost	9,833,279		
less depreciation	4,359,826		5,473,453
Goodwill, patents and trade marks			432,222
			6,490,906
Current assets:			
Stocks	1,825,036		
Debtors	1,232,111		
Cash and short-term investments	642,403		
	3,699,550		
Less current liabilities:			
Creditors	1,263,121		
Current taxation	596,112		
Proposed final dividend less income tax	200,000		
	2,059,233		
Working Capital			1,640,317

Exhibit 2. Ten-year statistical summary—balance sheet 1955-64 (£X000)

	1964	1963	1962 *	1961	1960	1959	1958	1957	1956 †	1955
Capital employed										
Ordinary share capital	4,000	4,000	4,000	3,000	3,000	3,000	3,000	3,000	3,000	2,000
Capital reserve	250	250	225	225	200	150	125	100	100	100
Revenue reserve	3,261	2,840	2,468	3,159	2,976	2,959	2,936	2,705	2,531	2,627
	7,511	7,090	6,693	6,384	6,176	6,109	6,061	5,805	5,631	4,727
Future taxation	620	600	510	450	180	120	250	250	175	150
	8,131	7,690	7,203	6,834	6,356	6,229	6,311	6,055	5,806	4,877
Employment of capital										
Tangible fixed assets	6,059	5,860	5,813	5,333	5,043	4,494	4,166	3,259	2,941	2,830
Goodwill, patents etc.	432	432	432	404	404	404	404	404	404	404
Working capital	1,640	1,398	958	1,097	909	1,331	1,741	2,392	2,461	1,633
	8,131	7,690	7,203	6,834	6,356	6,229	6,311	6,055	5,806	4,867
Expenditure on fixed assets	1,020	821	1,273	1,016	1,235	992	1,473	762	507	234

* Scrip issue of 1 share for 3 held on 31 March 1962.
† Rights issue of 4,000,000 shares at 5/- a share.

Exhibit 3. Ten-year statistical summary-revenue, expenses, profits and dividends 1955-64 (£X000)

	1964	1963	1962	1961	1960	1959	1958	1957	1956	1955
Sales	6,101	5,850	5,306	4,208	3,428	3,206	3,879	3,042	2,304	2,226
Expenses: materials	826	792	719	569	414	386	466	362	275	265
Wages, salaries	1,163	1,159	1,051	832	732	685	826	642	487	470
Manufacturing	1,433	1,383	1,263	1,002	892	871	932	725	551	532
Admin. sales	627	621	565	513	417	409	416	323	248	242
Depreciation	821	794	793	726	686	614	566	444	396	390
	4,870	4,749	4,391	3,642	3,141	2,965	3,206	2,496	1,957	1,899
Net profit before tax	1,231	1,101	915	566	287	241	673	546	347	327
Taxation	596	504	446	238	130	103	317	252	153	148
	635	597	469	328	157	138	356	294	194	179
Ordinary dividends: Amount	200	200	160	120	90	90	120	120	90	60
Percentage	5	5	4*	4	3	3	4	4	3†	3

* Paid on capital increased by 1 for 3 scrip issue.
† Paid on capital increased by 1 for 2 rights issue.

Exhibit 4. Ten-year statistical summary–share price, dividend and yield–1955/64

Year	Share price				Dividend data based on share price on 31st December		
	Years High	Years Low	Dec. 31st	Rate %	Gross Yield %	Div. Yield %	X covered
1955	5/3	3/5	3/6	3	12·8	4·3	2·98
1956[1]	6/4	3/6	5/10	3[2]	5·6	2·6	2·15
1957	5/2	4/-	4/6	4	10·8	4·4	2·45
1958	5/3	4/2	5/-	4	11·8	4·0	2·96
1959	4/8	2/3	2/6	3	9·3	6·0	1·53
1960	3/9	2/-	2/9	3	9·7	5·5	1·74
1961	3/8	2/6	3/6	4	15·6	5·7	2·73
1962	6/2	3/5	5/6	4[3]	10·9	3·7	2·94
1963	6/10	5/-	6/3	5	11·9	4·0	2·98
1964	7/8	6/-	6/-	5	13·3	4·2	3·17

1. Rights issue of 4,000,000 Ordinary Shares at 5/- per share on basis of 1 share for every 2 held on 31 March 1956. Quoted price at time of announcement 5/9d.

2. On capital increased by 1956 rights issue.

3. On capital increased by 1 for 3 scrip issue 31 March 1962.

Exhibit 5. Debenture and rights issue comparative figures

A. *Long-term capital to be raised–£1·5m.*

Alternative methods

(a) £1,500,000 7% Debentures redeemable in 20 years
(b) 7,500,000 Ordinary Shares at 4/- making total shares issued 23½m.
(c) 6,000,000 Ordinary Shares at 5/- making total shares issued 22m.
(d) 5,450,000 Ordinary Shares at 5/6 making total shares issued 21·45m.
(e) 5,000,000 Ordinary Shares at 6/- making total shares issued 21m.
(f) 4,280,000 Ordinary Shares at 7/- making total shares issued 20·28m.

Debenture issue (£X000)

Net profit before tax and debenture charges	750	1,000	1,500	2,000
Debenture interest	105	105	105	105
Net profit before tax	645	895	1,395	1,895
*Tax at 45%	290	398	627	845
Net profit after tax	355	497	768	1,041
Sinking fund	75	75	75	75
Income attributable to ordinary shares (16m)	280	422	693	966
Income attributable per ordinary share (pence/share)	4·20	6·33	10·4	14·5

Ordinary share issue (£X000)

Net profit before tax	750	1,000	1,500	2,000
*Tax at 45%	336	450	675	900
Net profit after tax	414	550	825	1,100

* The tax charge of 45% is an average figure after taking into account investment allowances.

Exhibit 5—*continued.*

Income attributable per ordinary share
  (pence/ord.) if rights issue

at 4/-	4·22	5·61	8·44	11·26
5/-	4·50	6·00	9·00	12·00
5/6	4·63	6·14	9·21	12·31
6/-	4·73	6·24	9·41	12·60
7/-	4·89	6·45	9·69	13·10

B. *Long-term capital to be raised—£2m.*

Alternative methods
(*a*) £2,000,000 7% Debentures redeemable in 20 years
(*b*) 10,000,000 Ordinary Shares at 4/- making total shares issued 26m.
(*c*) 8,000,000 Ordinary Shares at 5/- making total shares issued 24m.
(*d*) 7,270,000 Ordinary Shares at 5/6 making total shares issued 23·27m.
(*e*) 6,670,000 Ordinary Shares at 6/- making total shares issued 22·67m.
(*f*) 5,700,000 Ordinary Shares at 7/- making total shares issued 21·7m.

Debenture issue (£X000)

Net profit before tax and debenture charges	750	1,000	1,500	2,000
Debenture interest	140	140	140	140
Net profit before tax	610	860	1,360	1,860
*Tax at 45%	274	387	612	838
Net profit after tax	336	473	748	1,022
Sinking fund	100	100	100	100
Income attributable to ordinary shares (16m)	236	373	648	922
Income attributable per ordinary share (pence/share)	3·52	5·59	9·72	14·7

Ordinary share issue (£X000)

Net profit before tax	750	1,000	1,500	2,000
*Tax at 45%	336	450	675	900
Net profit after tax	414	550	825	1,100

Income attributable per ordinary share if
  rights issue

—pence/share 4/-	3·81	5·08	7·62	10·1
5/-	4·15	5·49	8·25	11·0
5/6	4·26	5·65	8·49	11·3
6/-	4·38	5·81	8·82	11·8
7/-	4·58	6·20	9·21	12·2

* The tax charge of 45% is an average figure after taking into account investment allowances.

Exhibit 5–*continued.*

C. *Long-term capital to be raised–£2·5m.*

Alternative methods
(a) £2,500,000 7% Debentures redeemable in 20 years.
(b) 12,500,000 Ordinary Shares at 4/- making total shares issued 28·5m.
(c) 10,000,000 Ordinary Shares at 5/- making total shares issued 26m.
(d) 9,100,000 Ordinary Shares at 5/6 making total shares issued 25·1m.
(e) 8,330,000 Ordinary Shares at 6/- making total shares issued 24·33m.
(f) 7,120,000 Ordinary Shares at 7/- making total shares issued 23·12m.

Debenture issue (£X000)

Net profit before tax and debenture charges	750	1,000	1,500	2,000
Debenture interest	175	175	175	175
Net profit before tax	575	825	1,325	1,825
*Tax at 45%	259	371	597	822
Net profit after tax	316	454	728	1,003
Sinking fund	125	125	125	125
Income attributable to ordinary shares (16m)	191	329	603	878
Income attributable per ordinary share (pence/share)	2·69	4·94	9·06	13·20

Ordinary share issue (£X000)

Net profit before tax	750	1,000	1,500	2,000
*Tax at 45%	336	450	675	900
Net profit after tax	414	550	825	1,100
Income attributable per ordinary share if rights issue–pence/share				
at 4/-	3·48	4·64	6·96	9·36
5/-	3·82	5·09	7·64	10·18
5/6	3·86	5·25	7·90	10·55
6/-	4·10	5·42	8·16	10·90
7/-	4·29	5·31	8·59	11·40

* The tax charge of 45% is an average figure after taking into account investment allowances.

Exhibit 6. Share price movements Jan. to Dec. 1964—Economist Extel Indicator (Jan. 1953 = 100) V Nocrode 5/- ord and shares of similar companies (Jan. 1964 = 100)

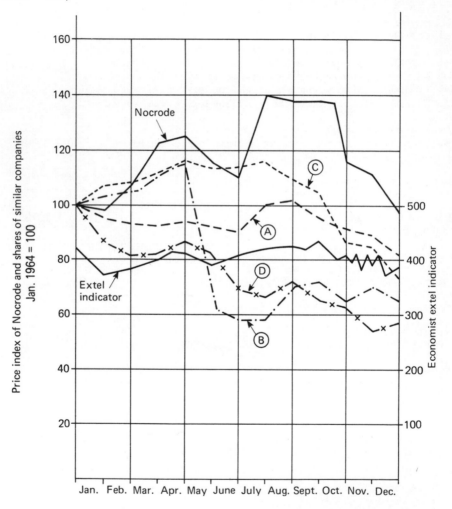

Exhibit 7. Comparative data on Nocrode Limited competitors

The data given below relates to companies which produce equipment competing with one or more Nocrode Limited products. There is, however, no other company manufacturing a strictly comparable range of products.

	Year	Share Price Dec. 31	Gross yield	Div. yield	X covered
Company A	1960	14/-	11·8	6·4	1·84
	1961	10/9	12·3	6·9	1·78
Main products—general	1962	16/-	9·0	5·4	1·67
engineering. Manufactures valves	1963	15/3	8·7	5·8	1·50
for the chemical industry	1964	12/6	9·7	6·3	1·54
Company B	1960	4/8	10·9	6·4	1·7
	1961	4/5	9·7	6·5	1·49
Pump manufacturers	1962	5/3	12·4	6·2	2·0
	1963	4/11	7·2	6·9	1·04
	1964	3/2	11·7	9·7	1·2
Company C	1960	52/-	11·6	4·8	2·4
	1961	50/-	11·1	5·3	2·1
Manufactures wide range of	1962	63/-	8·5	3·8	2·24
small stainless steel components	1963	61/6	7·2	4·2	1·7
	1964	44/6	9·1	4·5	2·0
Company D	1960	28/6	14·3	6·9	2·07
	1961	40/-	19·6	4·0	4·9
Manufacturer of hydraulic	1962	44/-	10·9	3·7	2·9
equipment mostly valves and pumps,	1963	37/-	12·0	4·0	3·0
some used in chemical plants.	1964	21/-	8·1	5·8	1·4

Art et Cuisine

M. Robin left the family furniture manufacturing firm in the centre of France after a disagreement with his two brothers who were co-directors. He then took an appointment as a Director of the Art et Cuisine factory in the Oise region of France.

Before accepting the appointment he visited the factory where he found a work force of 110 people producing kitchen furniture, particularly storage cupboards. The designs benefited from the application of many patents and the furniture was well finished, equipped with numerous gadgets and was selling well in spite of a high price. The sales catalogue contained eleven different items (see Exhibit 1) but offered a wide range of variations in the fittings to the standard designs-shelves, drawers etc. They were available in six different colours and the top surfaces which could be used as worktops were supplied in eight shades of Formica.

The factory personnel comprised the following:

(a) *Production personnel* :

Head of production	1	
Foreman in each workshop	4	
Panel finish machine shop	16	
Upright finish machine shop	22	
Paint shop	26	
Assembly	30	99

(b) *Staff*:

Accountants	2	
Order chaser	1	
Warehouse staff	6	
Typist	2	11

Total production and staff: 110

M. Robin then visited the Paris headquarters of Art and Cuisine where the commercial offices are situated. Here he found three high-class designers who adivise customers, draw up installation plans and design non-standard components. For example, if a customer required a wall panel measuring 1 m 95 cm his requirement could be met by fitting three standard 50 cm units and a special 45 cm unit. Often customers asked for tables with a non-standard layout. A recent management study had revealed that special items represented 212 million Francs out of a total annual turnover of 1,200 million Francs. Panels were sub-contracted to another company, Art & Cuisine being responsible for specifying the dimensions, finishing the edges and boring the fixing holes.

When discussing the factory with top management M. Robin was asked to concentrate his attention initially on the problem of delivery delays. Analysis of deliveries showed that:

 5% were on time
60% were 1-15 days after the promised delivery date
20% were one month after the promised delivery date
15% were over one month late.

These delays were particularly serious since most of the orders were for new accommodation and were required for installation after the painters, who also were often late, had finished the kitchen, and just before the purchaser of the house wanted to move in.

M. Paul Robin spent two weeks investigating the problem. He started by attempting to find out what was in stock and what units were being manufactured. This he found impossible. In following through an order he could nearly always find out when it was given, but was unable to form an overall assessment of stock levels and work-in-progress. M. Robin reported his findings to top management. He told them that, in his opinion, the staff should be left alone to manage as they had always done for the time being and that he should concentrate on reorganising the enterprise on a completely different basis within a year. The management expressed their confidence in him and asked him to make a detailed study and submit his recommendations to them.

M. Paul Robin started his study by examining the technical records. He discovered the results of a work study investigation which has been carried out on most of the jobs in the workshops except the assembly shop. He had at one time received work study training and was able to check some of the calculations from which he concluded that the studies had been done by an experienced work study practitioner. This man had worked for six months before leaving Art & Cuisine for another factory nearer his home. However none of his work had been implemented.

The procedure for documenting order was:

(*a*) A duplicate of the customer's order was prepared.
(*b*) The order chaser compiled a list of the components required (panels, doors, hinges, door stops etc.) from the catalogue description (Exhibit 2). These lists of units were typed with a copy for each workshop, one for the wood and panels warehouse manager, one for the head warehouse manager of the finished products section and one copy which he retained.
(*c*) The delivery note served as the basis for the invoice. M. Robin revealed a considerable number of errors. These arose because many customers informed the company, at a late stage, of changes to the specifications and the production control system failed to supervise the modifications effectively.

Foremen and workmen were paid on a complicated bonus system based on:

1. The number of hours worked in a month
2. The volume of wood used for manufacture
3. The number of orders for which delivery delays exceeded fifteen days.

The bonus system allowed a variation between 0 and 15% but was planned to provide an average bonus of about 6%.

The machinery was in very good condition. The buildings, however, were far too large. The works had previously been a textile factory employing 500 workers (Exhibit 3).

All the floor space was occupied but M. Robin observed that:

(a) The space occupied by wood stocks represented 10% of the available area. Art & Cuisine had an agreement with a firm which made prompt delivery of dry wood in small sections.

(b) The rough panels store was a quarter full of rough panels for obsolete models and a further quarter full of rough panels for current production.

(c) The four workshops were obstructed with current production.

(d) The hardware shop was far too large.

(e) The finished products store was half full. A large pile of standard units did not appear to have been moved for a long time.

(f) The wood store was used to store obsolete units.

M. Robin reviewed the results of his investigation and started to prepare his report and recommendations for the head office.

Exhibit 1. Annual sales in units–standard furniture

Code

PB3	Base units, standard type	15,620
PB6	Bread units	3,128
PB2	Base units, half size	6,432
AB1	Broom cupboards	1,454
AB2	Broom cupboards, half size	2,528
PB5	Duster cupboards	5,837
EV1	Sink doors (without frames)	7,535
PM2	Standard wall units	8,732
PM1	Wall units with concealed panels	5,829
TY1	Standard tables	1,425
	Normal sundries	5,432

Exhibit 2. List of catalogue items (Pieces which can be used to form a component)
PB3–Base Unit Standard Type

Components can be:

P	Permanent
F	Optional dependent on customer choice
FN	Optional in number dependent upon customer's wish
SM	Dependent on the assembly of joined component making up a part of the order.

Ref. mark	Quantity	Designation	Code no.
P	2	Side panels	1.227
P	1	Door panels	1.238
P	1	Normal door hinge	834
P	1	Hinge for spring door	845
P	1	Door handle	425
P	1	Bottom panel	1.224
F		Shelf for dishes	534
F		Bottle shelf	1.032
FN	4 x	Shelf blocks	497
FN	2 x	Guide blocks (2 per drawer and 2 per bottle shelf)	501
SM		Top panel: Formica colour:	See Special Code
SM		Plinth	,,
F		Drawer	612

Exhibit 3. Factory–layout (metres)

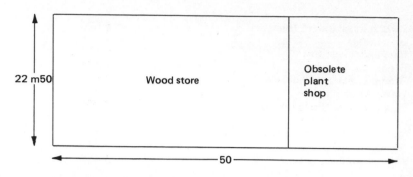

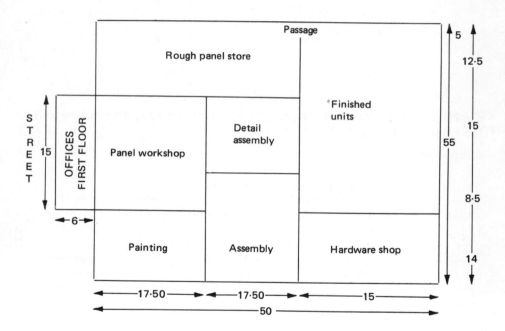

Gumish Tyre and Rubber Company

General facts about Gumish:

In 1950, it became evident that tyre manufacture in Israel was necessary, among other reasons, in order to reduce the Defence Ministry's dependence upon imports. Local demand was the incentive for setting up the Gumish Tyre and Rubber Factory, Limited by several groups and individuals from the United States and elsewhere. The capital for the company was raised by floating shares in Israel and the United States. Two of the largest buyers of Gumish shares were International Tires, and Israeli Investments. In March 1951, after the necessary capital was raised, construction began. It took fifteen months to complete the factory, and the first Israeli manufactured tyre was introduced on the local market in June 1952.

The following information was collected in Gumish during May 1970. Mr Zimroni, Assistant to the Managing Director, said:

'At first, the company's products were similar to those of International Tires because the Israeli staff had been trained by American experts. However, in the course of time, engineers and chemists were sent for training to other factories in the United States and these people gradually took over the plant. Since 1956, the factory has been operated by Israelis only. In 1953 it began to export in order to compete in world markets and started to produce European style tyres. Today, the factory produces about 500 sizes and different constructions and designs of tyre. They vary both in outward appearance and in strength. There are tyres of different shape and makeup, all according to the vehicles they are intended for. For example, a commercial van requires a stronger tyre for load-carrying than when it is used as a pleasure vehicle. Sizes range from those for small cars to heavy trucks.

'In addition to tyres, the company manufactures other rubber products such as tubes and tyre accessories. Eighty-five per cent of manufactured items are tyres, 10% tubes and 5% accessories.'

Exhibit 1 shows the increase in production from 1953-72.

Mr Galili, the Manpower Manager, explained the personnel setup in the plant:

'Altogether there are 580 people employed in the factory. 430 are daily workers, 130 are on a monthly basis and about 20 are senior employees. The monthly employees are the foremen, engineers, laboratory employees, technicians, quality inspectors, clerks and drivers. All the other production workers and technical works (excluding the foremen) are employed on a daily basis. The personnel breakdown shows that 350 people are employed in actual production processes and the rest are employed in maintenance and services. The salary of production workers is according to norms and premiums, and work is carried out in three shifts.'

Mr Zimroni stated that the production of the two tyre companies in the country was sufficient to supply all local demand. Therefore, future expansion lay in increased exports. There was an ever-increasing global demand for tyres which factories throughout the world were expanding their production to supply. Gumish too was in the process of doubling its production, practically all the increase being intended for export.

Demand and supply of the factory's manufactured goods

In speaking about the expansion of the plant, Mr Shamir, the chief engineer, said:

'In the world today there is a tremendous demand for tyres which existing factories cannot supply due to the growth in the number of automobiles on the roads. This is especially true in Israel. In the local market, there is a yearly growth in demand for tyres of 5-7%. However, we are expanding because of the increasing demand abroad for tyres. Our main problem in export markets is to make the price competitive. If we can succeed in producing goods which are competitive in price and in quality, there are no market limitations and any quantity we can produce can be sold.'

Mr Danieli, the sales manager, said:

'At this point, supplies are limited and plans are being made to expand the plant and to practically double production. Since the local price is higher than that for exports, there is a tendency to produce for the local market. However, this market is limited. It is not so simple to gain export markets, but our tyres have achieved a reputation for quality and service. At present the factory sells one half its volume abroad and one half to the local market. The proportions for value are different because of the much lower recovery abroad. For exports, the factory receives today a subsidy of fifty-five agorot* to the dollar whereas previous to the package deal, we received thirty-five agorot to the dollar. This additional subsidy of twenty agorot to the dollar will not cover the fringe expenses of the company and profitability will decrease.'

The principal countries to which tyres were exported from Israel were Britain, Germany, Ghana, and Australia. In speaking about export markets, Mr Danieli said:

'We also do substantial export to the United States, Iran, Greece, Kenya and South Africa. In some of these countries there are local factories, but either they cannot supply the demand or the quality is inferior. Another way of gaining clients is to grant exclusivity for Gumish products to one specific distributor. The distributor finds this preferable to representing a firm which has several other distributors in the country, in which case there is always the possibility that the customer will buy his merchandise from someone else next time.

'It is possible to expand existing markets abroad by granting credit assistance to the present distributor or by changing to someone else who is bigger and more

* 100 agorot = one IL. (Israeli Lira); the rate of exchange in 1970 was $1 = IL. 3·50.

established. In a new country, we are not always successful in attracting a large distributor because our products are not yet well known and the successful distributor is not interested. After a few years it becomes easier and convenient to attract a distributor who has good connections and wide marketing possibilities. In this manner it is possible to expand our exports, especially in the United States, Australia and Germany. The company does not intend to penetrate other markets, but is interested only in expanding sales in those countries to which it is presently exporting.

'There are several reasons why it is sometimes necessary to give up export markets. Turkey was one of our biggest export markets until it put up four tyre factories and then ceased to import. The Iron Curtain countries have practically stopped trading with Israel. The Yugoslav market was an important one until the Six Day War, but when Israel became part of the Free Currency setup instead of dealing in clearing, imports from Israel came to a standstill. In countries such as France and Italy, the local companies control not only the market, but also the distributor. In this manner, the company's export markets are often affected by political and economic factors.'

Mr Zimroni mentioned that both tyre companies in Israel manufactured a price controlled product, since the government had set a maximum price.

There had been a few instances of voluntary cooperation between the two companies. Thus, for instance, when it was impossible for one company to fill a large order for Yugoslavia, both companies worked together to get the order out.

Mr Danieli spoke about the difficulties of competition in selling the products. He said that to compete with other companies in foreign markets was difficult because credits abroad were generally cheaper than in Israel, and countries such as Japan had cheap labour which gave them an advantage in the export field. Competition was keen because the manufacture of tyres was a relatively simple process. Most countries were interested in producing their own tyres and the investment required was relatively small. Many of the large companies were setting up plants in underdeveloped countries. This made competition harder in spite of the fact that the market for tyres was expanding quickly.

The principal factor limiting the competitiveness of the plant was its small size and production had to be based on small batches. Mr Shamir said:

'Compared to other tyre factories in the world, our plant is small. Therefore, it cannot sign agreements with large automobile manufacturers to supply all their demands or even a small part of them. Dunlop, for instance, can do this because it has several factories and each one produces one type of tyre or whole sets of tyres. The factory can thus make long production runs which cut costs by saving time in specialization and in transferring from one production run to the next. In a small plant such as Gumish, we cannot produce in large runs.'

Mr Zimroni said:

'In our plant today, if we are to produce a certain type of tyre, we must set the machine to produce the necessary specification, such as width, strength, and ability, to withstand particular conditions. If a large amount of a certain type of tyre is manufactured, the production run is long, convenient, and inexpensive. However, our export markets demand short production runs, that is, the factory produces many models and only a small quantity of each model. The result is a conflict with the advantages of automation, a loss in the advantages of specialization, and an increase in production costs because of the necessity to set the machines every day or two for transfer from one run to another, from one type of machine to another. It takes about half a day to set the machines and this interferes with the continuity of production.

'Due to the economic and political situation in the country, we cannot allow ourselves to be dependent only upon certain customers, but must make every effort to spread our export markets even at the expense of producing small runs. If we could specialize on one model, we would be able to have bigger production runs and would cut down the time involved in the process of transferring from one run to the next.'

Mr Danieli said that it was dangerous for Gumish to concentrate on one market in spite of the advantages to be gained by increasing batch sizes. It was necessary to spread the risks. In connection with this, Mr Zimroni said:

'The company is forced to produce many types of tyre in accordance with the climatic and other conditions existing in those countries to which the products are exported, e.g. hot and cold climates, snow, speed, etc. Tyres manufactured for Ethiopia, for instance, must have been designed to withstand heat. On the other hand, tyres for Germany must withstand high speeds. The advantages of automation are lost in short production runs because the more improved and modern a machine is, the longer it takes to transfer its automatic operations from one setting to another.'

Mr Berkovitz, the Production Manager, said:

'There are two ways of increasing production runs: one is to affiliate ourselves with a car manufacturer and to supply all his demands; the second is to keep large inventories. To do the first is impossible because the plant is small, and the second cannot be done because keeping large stocks and inventories is an expensive process which the company cannot afford.'

Mr Zimroni, too, mentioned this fact:

'The company produces according to the orders it receives from clients and does not accumulate stocks. All production for export is in response to orders received. Production for local consumption is not by order, but the production department considers it as if it were by order. The way it works is for the Order Department (sales) to transfer orders to the production department. These instructions are not always identical to the orders actually received from the local client, since they take account of market demand estimates by type of tyre. The Production Department treats this type of order in the same way as one for export.'

Mr Danieli continued:

'The expansion of the factory does not mean that we will stock inventories, but that we will produce to fill existing orders from abroad. There is actually a doubt whether we will be able to fill them. Small factories cannot cope with the advances in technology and style, and their competitiveness is affected. By expanding the factory we will be able to offer the same quality at approximately the same price as other firms.'

Plans for expansion

Mr Zimroni explained the manufacturing process:

'The company uses various raw materials for manufacturing the tyre: rubber, carbon black, oil, chemicals, brass coated steel wire, rayon, nylon, and cotton. The rubber is placed into the mixer together with carbon black, oils and chemicals. From the mixer emerge rubber sheets.'

Mr Berkovitz explained the ensuing process:

'These rubber sheets go through three treatments: rubber, metal and fabrics. In the rubberizing process, the sheets pass through an extruder which creates the treads and the sidewalls of the tyre. In the material process, rayon, nylon and cotton are put into the calender which is a machine that coats material with rubber. This emerges in the form of rolled material which then goes into a diagonal slicing machine which cuts it on an angle and prepares it for the manufacturing bands. In the metal process, brass coated steel wire is covered with rubber to prepare beads for the tyre. These three processes merge together, and the treads, sidewalls with the beads and bands, to make the tyre which is then finally inspected and transferred to the warehouse.'

The processes for producing a truck and an automobile tyre are identical except that the former demands more physical effort on the part of the worker. (A sketch of the production process appears in Exhibit 2.)

Mr Shamir discussed the forthcoming expansion of Gumish:

'The expansion of the factory will not mean any changes in production processes. Generally speaking, there are no radical changes in the manufacture of tyres anywhere in the world. Changes in production methods for many years have been very small. In the first stage of expansion, this year, we intend to increase our annual output from 6,000 tons to 10,000 tons. The expansion of the factory will, of course, necessitate the renovation of the existing building, as well as building a new section, but essentially production methods are the same as those being used today. In the first stage of expansion, the factory area has been increased as a result of a new building which is now being erected and into which the new equipment is being put. There may be some changes in the siting of the machines in the factory when the expansion is completed.'

Mr Berkovitz when discussing the expansion said:

'Most of the changes will take place in the components preparation department. Because the machines in use in this department are relatively cheap, it is not worthwhile to run more than two shifts. It is preferable to buy a new machine for this department rather than to operate a night shift.'

Mr Zimroni stated:

'The total investment required for the expansion is about IL. 11,000,000. The principal investment is in a new mixer which will double output. Today there is one rubber mixer in the factory. The cost of this new mixer is about one quater of the total expansion cost. The purchase of the land and building costs accounts for another IL. 2,500,000. Together, this amounts to half of the new investment.

'After the mixer is installed, we will be faced with the problem of coping with the increased output. In the primary stages, the mixer and the building will not be fully utilized until the rest of the machines are delivered. Even today, there are some departments which do not operate at full capacity, and the installation of the new mixer will increase the capacity output of these departments.

'In the plans for doubling production, we have included a provision for purchasing new equipment and making improvements on existing machines. "The equipment operating in the factory is in good condition and has undergone improvements and adjustments." Practically none of the machines has been taken out of action. We have a machine which was manufactured in 1913. We made several improvements on it and it is a good machine. We have made many changes on machines in order to make the manual effort needed at the machine easier, and to increase its speed of production. The company contemplates additional improvements on the existing machinery and bringing in new equipment. This will decrease production costs because less manpower will be needed to work the machines, the efforts of the workers at the machines will be simplified—the work demands much physical effort—the speed of production will be increased, and there will be better quality control of the products. The quality of the product will be improved and, as a result, so will its competitiveness.'

Mr Zimroni then said:

'Some of the new equipment will replace the old. The new equipment is modern and has electronic control systems. The decisive factor in our bringing in this new equipment is that it makes the work easier at the machine. Some of our workers are getting older and cannot produce as much as in years gone by. It will be possible to produce a larger amount of work with less physical effort. For example, previously a worker had to lift a layer of rubber by himself and put it into the machine. Today, by pressing a button, the machine lifts the layer and puts it into place. Moreover, this increase in the production balance will enable more stations to work three shifts.'

Mr Zimroni finally stated:

'A general outline of the development and expansion programme of the company was brought before the managerial and senior administrative staffs. These people have the necessary knowhow because of the positions they occupy in the company and their knowledge of production. Those who are responsible for the expansion programme are well aware of what is going on. The technical department did most of the work on the expansion programme. It decided to a large extent what equipment to purchase and where, taking into consideration the points laid down by International Tires in matters of standardization, type of machine, delivery date and price.'

Mr Galili said when discussing the effects of the expansion on manpower:

'The expansion programme of the company will necessitate an increase of 80-100 people, of whom fifteen will be technicians. It will be necessary to employ people who are on a higher professional and technical level than those currently employed in the factory: workers with a vocational or technical high school education. At least one member of a machine crew should have a high school education.'

Dealing with the same subject, Mr Shamir said:

'The new workers should be trained on the job. Every machine operator needs a training period of one to three months, depending on his ability to acquire the necessary skills, while at work. It is assumed that more time will be spent on teaching the worker how to operate the new machine. A small group of potential foremen will have to be trained abroad for several weeks.'

However, Mr Shamir maintained that the lack of available manpower will disrupt the expansion programme. The Personnel Manager, Mr Galili, stated that due to this serious shortage in available manpower, it would be difficult for the plant to absorb new workers as planned. Although the work itself was not attractive, the system of wage incentives enabled the worker to earn high wages.

Mr Galili said:

'In certain jobs a good worker can, with premiums,* earn a daily wage of IL. 35-40.† Still the company is faced with serious difficulties in finding suitable employees and I am afraid this will affect the production and expansion programme to such an extent that we will be unable to fill the orders we have on hand.'

Mr Berkovitz stressed the difficulty of finding workers for the plant. He said:

'In the existing situation in the employment market, it is difficult to get workers for the factory. The work in the factory is hard. It is hot and demands physical effort. The working conditions are much pleasanter in other factories. In addition, we run shifts, and this is another drawback. It is even more difficult to get professional people: engineers, technicians and skilled workers for the technical department. Because of the shortage of available manpower and for the above reasons, the plant is not succeeding in attracting the necessary personnel and this may affect the expansion programme.'

Mr Shamir was in favour of making changes in the production standards for wage incentives. He said:

'The new equipment will automatically bring about an increase in the output of the worker because the machines are more modern; this irrespective of the increase in productivity. The machines are larger and modern and these advantages should bring about an increase in the present production standards. However, this will undoubtedly be a point of hard bargaining with the Workers Committee which does not easily agree to any changes in the standards.'

Mr Berkovitz stated his opinion on the subject. He said:

'The expansion will bring about only a small increase in output per worker in the production department. On the other hand, in the stock preparation department, the new equipment to be installed will likely increase the output per worker by about 50%.'

As to the present situation at the plant where work is measured according to production standards and premiums, Mr Berkovitz said:

'In the production department, the work at the machine demands great physical effort and attention. The worker can seldom make more than the standard and his wages are more or less the same every month. On the other hand, in the tyre department, where the work is done by hand, the worker can, in accordance with

* Based on wage incentive schemes.
† The rate of exchange in 1970, was $1 = IL. 3·50 (Israeli Liras).

his dexterity, make more than the standard. Therefore, when the new equipment is set up, particularly in the stock preparation department, it will be necessary to re-evaluate the standard.'

Several managers of Gumish felt that there was no intention to introduce any organizational changes. Mr Berkovitz said:

'There is no intention of making any changes in the organization of the production department and the various subsections, with the exception of enlarging the staff of foremen. This is made necessary because of the expansion.'

He said that, even with the addition of personnel, the same setup of workers would remain, except that their standard would be higher. On the other hand, Mr Zimroni said that it was not known how and where the new production processes would influence the organizational setup. He also maintained that the company would make changes as they became necessary in the course of time. As to the present situation, he said:

'There is a system of job analysis for workers, but not for secretarial services. Job grading, upon which basis people are employed, was created by historical developments. To continue grading job qualifications on this same basis would perpetuate those standards. If we continue to grade qualifications as they are being done today, we will perpetuate that system whereby workers are rated according to those standards set by the people presently working at those jobs.'

In his opinion, there was no sense in continuing this system. He said:

'On the other hand, there is no sense in doing it the other way. The solution is in analyzing the jobs and adjusting personal grades and differences.'

In conclusion, Mr Zimroni stated:

'The company is included in the government programme for encouraging investments in plant and equipment manufacturing for exports, and its expansion plans are designed to supply the export demand for rubber products. On the other hand, the company is cutting down on its imports of raw materials as much as possible. Some of the materials formerly imported from abroad are purchased today from the local Rogozin factory and carbon black is purchased from the local Petro-Chemicals Company. We do this in spite of the fact that purchases made in the country are not cheaper. However, it is sometimes more convenient to work with a local supplier than with one from abroad.'

Exhibit 3 presents some extracts from Israeli newspapers dealing with the Gumish expansion plans.

Exhibit 1. Growth in production 1953-72

Year		Number of tyres produced	Number of tubes produced	Production in tons
1953		65,000	50,000	1,600
1957		100,000	110,000	3,000
1961		150,000	140,000	4,600
1962		200,000	180,000	6,000
1969	app.	250,000	230,000	6,500
1972	est	–	–	10,000

Note: The first four lines of this table were taken from the advertising booklet of the company 'Twenty Years of Progress—1952-1972'. The last two lines were compiled from the figures presented by the people interviewed.

Exhibit 2. Outline of production process

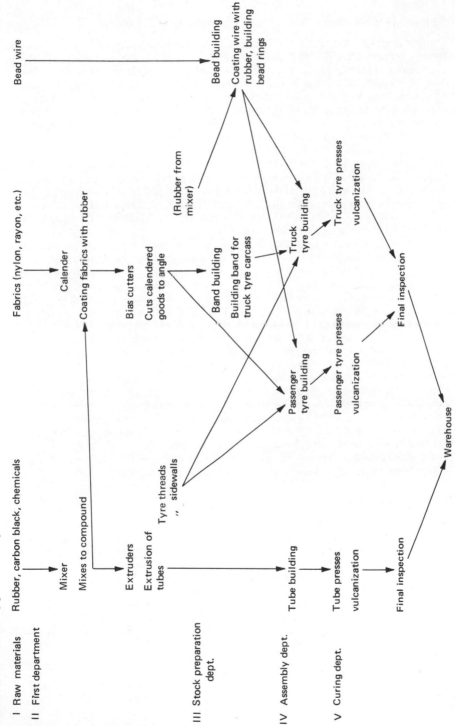

Exhibit 3. Increased production and profits at Gumish

12 Million for expansion: Doubts as to Profitability of Export*

On the morning of 5 June 1967, while the Israeli Defence Forces were crossing Israel's border, Mr Uri Ronel stepped in as General Manager of the Gumish Tyre Company in place of Mr Robert Ron. Mr Ronel was the former Assistant Manager and, previous to that, had served in the army. In taking over the management he was faced with several problems. The principal ones were to increase production by exploiting the full capacity of the equipment which had heretofore not be utilised, to transfer production lines from truck tyres to light cars, and all this together with increasing efficiency and enlarging the number of workers employed in production.

Since that time, some of these objectives have been attained. Sales, which in April 1967 amounted to IL. 20,000,000 reached IL. 24,000,00 in 1968 and toppled IL 28,000,000 in April 1969. Profits increased from IL 150,000 net in April 1967 to IL. 1,700,000 in April 1968 and IL. 2,500,000 in April 1969. Taking into consideration earned profits of IL. 6,500,000 (total profit possibilities 11 million) and fixed assets (after depreciation of IL. 7,000,000 investment value IL. 20,000,000) these are excellent results.†

Mr Ronel pointed out the fact that the main reason for this encouraging picture was the general conditions prevalent in the country today, especially as regards the increase in use of rubber tyres. However, his assistant pointed out that even before Israel's economic slowdown of 1965-67 Gumish has sold whatever quantities it manufactured, and the difficulty was to increase production in order to exploit investments to the utmost. In 1964/65 IL. 3,000,000 was invested in expansion, but this investment was not exploited until 1967. Now, having reached full capacity of production, Gumish is about to embark on a large expansion program of IL. 12,000,000. Of this sum, IL. 1,750,000 is earmarked for expanding production for the Defence Ministry, and the rest is earmarked for civilian production. There will be an increase in the production of all types of automobile tyres, including radial tyres. Gumish is not going in for developing fibre glass tyres, as the second Israeli Tire Company is doing, because it is not certain about the future of this type of tyre. However, it will be possible to make a quick transfer to production of fibre glass tyres. In addition to tyres, the department of rubber products will be expanded, especially for those items demanding wide knowhow. There is a possibility that this department will be separated from the plant and become an independent unit.

Workers are needed

The bottleneck in increased production is finding employees. Today 600 people are employed at Gumish. Working at tyre making is hard and dirty (from the carbon black) and there is a steady drain of workers. There were many difficulties during the Six Day War and in the following period. Workers come and go and the setting up of a permanent staff is a slow process. If a worker holds out for five years, he generally stays on permanently, mostly because he has a responsible job and his social benefits are accumulative. Today, Gumish employs workers who come from an area spreading as far as fifty kilometres away. There is still a shortage of workers and with the expansion, the shortage will be even more severe. Whether the firm will be able to fully take advantage of the expansion will depend on their successful efforts to keep this work staff together.

* Reprint from *Haaretz* (mid 1969).

† All these figures are annual figures. The financial year in Israel is sometimes from April 1st to March 31st of the following year; thus the above 24,000,000 in 1968 is for 1967/68 (from April 1st, 1967 to March 31st, 1968).

The salary is one of the luring factors and, as pointed out by the management, a worker who has been employed in the plant for seven years and is trained, can earn (with premiums) as much as IL. 800 per month net. The new and modern equipment which is to be installed will make the work at the machine less dependent on the operator.

Approximately half of the products produced by Gumish are sold in Israel to transport firms and the Defence Ministry and the local market, the rest are exported. When the expansion programme is completed, 70% of the products will be exported. Mr Ronel pointed out that it is not worthwhile to export. A ton of tyres costs about $1,000 abroad (prices vary from $750 to $1,000 per ton) and tyres are sold for IL. 6,000 per ton in Israel. Mr Ronel says that as long as there are custom discriminations against Israel in the Common Market and in EFTA, exports will not be profitable. The customs duties in EFTA are lower and therefore most of the export is directed to these countries, mainly England. Therefore, the local market must bear the burden of the expansion effort. There was a drop in profits from sales to EFTA countries because of the devaluation of the pound sterling. Our exports to EFTA are made through an English firm, so that the returns to Gumish for these sales dropped 15%.

Rubber from Singapore

Gumish imports raw rubber from Singapore. This gives it an advantage over European countries because transport to Israel is cheaper. Synthetic rubber is purchased on international markets. However, the main components of the tyre—carbon black, rayon, and nylon, must be purchased in Israel from the Petrochemicals Company and from Rogozin. According to Mr Ronel, the price of the materials bought locally is at least 5% higher than abroad, and this costs the firm more than half a million liras a year.

As of July 1st, 1969, imports of tyres will be permitted at the customs rate of 65% or not less than IL. 4·50 per kg. for automobile tyres and 35% or not less than IL. .50 per kg. for truck tyres. Mr Ronel is of the opinion that customs protection per kilogram is necessary in order to prevent import dumping from such countries as Czechoslovakia. He is not concerned about imports from developed countries because the price of their tyres is similar to the Israeli ones. Naturally these companies also export at a lower price, as does Israel. For example, a tyre for the Lark automobile, 560-15, costs IL. 40 in Switzerland. The same tyre at the factory in Israel costs IL. 44.43 without tax and IL. 55.30 with tax. The wholesale price is IL. 57.71 and the tyre retails for IL. 60.06.

Exhibit 4. Gumish tyre factory to invest IL. 12 million in expansion and development[1]

The Gumish Tyre and Rubber Factory will invest IL. 12,000,000 in expansion and development of the plant in order to enlarge its export capacity by 50% in 1971.

According to he plans, IL. 2,500,000 will be invested in land and buildings and IL. 9,500,000 will be spent for new equipment. The company intends to finance this expansion programme with the help of an IL. 4,500,000 loan from the Industrial Development Bank and a grant of IL. 1,800,000 given by the Government to encourage investments. The rest of the sum—IL. 5,700,000—will be financed by the firm from its own sources. It has become known that the management intends to float additional shares to raise part of the money needed.

1. From *Shaar* (mid 1969)

The expansion programme has been submitted to the Investment Centre and is awaiting approval of the Centre's management.

The expansion will enable Gumish to manufacture more types of products, among them products for the Defence Ministry. With the conclusion of the expansion programme, the company will add another 200 employees to its payrolls, in addition to the 550 already employed.

Sales of Gumish products have increased in 1968/69 and reached IL. 29,500,000 as against IL. 24,300,000 the previous year. Exports remained at the same level as the previous year and totalled IL. 11,300,000.

The profits in 1967/68 were IL. 948,000 as against IL. 122,400 in 1966/67. It is estimated that this year there will be a 100% increase in expected profits.

Hadar Products (A) Ltd.

In January 1968, David Rabinovitch, the production engineer of Hadar Products, Ltd., realised that his work scheduling for the Grapefruit Canning Department had been faulty.

The canning of grapefruit segments has been one of the main lines of Hadar Products, Ltd. for many years. The Grapefruit Canning Department is composed of three sections: peeling, slicing, and packing. The furit is brought into the department straight form sorting at the citrus packing houses. It is then warmed in hot water and passed through the three operations—peeling, slicing, and packing—during which time it also receives chemical and heat treatments. Finally, after packing, the cans are closed, heat treated, dried, labelled, put into cartons and, after being stacked in a warehouse, sent on pallets to Haifa Port to be shipped for export (mainly to Britain).

Mr Rabinovitch, the production engineer, called 'David' by everybody, was a comparative newcomer to the plant. He was graduated from the Technion in 1966, at the top of his class, and had been working in Hadar Products for one year. He had quickly proved himself capable and he had been complimented on the way he had planned the 1968 work schedules of the Grapefruit Canning Department. On 14 January 1968, in the beginning of the third week of the seasonal production of grapefruit segments, Mr Rabinovitch was urgently called to the factory floor.

There he found that a serious bottleneck had developed between the grapefruit peeling section and the grapefruit slicing section. The latter was understaffed with the result that the workers were nervous and under strain, and there was a backlog of several hundred trays of peeled grapefruits to be processed. At the same time the workers in the packing section were taking it easy, with less work than they could comfortably handle. The peeling section was operating normally.

On the basis of its past experience, Hadar's sales forecast for 1968 was 1,500,000 grapefruit segments cans. Steady supply of grapefruit could be counted on because the Citrus Marketing Board[1] had undertaken to supply fruit regularly and within a specified range of quality and size. A month before the scheduled start of the season, Mr Harel, the production manager, gave the production engineer some general information concerning the 1968 season and said to him:

---

1. A central organisation which controls all sales of citrus fruit in Israel with the prime purpose of insuring the export of the fruit in sufficient quality and quantity.

'David, you have all the data for the 1967 season; the methods will remain the same. I should like to plan the production in such a way that within a month we can reach a minimum production of 12,000 cans per shift. The labour capacity of the department must grow slowly until it reaches a peak of approximately 100 workers: I hope that we shall not need many more than 100 workers to produce 12,000 cans per shift.'

'What about the size of the grapefruit?' asked David.

'They will be larger than last year, but I cannot predict the exact size in number of grapefruit packed in one can.'

David, being careful not to overestimate the size of the fruit, decided to base his calculations on 3·5 grapefruit packed in one can (the figure for 1967 being four grapefruit per can).

He took his standards table (Exhibit 1) and calculated the number of workers in the three sections on the basis of the standards for size 3·5 per can. He computed the influence of acquiring skill (Exhibit 2) on the output of the first four weeks and constructed a table for manpower needs.

The table showed the number of workers in each unit (peeling, slicing, and packing) and for every week (first, second, third, etc.). His table was based on the following output:

During:	1st week		3,000 cans per shift
	2nd ,,		6,000 ,, ,,
	3rd ,,		9,000 ,, ,,
	4th ,,		11,000 ,, ,,
	5th ..	and onwards	12,000 ,, ,,

He gave the table to Moshe, the head foreman, and a copy to Avraham (foreman of Grapefruit Canning Department) to whom he explained his calculations.

Things went according to schedule for two weeks, until 14 January, when David found himself called to the disorganized department.

He inspected the grapefruit and found that their size had changed so that now only 2·5 fruits were needed per can. David immediately set about correcting the work schedule.

Exhibit 1. Standard times in minutes for different sizes of grapefruit

Section	Unit	Size* 2·0*	2·5*	3·0*	3·5*	4·0*
Peeling	per 1 grape- fruit	0·50	0·45	0·42	0·40	0·40
Slicing	,,	0·40	0·40	0·40	0·40	0·40
Packing	per 1 can	1·00	1·10	1·20	1·25	1·30

* In units of number of grapefruit packed in 1 can.

Exhibit 2. Acquisition of skill (in percentages of 100% normal skill)

Section	1st Week	2nd Week	3rd Week	4th Week	5th Week
Peeling*	55	80	95	95	100
Slicing	40	75	90	95	100
Packing	40	75	90	95	100

* Skill is acquired quicker because most workers were on the same job during at least two seasons.

Suggested questions for use of discussion leader

1. What was the manpower distribution when David entered the department on January 14?
2. What was the manpower distribution during the first two weeks?
3. What should be done in the department? (What should be the manpower distribution for size 2·5 for skilled workers? What should it be on the third and fourth weeks of production?)
4. What will be the final manpower distribution for 12,000 cans per shift if nothing changes in the department after 14 January? What if the grapefruit size changes to 2·0, 3·0, or 4·0 per can?
5. Construct acquisition of skill graphs for peeling, slicing, and packing.
6. What other reasons than the size of fruit could have caused the bottleneck on January 14?

Tiferet, Ltd.

In January 1968, Mr Talmi, Sales Manager of Tiferet, Ltd., claimed that his department was working under a severe handicap because the production department was incapable of fulfilling the orders submitted to it.

Tiferet, Ltd., a foodstuffs factory in the Tel-Aviv area, has been expanding steadily during recent years. Mr Livneh, General Manager, felt that the products as such were well received by the public. However, while sales had somewhat increased, the efficiency measured in man-days per ton (total man-days divided by total weight of products) was dropping as measured by the monthly efficiency figures.

On 9 January 1968, Mr Livneh received a written complaint from Mr Talmi, his sales manager, directed at the production department. Mr Talmi listed a number of products ordered by sales which had been delivered behind schedule, thereby causing losses to his department.

Mr Livneh asked Mr Weiss, Technical Manager of Tiferet, to try to clear up the situation.

Mr Weiss first called in Mr Levy, the man in charge of sales and production statistics, and asked him to submit sales figures for the years 1964-1967.

Then Mr Weiss called Mr Shlomo Cohen, Manager of the production department, to his office. Mr Weiss explained to Mr Cohen in general terms the problem at hand, then went on to say:

'I know, Shlomo, that the plant has grown and I am the last one to put all the blame on you, but these clashes and the drop in efficiency cannot go on. What is wrong'?

'I don't know exactly what is wrong,' answered Shlomo Cohen. 'All I know is that Talmi comes to me every day, sometimes even more than once a day, and puts in small orders of many types of products. It is always urgent, urgent, urgent!'

'But, Shlomo,' interrupted Weiss, 'we agreed that he would submit to you each Friday a weekly order for the next week. What about it'?

'Apparently he does not know what he needs,' explained Shlomo, 'and he changes his weekly orders so frequently that they are entirely useless to me and I would rather not have them at all. Because of him there are days that I work on all our products at once, and I just can't cope with the load with my regular number of thirty-five workers.'

He thought for a while and added: 'I feel I could have raised the efficiency if I had worked on less products a day.'

All rights reserved to T. D. Weinshall. This case was prepared in the Kaplan School of the Hebrew University.

When Cohen left, Weiss called in Talmi and told him that he had been asked by Livneh to try and clear up the situation. 'First of all.' added Weiss, 'I would like to know whether it is true that you are not able to submit a monthly or even a weekly order'?

'Yes, that is correct,' answered Talmi, 'how can I know what our agents are going to order and what the customers will want to buy in grocery shops?' (See Exhibit 1).

Mr Weiss put before Talmi the figures which he had obtained from Mr Levy concerning data for earlier years and said' 'We are a seasonally-producing factory; surely there are some regular trends in the demands for our various products.'

'Well, I don't know,' answered Talmi. 'Anyway, there is nothing I can do with these figures, and I don't know why we should waste time in collecting such detailed sales data. As far as I am concerned, I have only to know the monthly sales volume in Israeli Liras for each agent and the total annual amount of sales of each product.'

Why do you need the annual sales quantities of each product?' asked Weiss.

'That gives me some idea of the sales volume next year, so that I might give you my yearly sales forecasts.'

After Mr Talmi had left, Mr Weiss thought about the situation for a while. It seemed to him that this problem of planning production could be solved. Accordingly he obtained the production standards and the statistics showing the number of direct man-hours required for the production of each item (Exhibit 2). Using these data in conjunction with the company's sales statistics (Exhibits 3 and 4) he set to work.

Exhibit 1. Sales procedure

Travelling agents and central stores

Tiferet has twenty-one travelling agents who sell Tiferet products exclusively. These agents are supplied from eight distribution stores throughout the country. Some of these stores are under the management of the agent himself, while the big ones are run by district sales managers (in Tel-Aviv, Jerusalem, Haifa).

Distribution

Each of the travelling agents operates in an area covering from 250 to 300 retailers (mostly grocers). The agent travels in a delivery van belonging to Tiferet. He plans his route himself and also the frequency of his visits to the retailer. The agent tries to sell as much as he can to a retailer and to fill the retailer's stock with Tiferet's products. He collects from the retailer empties and spoilt-returns (most of Tiferet's products have a comparatively short 'shelf life'). The distribution from the factory to the central stores (often to several stores on one route at a time) is performed by large vans, and Tiferet's policy is not to send out a van uless it is more or less full.

Sales orders

Each store manager (whether an agent in the small distribution stores or a district manager in the big ones) orders various products from Tiferet's sales department, whenever he feels he has to replenish his stock.

The sales department is supposed to submit weekly orders to the factory based on the orders they receive. However, as the policy is to supply the distribution stores' managers with goods as quickly as possible (and the orders pour in continuously), the sales department is forced to order from the factory several times weekly. The factory has a small store which serves mostly as a transit store.

Commissions and spoilages

The travelling agents received a varying commission, depending on the product, based on the tonnage sold. The quantities of 'spoilt-returns' which they transfer back to the factory are deducted from the goods they sold, for the purpose of calculating commissions.

Exhibit 2. Production standards

Product	Package	Number of workers in production line	Number of man-hours per 100 kgs
Baking powders 'Universal'	50 gr. pack.	10	22·4
,, ,, ,,	100 ,, ,,	10	22·1
	in bulk	7	10·0
,, ,, Chocolate	0·5 kg. pack.	7	9·3
,, ,, ,,	50 gr. pack.	10	45·6
Marmalade 'Tifmar'	0·6 lb. jars	9	18·0
,, ,,	1·0 ,, ,,	22	17·7
,, ,,	2·0 ,, ,,	22	18·0
,, ,,	4·0 ,, ,,	20	7·0
,, ,,	A$_{10}$ tins	10	4·1
Jam 'Tiferet'	1 lb. jars	6	16·3
,,	2 ,,	22	18·0
,,	4 ,,	20	7·4
,,	A$_{10}$ tins	10	3·6

Exhibit 3. Annual totals and monthly sales fluctuations (1967–1968)

Table 1. Baking powders (all packs)

Year		Total Sales	Jan.	Feb.	March	April	May	June	July	Aug.	Sep.	Oct.	Nov.	Dec.
1964	Kgs.	71,631	6,893	8,180	17,173	8,639	6,493	2,941	1,247	1,720	1,710	5,450	6,909	5,691
	%		9·6	11·4	23·9	12·0	9·1	4·0	1·6	2·4	2·3	7·6	8·4	7·8
1965	Kgs.	40,088	4,606	3,949	3,792	2,196	1,681	1,253	844	1,203	1,366	2,039	6,492	10,407
	%		11·6	9·8	9·6	5·6	4·2	3·2	2·3	3·1	3·4	5·0	16·4	25·9
1966	Kgs.	79,156	8,358	7,095	7,025	6,064	3,841	4,018	1,490	2,954	4,611	6,280	12,919	10,904
	%		10·8	10·5	8·9	8·7	4·9	5·0	1·9	3·8	5·9	7·9	16·5	13·9
1967	Kgs.	134,708	13,686	12,224	9,891	9,103	9,742	7,629	8,166	8,836	10,791	12,192	15,828	17,171
	%		10·2	9·1	7·3	6·7	7·2	5·6	6·1	6·6	8·0	9·0	11·6	12·6
1968	Est.	186,000	20,274	18,972	16,182	13,020	10,044	8,556	6,510	8,370	11,532	13,206	27,528	32,550
	%		10·9	9·8	8·7	7·0	5·4	4·6	3·5	4·5	6·2	7·1	14·8	17·5

Exhibit 3 (continued)

Table 2. Marmalade 'Tifmar' (all packs)

Year		Total Sales	Jan.	Feb.	March	April	May	June	July	Aug.	Sep.	Oct.	Nov.	Dec.
1964	**Kg.**	146,023	9,355	7,940	10,937	12,312	11,670	11,943	11,071	13,417	18,179	14,763	12,489	12,212
	%		6·4	5·4	7·5	8·4	8·0	8·1	7·6	9·2	12·3	10·1	8·6	8·4
1965	**Kg.**	121,400	8,542	8,668	12,356	8,584	8,784	11,072	9,236	11,936	11,719	9,299	9,520	10,725
	%		7·1	7·2	10·4	7·2	7·5	9·3	7·6	9·8	9·6	7·6	7·8	8·8
1966	**Kg.**	124,394	8,624	8,300	11,927	8,104	9,404	12,222	10,472	11,996	13,084	10,264	8,487	10,224
	%		6·9	6·7	9·7	6·6	7·8	9·8	8·4	9·8	10·8	8·4	6·8	8·4
1967	**Kg.**	154,935	10,241	8,840	10,339	15,345	12,303	12,819	14,092	15,997	16,331	15,807	9,929	11,843
	%		6·7	5·3	6·8	9·9	7·9	8·4	9·2	10·4	10·6	10·2	6·5	7·6
1968	Est.	145,000	9,715	8,990	12,325	12,325	11,165	13,195	11,745	14,065	15,515	13,195	10,730	12,035
	%		6·7	6·2	8·5	8·5	7·7	9·1	8·1	9·7	10·7	9·1	7·4	8·3

Exhibit 3 (continued)

Table 3. Jam 'Tiferet' (all packs)

Year		Total Sales	Jan.	Feb.	March	April	May	June	July	Aug.	Sep.	Oct.	Nov.	Dec.
1964	Kg.	137,716	12,815	10,479	11,979	7,883	10,027	9,307	8,170	9,123	14,008	14,432	15,545	13,934
	%		9·3	7·6	8·7	5·7	7·3	6·7	5·9	6·5	10·2	10·5	11·3	10·2
1965	Kg.	143,649	9,445	12,008	16,554	10,073	12,804	14,792	10,086	12,905	11,926	10,051	9,758	10,593
	%		6·8	8·4	11·5	7·5	8·9	10·5	7·2	7·6	8·5	7·5	6·8	7·5
1966	Kg.	127,677	10,328	10,648	10,224	10,594	10,368	11,613	10,142	10,483	11,525	10,590	10,888	10,664
	%		8·1	8·3	8·0	8·3	8·1	9·1	7·9	8·1	9·0	8·3	8·5	8·3
1967	Kg.	137,603	12,412	10,667	10,416	9,566	12,487	13,297	12,205	11,696	12,473	11,964	9,525	10,793
	%		9·0	7·8	7·6	7·0	9·1	9·7	8·8	8·5	9·1	8·7	6·9	7·8
1968 Est.	Kg.	145,000	12,035	11,600	13,050	10,440	12,180	13,050	10,875	11,165	13,340	12,760	12,180	12,325
	%		8·3	8·0	9·0	7·2	8·4	9·0	7·5	7·7	9·2	8·8	8·4	8·5

Exhibit 4. Distribution of monthly sales according to types of each product line

Table 1. Baking powders

Month	'Universal'						Chocolate				Total	
	50 gr. kg.	Packs %	100 gr. kg.	Packs %	In kg.	Bulk %	0.5 kg.	Packs %	50 gr. kg.	Packs %	kg.	%
1966												
I	4,764	57	1,632	20	1,957	23			8,353		8,353	100
II	4,425	56	1,705	22	1,765	22					7,895	100
III	2,892	41	1,017	15	1,875	27	1,182	17			7,025	100
IV	3,228	48	405	6	1,843	28	1,188	18			6,664	100
V	1,394	36			1,176	31	1,271	33			3,841	100
VI	1,765	44			996	25	1,257	31			4,018	100
VII	830	28			783	26	1,356	46			2,969	100
VIII	851	29			935	31	1,168	40			2,954	100
IX	1,759	38			1,100	24	1,752	38			4,611	100
X	3,160	50			1,303	21	1,817	29			6,280	100
XI	6,248	49	1,974	15	2,231	17	2,466	19			12,919	100
XII	5,529	46	1,882	16	1,497	12	1,996	16	1,264	10	12,168	100
1967												
I	5,243	38	1,623	12	1,626	12	2,143	16	3,051	22	13,682	100
II	4,773	40	1,088	9	1,516	13	2,273	19	2,205	19	11,855	100
III	4,053	41	782	8	1,115	12	1,963	20	1,880	19	9,793	100
IV	2,071	29	414	6	1,148	16	2,130	30	1,306	19	7,069	100
V	4,543	39	266	2	1,362	12	3,203	28	2,268	19	11,642	100
VI	2,523	35			886	12	2,379	33	1,487	20	7,275	100
VII	1,878	25			1,148	15	3,193	41	1,491	19	7,710	100
VIII	2,178	25			973	11	3,847	45	1,674	19	8,669	100
IX	2,760	29			908	10	3,607	37	2,356	24	9,642	100
X	3,723	31	978	7	1,169	10	4,133	35	2,781	24	11,830	100
XI	3,555	28	646	6	1,385	11	4,456	35	2,434	19	12,808	100
XII	3,204	30			1,237	11	3,247	30	2,624	23	10,958	100

Exhibit 4 (continued)

Table 2. Marmalade 'Tifmar'

Month	Jars 0·6 lb kg.	%	Jars 1 & 2 lb. kg.	%	Jars 4 lb. kg.	%	Tins A_{10} kg.	%	Total kg.	%
1966										
I	1,286	15	5,416	63	1,705	20	217	2	8,624	100
II	1,259	15	5,343	64	1,691	20	7	1	8,300	100
III	1,309	11	7,226	61	3,021	25	371	3	11,927	100
IV	1,202	13	5,909	65	1,912	21	112	1	9,135	100
V	1,239	13	6,116	63	2,287	23	77	1	9,719	100
VI	1,680	14	7,659	62	2,645	22	238	2	12,222	100
VII	1,587	15	6,683	64	2,167	20·7	35	0·3	10,472	100
VIII	1,604	14	6,992	59	2,912	25	308	2	11,816	100
IX	1,891	15	8,404	64	2,649	20	140	1	13,084	100
X	1,421	14	6,576	64	2,197	21	70	1	10,264	100
XI	1,232	14	5,326	63	1,859	22	70	1	8,487	100
XII	1,390	14	6,445	63	1,839	18	560	5	10,244	100
1967										
I	1,305	13	6,544	65	2,048	20	210	2	10,107	100
II	1,016	12	5,558	63	1,806	20	420	5	8,800	100
III	1,090	11	6,596	66	2,027	20	252	3	9,965	100
IV	1,545	12	7,514	60	2,973	24	441	4	12,473	100
V	1,803	12	9,644	63	3.323	22	434	3	15,204	100
VI	1,595	12	8,171	64	2,443	19	665	5	12,874	100
VII	1,867	12	10,139	63	3,148	20	833	5	15,987	100
VIII	1,637	12	8,739	61	2,903	20	976	7	14,255	100
IX	1,779	12	9,441	62	3,705	25	196	1	15,121	100
X	1,926	12	10,119	64	2,898	19	767	5	15,807	100
XI	1,180	11	7,110	64	2,168	20	578	5	11,189	100
XII	1,416	13	6,326	60	2,445	23	416	4	11,843	100

Exhibit 4 (continued)

Table 3. Jam 'Tiferet'

Month	Jars kg.	1 lb. %	Jars kg.	2 lb. %	Jars kg.	4 lb. %	Tins kg.	A_{10} %	Total kg.	%
1966										
I	1,723	17	5,238	51	1,231	12	2,136	20	10,328	100
II	1,760	17	5,025	47	1,207	11	2,656	25	10,648	100
III	1,187	12	5,303	52	942	9	2,792	27	10,224	100
IV	2,094	18	4,483	40	1,334	12	3,408	30	11,319	100
V	1,745	18	3,987	40	1,137	12	2,981	30	9,850	100
VI	1,959	17	5,289	45	1,265	11	3,100	27	11,613	100
VII	1,812	18	4,159	41	1,235	12	2,936	29	10,142	100
VIII	1,838	17	4,553	44	1,228	12	2,864	27	10,483	100
IX	2,098	18	5,162	45	1,201	10	3,064	27	11,525	100
X	1,759	17	4,404	42	779	7	3,648	34	10,590	100
XI	1,235	12	5,117	49	636	6	3,502	33	10,488	100
XII	1,524	14	4,861	46	711	7	3,568	33	10,664	100
1967										
I	1,442	11	5,228	42	619	5	5,213	42	12,472	100
II	1,277	12	4,453	42	521	5	4·416	41	10,667	100
III	1·362	13	4·551	44	551	5	3,940	38	10,404	100
IV	867	9	3,993	42	338	3	4,368	46	9,566	100
V	2,172	14	6,394	42	891	6	5,712	38	15,169	100
VI	1,613	15	4,509	42	731	7	3,864	36	10,717	100
VII	2,049	17	5,320	44	748	6	4,088	33	12,205	100
VIII	2,085	17	5,500	46	666	6	3,642	31	11,893	100
IX	2,254	19	4,584	39	708	6	4,272	36	11,818	100
X	2,296	19	4,768	40	700	6	4,200	35	11,964	100
XI	1,697	18	4,204	44	474	5	3,152	33	9,525	100
XII	1,539	15	3·732	36	382	5	4,640	44	10,793	100

Part 3
Production in the human resources system

5

Production and personnel

There are three human factors involved in a manufacturing organisation—production managers, workers and trade unions. Production managers are, to a great extent, directly responsible for the continued cooperation of these three factors with the organisation. The managerial responsibility[1] of production managers with regard to trade unions will be discussed in the next chapter. This chapter is devoted to the managerial responsibility of production managers in securing the continued cooperation of the workers and themselves, the production managers, with the organisation.

Production managers share their managerial responsibility for manufacturing employees with both the personnel and the general management functions. The personnel function usually undertakes some managerial responsibility towards the workers, such as recruitment, training, and wages, General management may assume managerial responsibility for higher levels of production managers with regard to recruiting, training, and salaries. However, the major managerial responsibility, *vis-a-vis* all the manufacturing employees, workers as well as managers, rests with the production management.

The role of production management with regard to personnel, has changed considerably since the first appearance of Scientific Management at the turn of the twentieth century. Taylor, in his *Shop Management* had foreseen neither a competition for trained employees, nor a situation in which technical knowledge and skill requirements would change at such a speed that skills and professional knowledge had to be relearned every five to ten years. Taylor thought that 'men will develop faster than new positions open for them' (Taylor 1911, page 142). The one problem he saw in recruiting 'the best class of men' for an organised manufacturing plant was that 'only a few employees were sufficiently broadminded to adopt this policy. They dread the trouble and temporary incident to training new men'.

One of the consequences of the Industrial Revolution was the division of labour, which became necessary as a result of the ever-growing capital intensification of plant and equipment. This capital intensification meant that the relationship between operating expenses of plant and equipment on the one hand, and manpower expenses of salaries, wages and social benefits on the other hand,

1. The term 'managerial responsibility' is used in this book only in one sense—the responsibility of managers for the continued cooperation within the organisation of individuals and groups of people belonging to one or more of the integral factors of organisational decision-making, i.e. human groups whose cooperation is necessary for the organisation's survival.

changed considerably. The ratio of manufacturing manpower costs to plant and equipment costs, which might have been 5:1 or more before the Industrial Revolution, had reduced to approximately 1:1 in many industries by Taylor's time. Since then this ratio has changed considerably further, and may reach, in some technologically advanced organisations, figures as high as 1:10 or 1:100; so too have the requirements and problems of personnel in the manufacturing function changed considerably. These changes have occurred as industry has been moving first to mechanised unit production, then to mass production, and, finally, to automation, or process production.

We shall, consider therefore, personnel requirements and the problems involved in carrying out managerial responsibility, *vis-a-vis* manufacturing in each of the three main levels of technology, which have evolved in industrialised countries. We shall also consider separately managerial responsibility towards three levels of manufacturing employees—the workers, foremen and other production managers. The part concerning the workers is the longest, and covers also those aspects of manufacturing personnel management, which are common to workers, foremen, and other production managers.

5.1   Workers

Most of our notions about recruiting, training and motivating workers evolved from the Scientific Management School and its 'principles'. Unfortunately, we still find some industrial organisations which have not even advanced as far as adoption of these 'scientific management' principles. It seems to us even more unfortunate that many of the industrial organisations which underwent 'scientific management' are stuck with it, unable to cope with the inevitable changes necessary in the managerial responsibility towards workers. The principles of 'scientific management' first appeared in Europe and in the US more or less simultaneously (Taylor, 1911), (Fayol, 1949). However, it was not until the 1930s that they penetrated some European industrial organisations. The spreading of the 'scientific management' gospel was precipitated by Europeans who undertook to expose their fellow countrymen to the scientific management concepts of Taylor and his colleagues, and the administrative concepts of another American, Mary-Ann Follet (Urwick, 1956).

Only after the Second World War did the scientific management concepts penetrate Western Europe, as they had spread over US industry, over twenty years earlier. These principles, however, are mainly applicable as long as the manufacturing is being performed in a unit production system (as we have referred to the lower levels of mechanisation previously in the book, Chapter 1) and, sometimes, in mass production (the middle, pre-automation, levels of mechanisation). Once manufacturing is carried out by a process production method, in the automated, higher levels of mechanisation, the usefulness of these principles drops significantly, and in many cases some of these principles may do more harm than good. It is important, therefore, to consider and speculate how advancing technologies affect both the environment outside the manufacturing organisations, and the conditions within them. For it is evident that some of the things which were designed to help in managing the workers in Taylor's time are becoming increasingly inappropriate nowadays in the technologically advanced countries of Europe and, especially, in Taylor's native country, the United States. Let us consider some of the changes in the management of production workers, consequent upon the movement of manufacturing to more advanced technologies. This we shall do by examining how

- changes occur in worker *skill* requirements
- worker *job content* changes
- workers *educational requirements* change
- *wage incentives* based on piece rates are becoming obsolete, and
- *overtime* does not suit changing conditions.

One other phenomenon, in addition to the advancing technology, had a decisive effect on the management of workers. We refer to over-employment or a general manpower shortage, a phenomenon which was unknown before the Second World War. In order to illustrate the effects of this phenomenon, which we shall discuss in more detail in our next chapter, the principles which have hitherto guided us in manufacturing personnel management, and how for example, job evaluation does not make sense in times of manpower shortage.

We chose these areas in order to illustrate how the principles by which production managers manage the workers change when manufacturing moves from unit production to mass production and from there to process production. The following are only a few examples to show how 'scientific management' principles based on the individual physical contribution of workers as parts of a production system, are being replaced by a more appropriate approach, based on considering the overall contribution of workers as part of the large human system which constitutes an organisation.

This emerging approach is based on sociological as well as psychological considerations. We shall, draw therefore, in our examples, not only on research findings regarding relationships among the workers themselves and between them and other members of the organisation, but, likewise, citing findings relating to the individual behaviour of workers in modern manufacturing.

Skills

The skills required of workers in the more advanced levels of mechanisation are completely different from those in the lower levels. Figure 5.1 presents the skill requirements of workers in the different levels of mechanisation. We see that the higher the technology the less the skill required of the workers. When we reach the highest levels it becomes impossible to measure the individual effort and contribution of workers and to reward them accordingly. Indeed, when we reach these higher levels of mechanisation, the people who attend automated equipment can no longer be referred to as 'workers' or even as 'operators', because they neither work nor do they operate anything. They should rather be called 'watchers', because the major part of their duty is observing boards, dials and signalling lights—watching for any possible indications of malfunctioning of the process.

Thus the training of workers depends on the level of technology at which the plant is operating. In the unit and small batch production system, many of the operators of such equipment as machine tools would have passed through trade schools before being employed in a factory. In large batch and mass production the workers would, in most cases, be unskilled on entry and undergo training within the factory. The 'watchers' in the automated process production plants would probably require a special alertness training. In any case, the degree of attention to human relations required by superiors to their workers in the three production systems, increases as the technology advances. One of the reasons for this is undoubtedly that the amount of and the opportunities for interaction among the workers themselves, decrease the more advanced the technology.

Job content

The variations in the flow of materials from one worker to another in Unit Production (see Fig. 5.2) afford the workers many opportunities for interacting amongst themselves. In this system, the worker has also a greater opportunity for wandering away from his working place for short intervals, whenever he feels like it.

In mass production, on the other hand, every worker has, at best, only one worker on each flank. These are the only people with whom he can interact during manufacturing because he cannot usually leave his working place. The control over the worker's production, the quantity and, sometimes, the quality control, is performed by the two workers on either side. They try to make him work at a speed in harmony with themselves. However, as the natural working speed differs from one person to another, friction and conflicts are bound to occur on a mass production line. All this limits the voluntary interaction in a mass production system.

In process production the opportunities for free interaction with other workers are even more restricted. The total number of 'watchers' in an automated plant is smaller than the number of workers in plants manufacturing in the two other systems. The few 'watchers' are dispersed far apart from each other. It would not usually be necessary, from an operational point of view, to have more than one 'watcher' in a working place. Thus the 'watchers' of the process production system are more isolated than their counterparts in the other two systems.

While the interacting opportunities are diminishing, the more advanced the technology, the greater the need for human interaction because the job content becomes 'poorer'. In unit production the jobs are comparatively heterogenous and one worker performs a variety of tasks. There is usually less need for 'job enrichment' under these circumstances. In mass production, on the other hand, the worker is usually limited to one task, which generally means performing one operation only, repeated for long periods of time.

Fig. 5.1 *Changing contribution required of operators with advances in levels of mechanisation*

Worker contribution or sacrifice traditionally receiving compensation*	Mechanisation levels			
	1–4 Hand control	*5–8* Mechanical control	*9–11* Variable control signal response	*12–17* Variable control action response
Physical effort	Increasing-decreasing	Decreasing	Decreasing-nil	Nil
Mental effort	Increasing	Increasing-decreasing	Increasing or decreasing	Decreasing-nil
Manipulative skill (dexterity)	Increasing	Decreasing	Decreasing-nil	Nil
General skill	Increasing	Increasing	Increasing-decreasing	Decreasing-nil
Education	Increasing	Increasing	Increasing or decreasing	Increasing or decreasing
Experience	Increasing	Increasing-decreasing	Increasing-decreasing	Decreasing-nil
Exposure to hazards	Increasing	Decreasing	Decreasing	Nil
Acceptance of undesirable job conditions	Increasing	Decreasing	Decreasing-nil	Decreasing-nil
Responsibility†	Increasing	Increasing	Increasing-decreasing	Increasing, decreasing or nil
Decision-making	Increasing	Increasing-decreasing	Decreasing	Decreasing-nil
Influence on productivity‡	Increasing	Increasing-decreasing or nil	Decreasing-nil	Nil
Seniority	Not affected	Not affected	Not affected	Not affected

Source. Bright, J. R. 'Does Automation Raise Skill Requirements?', *Harvard Business Review*, July/August, 1958.

* Refers to operators and not to setup men, maintenance men, engineers, or supervisors.

† Safety of equipment, of the product, or other people.

‡ Refers to opportunity for the worker to increase output through extra effort, skill, or judgement.

Fig. 5.2 The layouts of the three systems

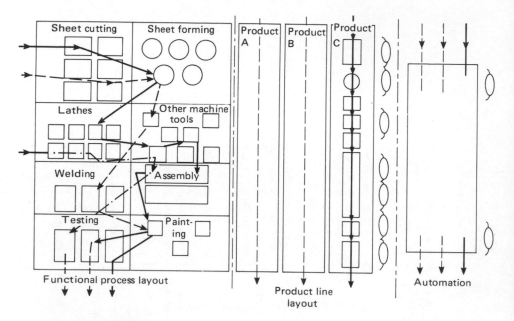

In process production the 'watcher' does not even have the opportunity of contributing his skill to the quality and quantity of the products manufactured. The more advanced the technology the less the 'watcher' contributes. In the lower levels of automation he may perform some maintenance duties, but in the higher levels he is just supposed to watch the dials (in the highest levels there is, theoretically at least, no need for human presence at all). The responsibility of the watchers, as we have seen in Chapter 1, Vol. 1, is enormous; however, it is not a positive contributing responsibility but a responsibility for preventing negative occurrences. This responsibility entails vigilance and mental stability, because the only two cases where the 'watcher' does not discharge his responsibility is when he fails to read and react upon the signals, because of negligence, or when he could deliberately sabotage parts of the equipment, because of a mental disorder.

The above means that the more advanced the technology, the more need for human attention towards the workers. This could mean that the jobs of workers should be 'enriched' by adding to them tasks which are surplus from a manufacturing process effectiveness point of view. Another way to do it is to change the length of the shift (i.e. one stretch of work) for this type of work and let the workers have long breaks after relatively short periods of work (say two to four hours); or to rotate the workers from one task to another every few hours or days. All such solutions will mean lower rates of task specialisation and of machine utilisation; however one solution which does not interfere with either specialisation or machine utilisation, is the improvement of the human relations between management and workers. We shall return to this aspect later in this chapter.

Educational background

The effect of the level of technology on the workers' skill is manifest as we have already pointed out, in the training of the workers. The knowhow of the workers has to be renewed every few years. However, the more advanced the technology, the less the technical knowledge required of the workers within the organisation. In unit production many of the workers are skilled workers who passed through trade schools in their elementary or secondary levels of education or underwent long periods of apprenticeship training. In mass production most workers need only to go through training programmes within the industrial organisations, e.g. the US method of TWI (Training Within Industry), the Swiss-Dutch method of Accelerated Training, or similar programmes. In process production there is only a limited need for regular technical training, either outside or within the industrial organisation. What is needed in process production, are people who have received a general education at the primary and secondary levels. It seems that such general education programmes could equip people with two main pre-requisites for a more technologically advanced society.

Firstly, they should provide an appropriate training for assuming increasing responsibilities, within a framework of doing ever diminishing amounts of physical or mental work. Secondly, such general education in the liberal arts and humanities, would equip the workers with interests and capabilities which could carry them through the longer periods of leisure that advanced technology provides in industrialised nations. It seems that the most industrialised country in the world, the US, already does not have sufficient work to offer to its inhabitants within a five-day working week. This might mean that work will soon become a generally sought after commodity. In order to divide it justly between all, it will be necessary within a comparatively short period of time of, say, thirty years, for the more industrialised countries to reach a time distribution of something like fifty per cent work and fifty per cent leisure. Thus, for example, people's time could alternate between *three days'* work and *three days'* leisure, and recreation centres (i.e. week-end resorts, theatres, cinemas, sports fields, libraries, beaches,) which have been hitherto used to undercapacity for only two out of every seven days would be more fully utilised. Likewise, it would, to a great extent, be a solution to the 'job enrichment' required in the more advanced technologies, because every two or three days the workers would stop doing their limited task in manufacturing and change over to a variety of pursuits of a completely different nature. Elementary and secondary education will need to prepare people to follow these pursuits.

Therefore it seems to us that while some of pre-university education will need to provide for the evergrowing demands in the sciences, e.g. mathematics and physics, the great majority of children will require to be better prepared and equipped in the humanities and arts in order to give them spiritual contentment and comfort in a world which in some ways, at least, would resemble the one which George Orwell predicted for *1984*.

Motivation

One worker management field in which major changes have occurred is that of the motivation of workers. Since the early 1950s behavioural scientists have pointed out that wage incentive schemes, relating the wages to the individual outputs of workers, seem in many cases to do more harm than good (Whyte, 1970). Such wage incentive schemes harm the social structure and elicit negative reactions towards the organisation in general and, in particular, towards the manufacturing process. Piece-rate incentive schemes perpetuate existing manufacturing methods, and prevent the introduction of methods improvements, and other changes. Workers on wage incentives can be expected to show more resistance to change than those who have not been exposed to such schemes (unless the changes are directly related to the incentive scheme, and the scheme is made conditional upon the introduction of the changes).

The opposition to wage incentive schemes appeared from various schools of organisational behaviour. The heads of the Glacier Project in Britain, the largest contribution of which was probably the notion of the measurement of responsibility by way of differences in the time span of discretion, have believed that remuneration should be correlated with the degree of responsibility. This is why they have opposed any wage incentive schemes which would disrupt what they consider equitable payment (Jaques, 1961).

Another group which has not accepted the role of wage incentive schemes as motivating workers to work, are Frederick Herzberg and his associates (Herzberg *et al.*, 1967). This group claims that wage incentives are a 'health maintenance' factor, i.e. that you have to keep on with it in order to avoid an unhealthy situation, rather than it being a motivating factor. However, it seems that wage incentives cannot be regarded as a 'health maintenance' factor, because sticking with a wage incentive scheme does not maintain a *status quo*. In many cases, it leads eventually to the deterioration of the existing situation. In all cases it causes a slowdown in the introduction of changes necessary for the progress of manufacturing and of the organisation as a whole. Indeed, whether one supports wage incentive schemes or whether one does not, the more advanced the technology, the more obsolete the whole idea. Even according to several 'scientific management' principles of wage incentive schemes based on piece rates, the introduction of such schemes is illogical in the more technologically advanced organisation. Let us first list, therefore, several industrial engineering principles relating to piece-rate wage incentives, and subsequently consider the relevance of these principles in the three productive systems.

These principles could be phrased as follows:

(*a*) *A wage incentive scheme should be based on time standards for cyclic operations*, which could be measured and established in advance of the introduction of a wage incentive scheme.

(*b*) *An overwhelming part of a working day based on a wage incentives scheme should be spent on measurable cyclic operations.* The reason for this is that in order to avoid time-keeping, when the worker is changing from one operation to another and from one batch to another, it is essential that practically his whole working day should be accounted for by piece-rate calculations (Fig. 5.3). The entries of these calculations are usually made by the workers themselves. The length of time worked on every item or batch does not come into these calculations. However, if during the day a worker has one or more comparatively long periods in which he is not working on wage incentives (i.e. being assigned to a task for which a standard time could not be or was not established) this time has to be deducted from the length of his working day in order to arrive at the actual time worked on wage incentives (e.g. the thirty minutes deducted from 480 minutes in Fig. 5.3).

This, in turn, means closely controlled time-keeping, usually performed by the foreman and, in some cases, by special full-time time-keepers (it has been claimed that at one stage in Yugoslavia's efforts to 'wage incentify' the whole of it's industry, one could find plants which had, on the average, one time-keeper, for every two manufacturing workers). One cannot leave time-keeping to the workers themselves because it would be too much of a temptation for most human beings not to cheat with time registering in a way beneficial to themselves, since their wages are directly affected by the time-keeping (i.e. the larger the registered length of time not worked on wage incentives, the larger the premium gained by the worker).

On the other hand, when the time-keeping is performed by foremen this adds an additional factor for friction and conflict between them and the workers. Consequently workers on piece rates should spend an overwhelming part of their working day on piece-rate work.

(c) *A great majority of the workers in the organisation should be working on wage incentives.* Wage incentives may mean an average increase of wages between ten to forty per cent over and above the previous regular wages. Workers who are not on wage incentives will, by and large, become jealous of those who receive a substantial increase in their wages, and demand a similar increase for themselves—or else such workers may start putting pressures on their fellow workers, as well as on management. Considering that a worker who is on incentives should work most of the day (according to item *b*) on cyclic operations that could be measured in advance (according to item *a*) manufacturing management has to ensure that the great majority of workers are indeed complying with such requirements. Otherwise management will be under pressure to include everbody else on a fictitious 'wage incentives scheme', i.e. paying people premiums unrelated to any increases in productivity. This means that:

(d) *The additional payment according to the wage incentives scheme should be related as much as possible to the individual performance of every worker,* so that he can recognise in the premiums he receives a direct connection with his efforts. Therefore, schemes based on individual piece rates should be preferred to those based on group piece rates.

(e) *The marketing function should be able to distribute and pass on to the customers as much as the workers produce.* Production engineers know they should make sure that the quality will not drop as a result of pressures for higher quantity. However, they do not always realise that before introducing a wage incentives scheme, one should ascertain that the customers will not only accept the quality of the products, but indeed absorb the increased output, which sometimes might exceed by fifty per cent or more the output prior to the introduction of the wage incentives. The flow of materials from the suppliers, through the manufacturing and finally, in a transformed shape, to the customers, is as much a 'balancing problem' as 'line balancing'[2] in industrial engineering. It is indeed a much more crucial sort of 'balancing' as far as the survival of the organisation is concerned.

Fig. 5.3 Example sheet of wage incentive calculations

Name: *Jack Jones*			Date: *21-3-72*	
Batch No.	*No. of pieces*	*Standard time (in minutes) per piece worked*		*Remarks*
0023	30	3·3	99	
0192	150	2·4	360	
0075	63	2·1	132	*Remaining 137 pieces of the batch for 16/4/71*
Total standard worked			591	
Actual time worked on wage incentives: Total clocked working time 480 Time worked on non-piece rate jobs 30			450	
Time gained in premiums (minutes)			141	

Figure 5.4 shows the degree of relevance of the above principles to the Unit, Mass and Process Production systems of manufacturing. We see that even if we consider only what we referred to as 'scientific management' principles, and ignore

2. 'Line balancing' is a work study technique which deals with appropriating the correct, balanced, number of workers (and the correct number and size of equipment which they operate) for each of the operations or 'stations' on the production line through which the materials and parts on which they work flow.

the negative social consequences that wage incentives could bring about, wage incentive schemes based on piece rates can be introduced only in unit production manufacturing and only in industrial organisations where all the principles listed in Fig. 5.4 apply. Wage incentive schemes are completely irrelevant to process production plants. Neither are they relevant to mass production manufacturing although some of the principles could be applicable in this case. This is because the moment one principle in Fig. 5.4. is irrelevant, all the others also become irrelevant too, because it would mean that piece rate wage incentives are unsuitable for such a production system.

Fig. 5.4 The relevance of wage incentive schemes in industrial organisations with different technology levels

Principles of piece rate wage incentives schemes	The production system		
	Unit production	*Mass production*	*Process production*
a. Measuring the cyclic operations in advance.	Relevant*	Relevant	Irrelevant
b. An overwhelming part of the working day should be spent on measurable cyclic operations.	Relevant*	Relevant*	Irrelevant
c. A great majority of the workers in the organisation should be working on wage incentives.	Relevant*	Relevant*	Irrelevant
d. The wage incentive scheme should relate the individual's efforts to his premiums.	Relevant*	Irrelevant	Irrelevant
e. The marketing function should be able to distribute to customers as much as the workers produce.	Relevant*	Irrelevant	Irrelevant

* Not in all tasks and in every industrial organisation.

Thus in a mass production system where output is based on the special effort of only one or a few of the slowest individuals working on the line, the premiums are unrelated to the efforts of the majority of the workers some of whom work at their usual speed while others have to work more slowly than their usual speed. This means that the majority of the workers do not make any special effort, and that they do not feel any relation between the premium they may receive and their individual effort (Principle *d* on Fig. 5.4). It also means that the speed at which workers work when on incentives, is not very different from the one at which they would have worked without incentives. Consequently, the marketing function does not have any special problem 'to distribute to customers as much as the workers produce' (Principle *e* on Fig. 5.4). In other words, there is no sense in introducing wage incentives in mass production manufacturing plants, even when considering only scientific management principles. That is to say that in more and more plants, wage incentive schemes based on piece rates make less and less sense, even to industrial engineers and not only to behavioural scientists, many of whom have felt since the Second World War that such schemes have done more harm than good in all types of factories.

One can indeed notice a steady and relatively rapid de-incentification trend in the US. In Europe this phenomenon is mostly evident in industries which went over to process production. De-incentification should, however, be regarded as a process in which the workers are involved rather than an arbitrary decision by management.

Workers could usually be earning through wage incentives some ten to forty per cent above their regular wages. This addition becomes an integral part of a worker's wages on which he counts and which contributes to his family's budget. He should therefore be expected to insist that he earns this money even when not on incentives. A de-incentification move should therefore desirably constitute part of a wider agreement with the workers, which, among other things, would provide for them to continue to earn more or less the same as before.

Overtime

Another area which has been a consequence of the unit production industrialisation which followed the Industrial Revolution, is the phenomenon of overtime. Overtime has been one of the 'scientific management' solutions to the ever-growing pressures, to utilise fully increasingly expensive equipment. However, this solution, like the solution of wage incentive schemes, has turned out to be more damaging than helpful when applied in more advanced technologies, even when evaluated only on the basis of strictly economic considerations. Overtime, like piece-rate wage incentives, has been rejected by many social scientists who feel that workers should not work more than the length of a working day because of family reasons as well as personal health. Some social scientists feel that a worker should earn fair wages for a regular working day. It has been a known phenomenon that as long as overtime is part of the system, the workers would create the necessity for overtime even when they could have completed their work within the length of an ordinary working day. This phenomenon is only natural, considering that for many of the workers the overtime pay has become part of their contribution to their basic family budget.

However, when we consider the relation of overtime to its possible economic contribution in each of the three basic production systems, we discover that the more advanced the technology the less the potential contribution of overtime. Figure 5.5 presents some criteria by which we could evaluate the usefulness of overtime in each of the three production systems.

We see, for example, that using overtime in mass production manufacturing means that either the length of work of the whole production line is extended for some time (i.e. all the workers would have to put in another, say, two hours) or,

Fig. 5.5 Advantages and disadvantages of overtime in the three production systems

Production system	Unit	Mass	Process
Criteria for evaluation / *Usual length of operation every 24 hours*	*1 or 2 shifts*	*2 or 3 shifts*	*3 shifts*
1. Length of overtime period	Could be extended for any individual to any necessary length of time	Could either be extended for *all the workers* to any necessary length of time *or* be extended for *any individual worker to a whole additional shift*	Could only be extended for *any individual worker to a whole additional shift*
2. Labour cost	Higher	Much higher	Very much higher
3. Ability of one worker to replace another in a different job	Usually able	Usually unable	Almost always unable
4. The willingness, as well as the readiness of workers to work overtime	Usually willing	Usually unwilling when it is for a whole additional shift	Usually unwilling
5. The Need for management to plan for cases of a sudden need for an additional worker or group of workers	Not absolutely necessary	Absolutely necessary when one or more workers are missing	Absolutely necessary
6. The overall feasibility of overtime, and therefore the ability of production management to rely on overtime in cases of emergency.	Feasible	Usually unfeasible	Unfeasible

because one worker is missing for the second or third shift, another worker would be asked to work a whole shift.

This in turn would mean that the labour cost of manufacturing would be much higher than with regular pay because overtime pay is substantially higher than the regular pay. Likewise, because workers in mass production are semi-skilled and every worker becomes proficient only in his own task, a worker would usually be unable to replace another one without disrupting the output of the whole production line. Workers would usually be unwilling to work on overtime during a whole shift; it might also be difficult to persuade every one of a whole group of workers on the same line to work overtime for a shorter period of time. Consequently management has to plan for emergencies when a worker does not report for his shift on a production line, keeping reserve people in tasks from which they could easily be moved to replace those missing. For all these reasons, it seems that overtime is usually unfeasible in mass production manufacturing.

Process production plants, like refineries, where overtime makes least sense, have been gradually moving away from it. Moving out of overtime in a plant where it has been a regular practice is similar to moving out of wage incentives and cannot be done arbitrarily. For workers who have been accustomed to working overtime the additional payment they received for it became part of their expected and habitual remuneration, and they could not and should not be made to give up a substantial part of it.

Job evaluation

This is an area which has received a great deal of attention not only from 'scientific management' supporters but, likewise, from many social scientists. As with many other 'scientific management' innovations it contributed positively to many industrial organisations and even to whole economies (e.g. Holland, where job evaluations were established for all occupations in the Dutch economy). However, although job evaluation makes sense to many in that it lays down criteria for establishing levels of what seems to them to be fair wages, it has been criticised quite frequently in recent years and was found to be a burden more than an aid in periods of full and over employment.

The criticism of the logic and acceptance of job evaluation as such comes mainly from the so-called 'Glacier School' who insist, as we have already indicated, that the only criterion for the basis of establishing wages is the degree of responsibility. This is because people are promoted in the organisational hierarchy only on the basis of their added responsibility and not primarily because of any other criterion of job evaluation (responsibility is one of many criteria in most job evaluation schemes). The Glacier School likewise claim that the only wages which are accepted by employees as 'fair' are those which correlate with their degree of responsibility (Jacques, 1961).

They claim that the degree of responsibility can be measured by means of the time span of discretion. Although the notion of the degree of responsibility and its conceptualisation through the time span of discretion is an important contribution to our understanding of management, the actual measurement of the time span of discretion and its application to the establishment of wage scales has been rejected by many.

Whatever one feels about the logic of the various job evaluation schemes, it is absolutely evident that pressures of supply and demand are stronger than any predetermined wage scales. Thus, when a specific skill is in great demand, individual workers or groups of workers in that skill can easily obtain a wage increase over and above a pre-established, job-evaluated, rate. Management cannot afford resisting pressures for raising wages under such circumstances. The more critical the role of workers in the whole manufacturing process—the less management is able to resist their wage claims. Thus, in periods of over-employment, when a manpower shortage is experienced in all skills, trades, and professions, any pre-established wage-scales will crumble under the pressures of supply and demand. Under such circumstances management must be as flexible as possible in order to ensure the survival of the organisation. A dogmatic insistence on wage scales and policies can easily lead to the collapse of the whole organisation. In the following chapter we shall discuss in more detail, the dynamics of the effects of the employment market on the relationship of management—workers—trade unions.

The inability of management to stick to pre-established wage scales in times of employment market pressures, does not mean that management should not try to follow a logical wage structure. This structure should primarily be logical to the workers themselves. There is no doubt that relating wages to the degree of responsibility required in the job, would, as the Glacier people claim (Jacques, 1961), make a lot of sense to the workers. However if, say, the training for a specific essential job, is much longer than for another job—in which the responsibility is much larger than that in the long trained job—it would be necessary to compensate employees for the length of training (i.e. of education) too. Otherwise people would not undertake long training, and eventually the manpower shortage in a certain skill would anyway lead to compensating the employees for the previously unremunerated length of education. Similarly, it could be shown that the inclusion of additional factors of job evaluation (other than the degree of responsibility) could counteract short- and long-range supply and demand pressures on the wage structure. Thus, although the Glacier people might seem to be right in claiming that relating the wage structure to the responsibility structure makes sense to wage-earners, it appears that it would be sensible to continue basing the wage structure on other factors too, for pragmatic rather than for logical reasons.

Summary and conclusion (workers)

We have discussed several areas in which the traditional contribution of scientific management principles to the management of manufacturing workers, has been declining, as new phenomena changed the conditions which prevailed when Scientific Management was first propounded. The first phenomenon we have discussed, the technological developments, originated in the United States. European manufacturing organisations, can therefore learn from the US experience, regarding the effects of advancing technologies on the management of workers. On the whole we can say that the more advanced the technology:

- the less the skill of the worker
- the less heterogeneous his job content
- the less technical his educational background should be

- the less sensible the use of wage incentives
- the less suitable is overtime

The second phenomenon which we related to the management of the workers, the condition of overemployment, first appeared in Europe after the Second World War.

Overemployment is not an unavoidable outcome of technological progress. The best proof of this is the US which has not yet experienced overemployment. Overemployment is a consequence of one or more of the following:

- The educational system is not coping with the emerging manpower requirements of new technologies. Thus while in some skills there may be a manpower shortage, in others—obsolete skills—there could be unemployment.

- The population is not increasing at the same rate as the economic growth, in terms of the number of jobs available in the economy.

- The growth in the scope of decision-making process (DMP), which is a consequence of technological development, is not accompanied by the necessary parallel changes in organisational structure throughout the economy.

The United States has tackled on the whole, all these three points by adapting its educational system, absorbing a high rate of immigration and changing its organisational structures to fit them to the new scopes of DMP. European countries tried to solve the population requirements by employing foreigners from the southern European and other less developed countries with a surplus of labour. As for the educational and organisation structure requirements, the necessary changes have only now started to occur.

Some of the countries represented by case studies in this book have experienced the effects of overemployment on manufacturing organisations. One of the most drastic effects of overemployment is an escalation of wages and salaries. We saw that under such conditions a pre-established wage structure cannot withstand the pressures of employees for wage increases over and above any established scales. What is then the way to manage the manufacturing workers under conditions of advanced technology and changing conditions in the employment market?

It seems to us that one has primarily to prepare different kinds of workers and to care differently for them while they are employed. We have concluded that the workers should receive a more humanistic (i.e. liberal arts) education which would give them a spiritual lead and internal contentment to carry them through the emptiness of their jobs, starting with a mental idleness and followed by a physical one, which accompanies the transfer of jobs from unit production to mass production, and finally to process production. Such an education should also be at the disposal of workers during their leisure time, which will continue to increase as a result of technological developments, to a possible ratio of an equal number of working days to an equal number of leisure days, for workers in Europe, by the end of this century.

During the time that workers spend within the boundaries of the manufacturing organisation, there is an ever-growing need to offer them an opportunity for 'catharsis'. Catharsis is the process by which a person is relieved of the worries, tensions, troubles, etc., which weigh upon his mind—by way of relating his innermost feelings to somebody else. The need for catharsis is universal and well-known. The Catholic Church has offered confession to all its members for centuries, and, undoubtedly, this has been one of the organisational foundations of the Church. Sigmund Freud introduced the notion of catharsis into psychology and it has been the basis of psychoanalysis, psychiatry, psychotherapy etc. ever since. It is clear that the more complicated our life is, technologically and organisationally, the more we need catharsis. The more industrialised the country, the more the need for catharsis. This also means, although in a more remote sense, that generally speaking, the more industrialised the country, the more democratic it should be or, that the more democratic the country, the more advanced the technology it can absorb.

The idea of catharsis was first introduced into industry by Elton Mayo, Fritz Roethlisberger and their colleagues from the Harvard Business School, following what turned into the most famous organisational research of this century—the study of the Western Electric Company in Hawthorne. The only conclusion which followed the study reported in *'Management and The Worker* (Roethlisberger and Dickson, 1971), the 'bible' of all organisational research, was that psychological counsellors should be put at the disposal of the employees, workers as well as managers. These psychological counsellors should enable the employees to talk freely about their feelings, thoughts, etc.

This sole conclusion, followed a long and impressive list of findings, the contribution of which has served as a direct or indirect foundation to any worthwhile organisational theory, conceptual scheme, and research project ever since.

Strangely enough, or may be not strangely at all, it is also our conclusion following this analysis of the management of manufacturing workers—that the best way for securing the voluntary cooperation of the workers with the organisation, is to offer them an opportunity for catharsis. This could be done by putting at the employees' disposal well-trained psychological counsellors (i.e. non-directive interviewers) who should be as little as possible formally linked with the management organisation. These counsellors could help the organisation in one additional major way:

They could facilitate communication by reporting the general trends of attitudes, opinions and thoughts, that they discover in the *tête-à-tête* non-directive interviews with the employees at all levels, workers as well as managers. This they should report back to all levels, but primarily to the higher levels of management. However, they should make sure that the identity of 'who said what' would be strictly safeguarded.

The whole notion of catharsis in industrial organisations, is based on the factual situation that in a formal organisation a person is generally hiding many of his feelings, ideas, and opinions, from those above and below him, as well as parallel to him, in the hierarchy. The psychological counsellor (i.e. the non-directive interviewer) could both help the person maintain his 'mental hygiene' and help the organisation maintain its communication channels 'fully open'.

5.2   Foremen

Some of the aspects covered in the preceding part of this chapter, concern foremen as well as workers. However, there exist problems which are specific to foremen. The common denominator, and sometimes the source of all these problems, is that the foremen are the only managerial level which is permanently intermixed with the workers. We shall start our discussion by describing the managerial responsibility and status of foremen, in general. We shall then proceed to discuss the roles and leadership of foremen in the three production systems.

Let us first of all re-emphasise that the answer to the question 'are the foremen managers?' is 'definitely yes'. This follows our definition that (Chapter 1, Vol. 1) 'managers are all those members of the operating organisation (the employees) whose primary role in the organisation is to ensure the continued cooperation of a group of people'. The managerial responsibility of the foremen is to ensure the continued cooperation of the workers, exactly as the buyers are entrusted with the continued cooperation of the suppliers and the salesmen ensure the continued cooperation of the customers. The foremen have to ensure the continued cooperation of the workers, with whom they are employed in the same organisation.

Both parties, workers and foremen, are formally rewarded for their cooperation with the organisation in the same manner, by way of financial remuneration. The most important point for the manufacturing management to bear in mind in respect to the foremen is, therefore, how to help them fulfil their difficult role as the in-between people of the operating organisation (the employee organisation). This is a problem of identification: with which group does the foreman identify himself?; or, to put it in sociological terms: what is his reference group? In order to help him identify himself with the management, one should let the foreman feel he *is* a manager and that he *is not* a worker. The manufacturing management has, therefore, to make sure that the status of the foreman[3] is that of a manager, and not of a worker.

Following are several areas which constitute the foreman's status. We indicate in each of these areas what should be done, *if* the manufacturing management feels that the foremen have problems of identification with the management in that specific area.

Salary and wages

There should be a clear distinction between the financial remuneration of foremen and workers. This applies to several points:

The name. 'Salary' for foremen and 'wages' for workers.

The level. The gap between the two should be distinguishable. When the workers are on an incentive the gap should be between the total take-home wages of the great majority of workers—and the salaries of foremen.

3. Status as defined by Chester I. Barnard in *The Nature of Leadership,* Barnard, 1946.

Payment period base. The basis of salary calculations for foremen should resemble that of other managers—monthly or annual.

Premiums. The method of any additional productivity, profit-sharing or other incentive scheme—should be different for foremen and for workers. If managers are not on any incentive scheme—neither should the foremen be. If managers are on incentives—the foremen should have a similar scheme, resembling that of managers, rather than that of the workers.

Trade or professional affiliation. Unless there exist special unions for managers (like the unions for the 'cadre' in France) or unless there exists a general federation of trade unions to which everybody including chief executives (like the Histadrut in Israel) may belong, in which other managers of the same organisation are members, foremen should refrain from membership in trade unions. Foremen should be afforded working conditions which are appropriate for their roles and distinguishable from those of the workers. The more the foremen are inclinded to be confused about their managerial responsibility and role, the more important it is to introduce distinctions, such as special overalls for foremen. Whenever other managers of the organisation have special arrangements or privileges (e.g. special dining halls, no clocking-in,) the foremen should be granted the same (this does not mean, of course, that if the chief executive has a company car, cars should be given to the foremen!).

The above are only some of the points which one has to bear in mind when trying to make foremen feel and assume their managerial responsibility towards the workers.

By using the term 'should' when discussing the above areas, we intend to emphasise, rather than to insist. Organisations could survive without one or more of the 'shoulds' we have mentioned in specifying these areas. We likewise realise that within some socio-cultural environments, some of these 'shoulds' are not feasible, sometimes not even necessary.

Foremen roles and leadership in three production systems

The changing roles required of foremen in the three productions systems emerge from Fig. 5.6. The type of leadership of foremen can be deduced also from Fig. 5.7. We have compiled in Fig. 5.8, the main information from these two other tables in order to analyse foremen roles and types of leadership in the three production systems.

The information in Fig. 5.8 tells us the following about the foremen in each of the three production systems.

Unit production
The foreman here is at the head of a functional department (e.g. a machine tool shop, a paint shop, a welding shop). Since he is leading workers who are mostly in the same trade (e.g. painters, welders), it is usually expected that he will have

Fig. 5.6 Tasks or roles of supervisors in production process

| Task or role | Order ranking* as to scope of decision making (or as to relative time consumption) | | | | | |
| | Unit | | Mass | | Process | |
	Within production system	Compared with other systems	Within production systems	Compared with other systems	Within production systems	Compared with other systems
Within unit (towards their subordinates and equipment)						
Planning	High	(1)	Low	(2)	Nil	(3)
Materials handling		(1)		(2)		(3)
Quantity control		(1)		(2)		(3)
Quality control		(1)		(2)		(3)
Work instructions	Medium	(1)	High	(2)	Low	(3)
Human relations		(3)		(2)	Very high	(1)
Machine repairs and maintenance	Low	(2)	Medium	(1)	Very low	(3)
Worker training		(2)		(1)		(3)
Outside unit						
Communication with superiors and peers		(1)		(3)		(2)

* (1) Indicates the production system in which the task/role has the largest scope of decision making (i.e. the most time consuming).

(3) indicates the smallest scope of decision making.

(2) is between (1) and (3) in scope of decision making (i.e. in time consumption).

Fig. 5.7 Interrelation of three systems

Production system (Woodward)	Organisational structure (Woodward)	Scope of decision-making (c, below)	*Physical set-up**	
			Materials flowing through	Departmental layout (a, above)
Single unit and small batch	Centralised	Entrepreneurial and Functional	Multiple single units	Functional (process)
Mass and large batch	Decentralised	Decentralised	Lines	Product line
Process	Centralised	Functional	Single installation	Automation

* See above, Fig. 5.2.

Fig. 5.8 Foremen roles and types of leadership in three production systems

	Production system		
Factor	*Unit*	*Mass*	*Process*
Technical knowledge	Much	Little	None
Planning and paperwork	Much	Very little	None
Instructing and training	Much	Much	Little
Controlling quantity and quality	Much	Little	None
Communication with superiors and Peers	Often	Not often, but urgent	Rare but very urgent
Personal attention to workers	Much	Little	Very much
Mobility (Kilometrage or Mileage)	Much	Little	Much
Type of human leadership	'Functional subordinate' (dependent on other units)	'Decentralised Subordinate' (fully responsible for total results)	'Human leader'

considerable technical knowledge. In some countries like Germany, he is referred to as a 'meister', i.e. a master in his trade.

He is responsible for the planning of the flow of a variety of units and small batches through his shop. These orders are going through different routes and the foreman's task is to ensure that the various orders flow through as quickly as possible, while the workers and machines are as fully utilised as possible. This requires much planning and paperwork. It likewise requires a good deal of instructing the workers as to what and how are they going to produce each of the variety of units and small batches, which are allotted to them. Subsequently the foreman has to control the quantity and quality of work performed by each worker, according to a plan or to change it according to the actual results achieved.

The functional layout of unit production, makes it dependent upon the central planning of the flow of units and small batches through the plant, and the subsequent coordination of every department with other departments—in relation to the parts and materials they are going to receive from some departments and transmit to others.

Because of the nature of the work in a unit production system the foreman has to give much personal attention to his workers. Consequently he has to be mobile and cover a large kilometrage (or mileage). A recent study in a batch manufacturing factory, with a functional layout (Shur, 1969) found that the more mobile the foremen were, the better foremen they were considered to be, either when measured by conventional leadership tests (Fleishman, 1953) or according to the opinion of their peers and superiors. The totality of the foreman roles in a unit production system indicates that the type of leadership required of him is not dissimilar to the subordinate of the chief executive in a functional managerial structure (e.g. the head of marketing or the head of production in a functional structure).

Mass production

The foreman in this production system is at the head of a group of workers with different types of trades and skills who, unlike the workers of unit production, are continuously dependent upon the two workers flanking them on the right and on the left.

The foreman cannot have a thorough technical expertise in the skills of all his workers and indeed does not need to have much technical knowledge of the skill of any of them. Neither does the foreman need to do a lot of planning and paperwork, in order to prepare and report the daily performance of his group of workers. Only occasionally does he have to rearrange the workers, because somebody may be missing. He has however, to train new workers for their work in the mass production system.

Once they are on the mass production line, he does not have to control their output quantity because this is done by the workers themselves, who control each other. As for the quality, the foreman has to control only those workers, who are not controlled by those who follow them (i.e. when the following worker does not by the nature of his own operation, make sure that his predecessor performed up to the quality standard).

The mass production foreman does not usually have frequent communication with his superiors or peers. However, when he has to be in contact with them, the communication is of an urgent nature, because if something happens in a mass production line it usually affects the whole line and not just one worker or machine.

The personal attention the foreman gives to the workers is little, because usually nothing extraordinary happens and the work is carried out as if by itself. Because of the line layout of mass production the foreman can see most of his workers from one place and anyway, he does not have to attend to them as much as in the other two production systems. This is why he is not very mobile. On the whole, the type of leadership of the foreman in mass production, reminds one of the subordinate to the chief executive in a decentralised managerial structure. Like the head of a decentralised product line or of a decentralised area, the mass production foreman is fully responsible for the total results (of manufacturing the product).

Process production

The responsibility of the process production foreman is what one could refer to as 'preventative'. In other words, neither the foreman nor the workers in a process production can contribute positively to the manufacturing process (when we refer to workers in process production we exclude, as we have done in the other two production systems, set-up men, maintenance men and other workers who do not have to be present continuously at the equipment). The people who attend the process production equipment could not, as we have previously mentioned, be referred to as either 'workers' or 'operators'. They should preferably be called 'watchers'.

The foreman in process production is therefore a caretaker of 'watchers'. He neither needs any technical knowledge, nor does he have to plan, do paperwork or control the quantity and quality. All this is done by the equipment itself. However he does have to do some instruction and training. Likewise he is rarely in communication with peers or superiors. Moreover, whenever this does happen, it is usually in connection with a very urgent matter.

The main role of the foreman in a process production plan is to prevent as much as possible these very contacts with his superiors. In other words he has to make sure that his 'watchers' perform their work as best as they can, so that if something happens, it is entirely because of a failure in the equipment, and is brought to the attention of superiors in the shortest possible time. This means that the 'preventative' role of the foreman is to make sure that the 'watchers' are permanently on the alert and always mentally stable. Consequently he has to pay a great deal of personal attention to the workers and must be mobile, covering a great distance, so as to spend personally as much time as possible with each of his watchers. This is why we describe his type of leadership as the 'human leader'.

Summary and conclusion (foremen)

Many of the points we mentioned in relation to the personnel management of manufacturing workers apply to foremen also. We have primarily stressed, however, the difference between the two groups of manufacturing employees.

The foremen are managers and it is of cardinal importance that they be made to feel that they are indeed part of management. This is important because otherwise they would not be able to fulfil their managerial responsibility securing the continued cooperation of the workers with the organisation. Foremen should be given the feeling that they are managers, and they should be treated as managers by granting them managerial privileges and restricting them from doing things which are not acceptable to managers.

Subsequently we discussed the different roles of foremen in the three production systems. After analysing the different roles we arrived at the conclusion that the foremen in unit production resemble the heads of functions in a functional managerial structure, since they must have technical expertise, must control closely their subordinates and lead their workers in a formally centralised structure.

The foremen in mass production, on the other hand, are similar to the heads of decentralised product lines or geographical areas in a decentralised managerial tructure. They are responsible for the total manufacturing results of their workers, but do not control them closely.

Finally, the foremen in process production are completely different from their peers in unit or mass production, in as much as their subordinates cannot positively contribute in quantity or quality to manufacturing output. The role of the 'watchers' in process production is 'preventative'. The foreman has to make sure that his 'watchers' are alert so that they can react to and report any irregularity in the process. He also has to ensure their mental welfare. He therefore assumes the role of a 'human leader'.

5.3   Other production managers

We have already discussed many aspects of personnel management—with regard to the managers themselves. The effects of the changes in the employment market are similar with regard to all employees—workers or managers.

The particular situation of production managers in their being continuously involved with the human factor for the cooperation of which they are responsible— the workers—is similar to that of foremen, although the latter are more involved with the workers than other production managers.

Other production managers are, however, in some respects a group in themselves. We shall discuss two aspects in which the treatment of production managers as employees differs from the treatment of workers and formen, if not in essence then, at least, in degree. The first aspect is the effect of the production system on the requirements for production managers, while the second one concerns the effect of the type of business on production managers.

The effects of the production system on the requirements for production managers

Figure 5.9 presents the different requirements for the type and characteristics of production and technical managers in the three production systems.

Fig. 5.9 Different requirements of production managers in three production systems

Production system / Type of managers and of requirements	Unit	Mass	Process
Existence of types of production managers (except foremen)			
Line managers	Existent	Sometimes existent	Non-existent
Planning ,,	,,	Non-existent	,, ,,
Materials ,,	,,	,, ,,	,, ,,
Quality ,,	,,	Sometimes existent	,, ,,
Maintenance managers	,,	Generally existent	Generally existent
Existence of technical staff within other functions			
Size of staff	Small	Large	Very large
Association with production managers	Very close	Close	Usually remote (Extremely close in emergency)
Characteristics of technical managers (including production managers)			
Degree of specialisation	Regular	High	Very high
Rate of relearning	Regular	High	Very high
Organisational flexibility (mainly in relation to other functions)	Very high	High	Usually regular (Extremely high in emergency)

Type of production manager

The managers who are generally operating formally within the manufacturing function in addition to the foremen, are concerned with line duties, planning, maintenance, materials and quality. Other managers in technical areas, engineering and scientific managers, are usualy operating mainly within the engineering and research and development functions of the industrial organisation. Some technical managers may be found in the marketing and purchasing functions. The type of production manager operating within the manufacturing function varies from one production system to another. In unit production, where there is an organisation with a scope of decision-making process (DMP) which requires a functional structure,[4] one will usually find production managers specialising in the areas of line management—planning, maintenance, materials and quality.

In mass production one will sometimes find line managers and quality managers, and generally find maintenance managers. However, in mass production planning managers and materials managers are likely to be centralised outside the manufacturing department and are not concerned with day-to-day operations. In process production there will not generally be any production managers as such in addition to foremen, except for maintenance managers. We have already discussed in Chapter 1, Vol. 1, the reasons for the desired absence of managers between the foreman responsible for the 'watchers' and the Chief Executive (CE). The main reason for this is that the only essential communication between manufacturing and the top management in process production occurs in emergency cases, when it has to reach the CE; in such cases it must reach the CE as quickly and as authentically as possible.

Other engineering and scientific teams
The technical staff operating formally within other functions (e.g. engineering, R & D, marketing, purchasing), is usually relatively small in unit production, but is operating very closely with the manufacturing function. In mass production the engineering and scientific team is large and is operating closely, but not as closely as in unit production, with manufacturing.

In process production the engineering and scientific staff form the bulk of the technical personnel, including the manufacturing personnel of the organisation. However, they operate independently of the manufacturing function, usually separated geographically from them. Only in times of emergency, when the total technical organisation should be considered as a 'fire brigade' for the purpose of forming a task force to tackle the emergency, does this part of the organisation come in contact with manufacturing.

Characteristics of technical managers:
The technological characteristics of the three production systems require special characteristics in the degree of the technical manager's specialisation, rate of re-learning and organisational flexibility. In this context we refer to all technical managers, not only the production managers. The higher the level of technology, the higher the *degree of specialisation*, because the amount of specific knowledge in each separate area is growing. *Rate of re-learning* is also greater because, although technological innovation occurs in each production system, the rate of innovation is faster, the higher the level of technology. The need for *Organisational flexibility*, relates mainly to the technical staff operating within functions other than manufacturing. This staff, in the higher technological levels, operates, in a formal organisation, innovating for the existing technological systems and designing new ones.

4. When we refer to unit production in this text, we usually refer only to plants where the scope of DMP requires a functional structure and *not* small workshop types of unit production system which require an entrepreneurial structure of management where there is usually no managerial specialisation.

However, when an emergency occurs in a plant designed by the scientific-engineering organisation, the Chief Executive or the chief scientist has to make a quick diagnosis and form a task force of engineers and scientists chosen from throughout the organisation. Thus a technical organisation operating usually under regular conditions as a functional, formally centralised, organisation, has to transform into an entrepreneurial structure, 'fire brigade', type of organisation, when emergencies occur.

The effect of type of business on production managers

Business organisations could be categorised according to a 'hierarchy of service' typology, presented on Fig. 5.10(*a*). Industrial organisations will usually fall into one of the five upper levels of the Hierarchy.

Examples of industries	*Type of organisation*	*The customer and supplier factors*
Cars	1. Manufacturing for inventory	Customer and supplier separate.
Heavy electrical equipment	2. Manufacturing to order	,, ,, ,,
Textiles—Dyeing and finishing.	3. Manufacturing service to order	Customer and supplier the same
Shipping repair docks	4. Repair service for organisation	,, ,, ,,
Garages	5. Repair service for individuals	,, ,, ,,

Figure 5.10(*b*) presents the anticipated requirements of production managers in these five different types of business organisation. Generally speaking one can say that the more the type of business organisation requires the production managers to be in contact with managers in another function—the less knowledgeable they can afford to be in the intricacies of that function.

Thus the more service oriented the organisation is, the more involved the production managers are with the financial function, and the less knowledgeable they have to be in financial matters. The absence of a better knowledge of financial matters was probably one of the principal reasons for the crisis in Rolls-Royce, which operated in the two highest levels of the hierarchy of service. Likewise, the more service oriented the organisation, the less are the production managers likely to be involved formally with the marketing department since they have more direct contact with clients and therefore the more knowledgeable they should be in marketing. In this case the production managers assume a partial direct responsibility for the continued cooperation of the customers with the organisation. Under these circumstances the production managers must be well aware of the dynamics of the total organisation, and the crucial importance of the customer's cooperation with the organisation for the survival of the whole organisation.

Fig. 5.10 The effects of the type of business on production managers

(a) 'Hierarchy of service' Pyramid of organisations from the remotest to the most involved with the clients*

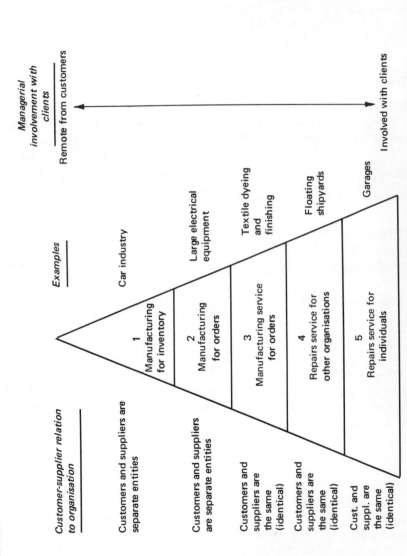

* This is only a partial 'hierarchy of service'. A full one would include non-manufacturing organisations in which the customer-suppliers are themselves also the raw material (e.g. ground transportation companies, barber shops etc.) in which they are physically involved (e.g. airlines, hospitals etc.), in which they are mentally involved (e.g. schools and universities) and spiritually involved (e.g. prisons and religious organisations).

(b) *The effects of type of business on production managers*

Requirement of production managers	Level in the hierarchy of service				
	1 *Manufacturing for inventory (customer, and suppliers separate entities)*	2 *Manufacturing for orders (cust. and suppl. are separate entities)*	3 *Manufacturing for orders (cust. and suppl. are the same)*	4 *Repairs for organisations (cust. − suppl. are the same)*	5 *Repairs for individuals (cust. − suppl. are the same)*
Involvement with clients	None	May know client's name	Know client's name and may have met him personally	Client has his managers visit from time to time	Client is waiting inside the organisation. Knows personally production managers
Contact with financial function	Almost none	Only a little	Not much	Much	Very much
Contact with marketing function	Much	Very much	Not much†	Only a little†	Almost none†
Contact with purchasing function	Very much	Much	Not much‡	Only a little‡	Almost none‡
Know how about human beings	About the operating organisation (workers and other managerial functions)		About the total organisation (the effects of factors of DMP, e.g. customers, suppliers, government, banks, etc.)		
Know how about financial matters	Very much required		Required to a lesser extent		
Know how about marketing	Required to a lesser extent		Very much required		

† In these types of organisations the marketing function is limited because one does not usually cater for customers.

‡ In these types of organisation the main object of manufacturing is provided by the customer-supplier.

Summary

We have discussed in this chapter some of the factors which affect the personnel management of the manufacturing employees. These employees consist of two main groups (or human factors of the decision-making process) workers and managers. The manufacturing management is responsible for the continued cooperation with the organisation of both the workers and the managers themselves.

We have already summarised previously in this chapter our discussions concerning the management of workers and the foremen, who are part of the manufacturing management. Let us now consider some of the similarities and some of the differences in the management of the three employee groups: workers, foremen and other production managers.

Figure 5.11 summarises some of the aspects previously discussed in this chapter. The only factor which has a similar effect on all three employee groups is the situation of the employment market. This is why it is in the interest of management to ensure that there are as few conditions of manpower shortage as possible. There are several ways in which management can counteract conditions of manpower shortage. It can first of all employ workers belonging to groups which have not previously been utilised. These could include such potential manpower sources as women, men in older age-groups and foreign workers who were specially brought into the country. The management should likewise consider possibilities for further mechanisation of the production processes, which would necessitate the employment of fewer workers, yet increasing the industrial output.

The other main factors affecting the manufacturing personnel management—the technological development and the service orientation of the organisation—affect the three employee groups in diverse manners. The technological development affects the skill requirements, but while the skill required of the workers is reduced almost completely, the specialisation required of technical managers (i.e. engineering and scientific managers in production and other functions) increases considerably.

As for the foremen, the skill required of them becomes less and less a skill in technical matters and becomes more and more a skill in human relations.

The same phenomena occurs in another area affected by technological development—leisure time. The more advanced the technology, the longer the leisure time for workers and foremen; but the other production managers, along with the technical managers in other functions, would become increasingly involved in new technological developments and innovations.

The last factor which we consider to be of major importance in its effects on manufacturing personnel management is the service orientation of the organisation. By arranging organisations according to their degree of involvement with their clients we arrive at a so-called 'hierarchy of service' pyramid of organisations. At the lower the level of the pyramid, the clients are more closely involved with he organisation, which consequently must become more service oriented. This aspect of the service orientation affects the three employee groups in a different manner.

While the workers are generally not affected by the service orientation, the production managers, foremen and other managers, become more involved with the customers, and assume a partial managerial responsibility towards them.

Fig. 5.11 Similarities and differences in the effects of environmental factors on personnel management of three manufacturing employee groups

Factor		Manufacturing employee group		
		Workers	*Foremen*	*Other production managers*
Similar effects on all groups	Employment market	The more full and over employment the more powerful small groups and individuals and the more difficult to ensure their cooperation with the organisation		
Different effects on different groups	Technological development affecting skill	The higher— the less skilled the workers	The higher— the less technical the supervision and the more human	The higher—the more specialisation and the technical knowledge
	Technological development affecting leisure time	The higher— the more leisure time	The higher— the more leisure time	The higher—no perceived difference in leisure time
	Service orientation of the organisation	Generally no effect	Some effect— similar to that of the other production managers	The more service oriented—the more involved the production managers with the customers

6

Production and trade unions

6.1 The role of trade unions—the union point of view

The relative power of the unions—in changing employment market conditions

One of the assumptions about trade unions which had prevailed for a long while but which has recently been refuted, is that in any power struggle the unions would be found in the same camp as the workers. This had, of course, originally been the case during the period immediately following the establishment of a trade union by a group of workers. However, once the trade union matures and becomes an organisation in its own right, it assumes organisational characteristics similar to those of any other organisation. Like every other organisation, the most predominant characteristic of a trade union or a group of trade unions is their desire to survive. This desire prevails even when it involves the undermining of the temporary interests of individual workers, groups of workers or even a whole working population.

The phenomenon of trade unions not aligning themselves with the workers in a power struggle can occur in one of two ways. Either the trade unions find themselves on the same side with management, or they find that they face a united front of management and the workers. In both cases the situation arises when the workers discover that they can further their cause better without the union than with it. Such situations usually occur as a consequence of employment conditions which make labour a scarce resource. However, even before the industrial world experienced conditions of full and over employment (i.e. conditions of manpower shortage) there were instances of the workers aligning themselves with management against trade unions. Examples of this have occurred when the management of an enterprise have offered their workers financial remuneration well above the union rates for the same skills in other organisations. In such cases the unions would put pressure on managements to withdraw the offer and will usually urge their members not to accept remuneration which would put them in demonstrably superior conditions to other union members with exactly the same skills. In many cases the working agreements with the union require that management will indeed pay the workers not more than the union rates. If the management is for various reasons, reluctant to follow a union policy of equal wages for equal skills, and the workers refuse to give in to the pressures of their union—both parties find themselves in a united front against the unions. Such a united front between management and the workers is often the case when trade unions try to unionise the workers in a factory where until then the workers enjoyed relatively better financial remuneration than that of their unionised peers of equal skills.

As we have already seen, worker pressures for better financial remuneration and other physical benefits and conditions, increase considerably during periods of full employment and become frequent, strong and persistent in periods of over-employment. As far as the trade unions are concerned, the outcome of these pressures is always to their detriment because of the bargaining power which individuals and small groups of workers accumulate. When these workers pressures on management are mild and management feels that by giving in they would ensure the cooperation of the workers without undermining management's capacity to maintain the cooperation of other factors (e.g. the cooperation of the shareholders and bankers, by way of achieving reasonable earnings) management would find themselves supporting the workers against the equal wages policy of the union, a phenomenon which could, as we have already seen, also occur in times of unemployment.

However, once these pressures intensify and are backed by an ever-growing shortage of manpower, management quickly reaches a point where succumbing to additional pressures could endanger their very survival. This is because, as a result of these pressures, prices may have to be raised and earnings cut to such an extent that the customers and the shareholders may, respectively, desert the organisation. Under these conditions management would mobilise the aid of the trade unions, as well as the government, to counter the worker pressures. Under such conditions of escalating wages, most governments, whatever the political tendencies, would introduce policies reducing the overemployment and combatting the effects of manpower shortage.[1]

The trade unions would tend to support policies countering the worker pressures, even if this meant lining-up with management against the workers. 'Under these circumstances', the trade unions would claim 'the future of the economy and, therefore, the economic fate of the workers too, is at stake'. While this and similar statements are factually true as such, one should also remember that the future of the trade unions is also very much at stake when it seems to many workers that they can do without them.

Let us consider how the so-called 'employment pendulum' moves from one extremity, unemployment, to the other extreme, over-employment. These movements and the change in the balance of power from the trade union factor to the worker factor in the organisational DMP (decision-making process), are presented in Fig. 6.1.

The employment pendulum remained for a very long period of time in the position of 'DMP in unemployment'. Only after the Second World War did the employment pendulum start to move from unemployment, through full employment, to over-employment and backwards, moving constantly to and fro. This phenomenon of the employment pendulum has occurred since the Second World

---

1. The governments of Great Britain and Israel introduced such policies during the mid-1960s in spite of the fact that in both countries the Labour Party was ruling at the time.

Fig. 6.1 The 'employment pendulum' and its cause and effect in the organisational decision-making process (DMP)

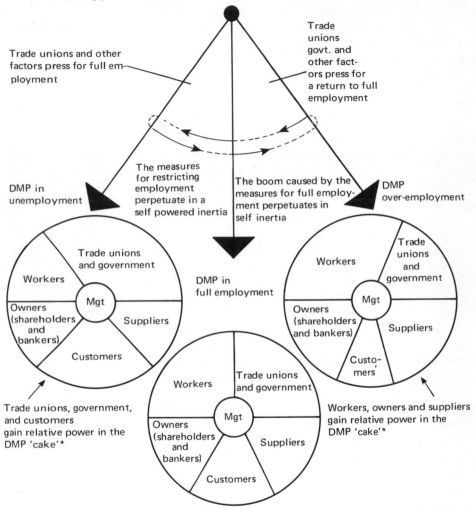

* 'Losing' or 'gaining' power in the DMP 'cake is identical to a resource being, respectively, in abundance or in shortage. Thus, for example, when the workers are in abundance, they lose power in the DMP 'cake'.

War only in European countries, (in the wider sense that Europe is considered in this book). The movements of the employment pendulum were fast in some countries (e.g. Israel) and slow in others (e.g. France). Let us follow the dynamics of these movements, as to the changes in the relative scope of decision-making process (DMP) of the management with regards to the various other groups forming the DMP (see Fig. 6.1).

DMP in unemployment

The workers are in a relatively weak power position in the organisation. Their bargaining power is limited, because losing their jobs could well mean unemployment. The workers put the fate of their employment in the hands of their unions. The unions have a relatively strong power position *vis-a-vis* management. So has the government, which is supporting those industries which follow its development policies.

Under these conditions the relative power of the owners in the DMP is small. The customer's scope of DMP is large because they are careful in their spending habits. Here management has to do all it can in order not to lose their cooperation. On the other hand, the suppliers are eager to sell whatever they can and, therefore, their relative scope of DMP is small.

DMP in full employment

An economic expansion policy, aimed at full employment, by the government, sometimes can be successful, within a relatively short period of time, perhaps in a few months. A high unemployment rate of then per cent can be turned into an unemployment rate of two to three per cent (which is considered as a full employment situation).

The scopes of DMP of the various factors in industrial organisations reach an equilibrium in a full employment situation. Confronting management now are workers and trade unions who have more or less the same degree of power. Likewise, the owners, customers and suppliers are in a relatively equal power position *vis-a-vis* management. The government would be content if this situation prevailed.

DMP in over employment

However, this situation of full employment cannot last for too long. Once the pendulum has been put in motion, it continues swinging to the other extreme—to over employment. The relative power of the various human factors are now in a reverse situation to their relative positions in unemployment. The scopes of DMP of these factors are, therefore, as follows:

Workers: Every small group of workers or even every individual worker feels that he has assumed a large amount of power. He can now put, by himself, the utmost pressure on management because he could easily find another job.

Trade unions: Under these conditions the need of the workers to rely on their unions diminishes considerably. The unions find themselves stripped of a great deal of their power and start losing many of their members.

Government: The government, facing an escalation in wages and salaries, together with a flooding of the internal market with consumer goods, introduces an economic contraction policy aimed at the reduction of overemployment, the reduction of internal consumption (and the expansion of exports) and halting other inflationary trends.

Customers: The purchasing power of customers grows considerably in times of overemployment, because everybody is employed and wages are high. The scope of DMP, which management has to devote to the customers is, therefore, considerably reduced.

Suppliers: On the other hand the suppliers have a lot of work on their hands and start to miss their delivery deadlines. Simultaneously, their prices rise and quality drops. All this increases the scope of DMP, with regards to suppliers.

Owners: All industrial organisations are growing rapidly in over-employment and the competition for new investment and working capital is severe. This is a period when interest rates are increasing and so are the pressures from shareholders for higher dividends and higher rates of re-investment of earnings. Simultaneously, as the government is taking measures against inflation, it becomes increasingly difficult to find investors, shareholders or banks, to finance the needs of the growing industrial organisation. All this increases the scope of DMP with regard to the owners.

The effects of the union structure—on its power and role

The first trade unions were formed in Great Britain in the middle of the nineteenth century. The historical consequence of this event on the trade-union movement in Britain has been one which could be referred to as the 'pulverisation' of this movement into '574 separate unions with a membership of 10,111,000. Unions vary in size from the twenty-seven members of the Jewish Baker's Union to the 1,482,000 members of the Transport and General Worker's Union' (Stettner, 1969, p. 130). At the other extreme one finds a country like Israel where, for all practical purposes, there exists only one large federation of trade unions. This federation, though divided formally into unions of trades (e.g. metal workers) or organisational affiliation (e.g. government employees), takes its major decision centrally. In between these two extremes, one finds there are other trade-union structures; for instance, a trade-union structure divided according to fields of industry (e.g. in Germany), a political union structure (e.g. in France), or even a religious union separation (e.g. in Holland) or a religious-political separation (e.g. in Italy).

The difference between these types of structure is in their ability to maintain their power and influence during fluctuations in the environmental conditions. Let us consider the effects of environmental conditions in the two extreme union structures found in the UK and Israel. The UK structure can better withstand the pressures of over-employment, than the Israeli federation of trade unions (the 'Histadrut'), because it is split into smaller unions which are more 'local interest oriented'. On the other hand, under conditions of unemployment the Histadrut structure is the stronger of the two.

One other important factor affecting the power and role of the unions is the degree of their involvement in economic and political activities. Here again one finds the trade unions in the UK and in Israel at the two extremities. In the UK the political affiliation of trade unionists, is sometimes known, but there is no formal political structuring within the unions. In Israel, on the other hand, union leaders and officials are elected on a political party platform. The parties participating in the Histadrut elections include all the parties in the political spectrum of Israel (while in Britain one could hardly imagine that in a union election many candidates would be acclaimed on a Conservative Party platform).

The economic involvement of the union has a large effect on its role and power, sometimes a larger effect than its involvement in politics. While in the UK trade unions are not formal owners of industrial or business enterprises, the Histadrut in Israel owns enterprises in every conceivable business field (e.g. industry, banking insurance, transportation). Although the trade unions activity is formally separated from the ownership activity of the Histadrut, the ambiguity of this duality is felt among all the employees from shop floor to the highest governing body—which controls the two activities.

This duality makes the Israeli trade-union movement stronger in many respects and primarily in its position *vis-a-vis* the government and in its ability to withstand long periods of strife and strikes. It also has a better grip on the workers who, even when not working in trade union-owned organisations, are medically insured by a trade union sick fund; the fees for the sick fund are deducted from the worker's wages together with their union dues. On the other hand, when the Histadrut has to confront the industrial employers in Israel on such things as bargaining for new collective wage agreements, the industrial ownership part of the Histadrut becomes an internal pressure group against the demands of the trade union part, because on the whole the Histadrut-owned industries are in the same position as their privately-owned industrial counterparts.

The role of trade unions—in changing technological conditions

We have discussed in the previous chapter, the effects of technological development on manufacturing personnel management. Some of these consequences of technological development directly affect the traditional pressure-techniques of unions *vis-a-vis* management. Two of the most common pressure-techniques used by unions throughout Europe are the discontinuence of work on the basis of piece rates and the discontinuence of overtime working. These so called 'work to rule' pressures usually precede the more extreme pressure of a straightforward strike. We have pointed out, however, that both piece rate wage incentives and overtime would probably disappear from mass and process production industries sooner or later. This means that if the trade unions do not want to embark directly upon their most extreme legal prerogative, the strike, in every conflict with management—they would have to devise some new means of pressure to replace the 'work to rule' measure.

A more severe problem for the trade unions, as a result of technological development, is that they would have to change their basic objectives or else their survival would be endangered. This we predict primarily because the people for whom the trade unions usually cater will not have in the advanced production systems any specific trades, nor would they be workers in the present-day sense of the word. Even the extreme pressure of a strike may not have the same effect in the more advanced technologically enterprises, as it has had up till now, because the workers (or 'watchers' as we have referred to these employees) do not contribute positively to manufacturing in a process production system. Indeed in the ultimate process production plants one would not even find any watchers.

It therefore seems to us that in order to survive, the trade unions will have to move into new 'product lines', and cater for employees in the managerial technical areas of engineering and the sciences.

6.2   The role of trade unions—the government point of view

The desirable union structure

When discussing the union point of view, we have touched on some of the problems of governments when confronting trade unions. Thus there is no doubt that the problems that the British Government has had with the unions in the early 1970s, originated from the very fragmented structure of the British trade-union movement.

It can be established that the larger and more encompassing the trade unions in a country, the more they would pay regard to the economy in resolving their problems. When the trade-union structure is split into large unions each covering an industrial field of activity (e.g. textiles, cars), as is the case in Germany, they would better understand the problems of the survival of the industry in which they operate. Such is the desirable trade-union structure with respect to the national interest. It prevents small trade unions, representing relatively few workers, from bringing to a standstill industries with, perhaps, hundreds of thousands of workers.

The way that governments have tried to buffer negative consequences to the economy from trade union pressures, has been through industrial relations bills, which would diminish the occurrence of strikes and thus reduce the damage to their respective economies. This we think is preferable to bringing in unskilled employees, in military uniforms or otherwise, to replace striking workers in key industries.

Political involvement of unions

We have already pointed out that the degree of trade unions political involvement varies from one country to another. This refers to both the internal structure of the unions and to the degree of their participation in the country's politics. Traditionally, the unions in Great Britain have been less political, compared with other European countries. This is also true of the unions in Germany. On the other hand the unions in France have been involved traditionally in their country's politics, each union belonging more or less to a political movement. Likewise in Israel, where the Histadrut is composed of more or less the same parties as those participating in the national political system, there appears to be some ambivalence in the system; on the one hand the Histadrut tries to assume powers which in other countries are traditionally part of the government, and on the other hand the political parties try to reinforce their position in national struggles, by maintaining the same position in the Histadrut, and vice versa.

The other factor influencing the involvement of unions in politics over and above their traditional role as the 'economic *avant garde* of the workers', is the degree of their ownership of business enterprises. Thus in Israel the Histadrut becomes a pressure group in politics concerning owners and employers, being itself one of the biggest owners and employers in the country.

Unions working with and against the government in changing employment conditions

We have already seen that the unions would pursue their role of the 'economic *avant-garde* of the workers' as long as this role does not interfere with their own survival. They would therefore strive for full employment and to raise the wages of workers, as long as the employment pendulum (Fig. 6.1) does not swing to the over-employment position. When this happens and general shortage of manpower descends upon a country, the unions rally to the government's support, trying to reduce the over-employment situation and to curtail the escalating wages.

The government may take various steps in order to counteract over-employment. These steps could be divided into three main groups. The first group includes policies aimed at slowing down the economic expansion. Secondly, come the policies aimed at continuing the economic expansion but simultaneously changing the technological structure of the economy—introducing manpower saving equipment. The third group of policies advocates the utilisation of additional manpower sources (women, men in older age groups, invalids, national minority group workers and foreign workers coming in temporarily from less developed countries), in order to continue the economic expansion without overemployment. These three types of policies are usually applied simultaneously by governments, trying to save their economics from the malfunctions of over-employment. The unions will usually support such policies.

This has already happened in countries like Britain and Israel, where socialist governments had to fight over-employment in order to avoid economic catastrophes. In Israel a prominent socialist cabinet minister said that 'in order to cure the economy we need a certain amount of manpower reserve'. A 'certain amount of manpower reserve' is a way of referring to what economists call 'slight unemployment'.

Therefore governments in Western Europe can usually expect the trade unions to oppose economic conditions which are accompanied by unemployment. However, when economic expansion leads to over-employment conditions, the unions would support the introduction of governmental anti-inflationary policies.

6.3   The role of trade unions—the management point of view

The conventional role of trade unions in an industrial organisation is to serve as the 'economic *avant-garde* of the workers'. We shall devote, however, our discussions to only two problems concerning the role of unions in the manufacturing function—their role in enabling catharsis among the workers and their institutional role in organising the workers.

The catharsis role of shop stewards

We have already described (in the summary of the previous chapter) catharsis and the need of people to disclose their innermost feelings to others. We, likewise, suggested that the best way to enable workers to have catharsis is to put psychological counsellors at their disposal. However, as long as such psychological counsellors are not available, people find other ways of relieving themselves from the thoughts and feelings which weigh upon them. Catholics perform their catharsis by way of confession. People find informal ways for their catharsis—by relating their innermost feelings to anyone who cares to listen. The people who care to listen to the workers on the production floor are the shop stewards, to whom any worker can disclose anything which is on his mind and in his heart.

There is good reason to believe that the link of the workers to their shop stewards is to a large degree connected with their ability to perform their catharsis through them. The same kind of link exist between a priest and his confessees and between a psychiatrist and his patients. These links create so-called 'dependency' situations.

There is no doubt that the introduction of psychological counsellors into industrial organisations would undermine the position of shop stewards and their links with the workers. This is because the workers could be expected to prefer catharsis with psychological counsellors rather than with shop stewards, who are both less qualified to perform it and are also formally related to the workers, a thing which is not conducive for thorough catharsis.

It is interesting to note that in a book, which strongly criticises the conclusion of the Hawthorne researchers* that psychological counsellors should be introduced into industry, many of the critics were people linked with the US trade unions (Landsberger, 1958). The introduction of psychological counsellors into the Western Electric plants proved to be successful. However, after several years of operation, the psychological counsellors were removed, probably because of pressures coming from sources not unsimilar to those who criticised the Hawthorne research.

The manufacturing management should take account of this catharsis role of the unions, when trying to elicit the cooperation of the workers. This should specially be borne in mind when trying to introduce into an organisation psychological counsellors, who would undoubtedly be perceived by the shop stewards, as competition to themselves.

The advantage of having unions

Following the analysis we have made of the role of the trade unions in industrial organisations, the question arises whether it is at all advantageous for manu-

* Primarily Elton Mayo and Fritz Roethlisberger (1941).

facturing managements for them to exist. This is an appropriate time to ask this question because, as we have seen, the role of trade unions is probably going to change in the not too distant future, if they are going to survive at all. So it is to a certain degree up to the managements of organisations in the industrial countries to decide whether they are going to support the trade unions in their coming struggle for survival.

It is our belief that there is a definite advantage for management in having the unions continue to play their role in industrial organisations. However, in order to derive the utmost advantage for the organisation, it is essential that the unions should not only represent the workers in their claims for better employment conditions but that they would likewise be well aware of the special conditions of the industrial organisations, of the fields of industry and of the economy as a whole. A 'pulverised' trade union structure like the one in Britain does not even enable a knowledge of the special conditions of the economy as a whole, let alone the awareness of a special conditions of industries and individual organisations. Structuring the unions according to political or religious divisions, may reduce the number of unions and increase the knowledge and awareness of national economic conditions, but does not contribute to the awareness of the special economic conditions of different industrial organisations and fields of activity. A structure in which unions are divided according to fields of industry, requiring them to be large enough to be knowledgeable and aware of the national economy requirements, should be the ultimate interest of management, government *and* the workers themselves. In a country like Britain, this could be achieved not only through the Industrial Relations Act, but likewise by direct contribution of the managements of large industrial organisations. By refusing to negotiate separately with a large number of unions, unrelated to each other, they would eventually force the unions to re-structure themselves and merge into unions affiliated to fields of industry and business. This would give the trade-union movement a new standing and strength it has never had before, accompanied by a feeling of national responsibility and serving the long-range interests of the workers, rather than their very short-range interests. The workers would have better security knowing that their unions would support their claims for the improvement of employment conditions, as long as the realisation of such demands would not completely undermine the survival of the organisations in which they are employed.

Some managements in Britain have already embarked upon this new approach, which is legally supported by the Industrial Relations Act. We believe that this is a beginning of a new era for the constructive role of trade unions in Britain. The creation of closer contacts between unions of the various Western European countries, and between them and the United States trade unions is closely linked with the spreading of multinational corporations. The US trade unions, similar to those in Germany, are split along lines of fields of industry. This, we believe, will spread not only into Britain, but also into countries like France and Italy, where the unions are larger, but split according to a political or political-religious structure.

6.4 Summary

There are two main factors which influence the role of the trade unions in industrial organisations and in the economy as a whole.

The first one is the power position of the trade unions, in the changing employment conditions. We have seen that when the economy experiences unemployment conditions, the workers fully support the unions as their 'economic *avant-garde*'. However, when conditions change to those of full employment and, subsequently, of over-employment individual workers and small worker groups discover they can struggle for themselves and, consequently, reduce the support for their unions, sometimes abandoning them altogether.

While the environmental employment conditions affect the position of trade unions in a similar way in all western democratic countries and probably in all countries, their internal structure creates differences in their roles and positions in various countries. In some countries, there are many trade unions, in others only a few. In some countries they are structured along political divisions, in others along industrial ones. Finally, in some countries they devote themselves exclusively to their trade-union role of representing the workers towards the employers, who are the managements of privately- and government-owned enterprises; however, in other countries they become, to smaller or larger extents, owners of industrial and other business organisations—turning themselves into employers.

We have concluded that for the benefit of all concerned—managements, workers and the national economy—the best union organisation should be along a division of industrial and business fields, only with a few large unions, rather than too many of them. By implication we have also concluded that unions should better refrain from, or at least restrict, their becoming owners and managers of enterprises employing workers whom they have to represent towards the imployers. We finally concluded that the role of the trade unions is and would continue to be important not only for the workers, but likewise for management and for the government. We suggested, however, that in order to enable them to play their important role, both the government and the managements of large industrial organisations should contribute towards re-structuring the trade-union movements along the lines we have proposed, in those countries where it has not yet been done. Governments could do this by introducing appropriate legislation, while managements of large organisations could refuse to negotiate with unions, unless they are large enough and affiliated to their respective fields of industry.

7

Preparing production managers for the future

7.1 Introduction

So far we have considered the organisational context within which the production manager works. We have also examined a wide range of problems arising from his relationship with other functions and groups of people within his company and with the trade unions. We have seen that these relationships are becoming increasingly complex and that they place considerable demands upon the manager's professionalism and judgement. It calls for more than just technical skills. The pace of development of European business shows no sign of slackening. Thus the pressures upon the production manager will continue to increase; his success can be expected to depend increasingly upon the skill with which he applies new concepts, introduces changes, assimilates new technology and above all the understanding and sensitivity he displays in handling human relations both within his own department and in his dealings with other departments.

Therefore, we shall now turn our attention to the production manager himself. We shall attempt to assess in a general way the level of attainment of production management in Europe at the present time and to identify the preparation the manager needs to face the challenges of the future.

The performance of production managers and consequently their calibre and managerial development determines the effectiveness of the production function. Therefore, if there are inadequacies in production management, and there are good grounds for believing they exist, it may be because:

- production managers are of a lower calibre than their colleagues in other areas
- the problems of production management identified in earlier chapters are inadequately appreciated
- The development of managers in the production function has been given too little attention, particularly in business schools.

7.2 Calibre of production managers

Any statement regarding the calibre of a large proportion of managers, representing approximately one-third of all managers is inevitably an over-generalisation. Thus the suggestion that the average production manager is of a lower calibre than his colleagues is open to criticism because it is difficult to substantiate. Yet, the view that production management fails to attract a high calibre of entrant is frequently expressed and cannot be ignored. It also accords with the personal view of the authors who consider that it should be of great concern to all manufacturing companies that they attract a higher level of recruit into production and provide him with the opportunity to develop his managerial potential so that a proportion can eventually play a substantial part in the general management of the company.

There are, however, wide differences between countries, industries and individual companies. The international comparisons probably reflect differences in culture, status and education. Brua found that in a sample of 600 European Chief Executives twenty per cent of the French considered that they had gained their most valuable experience in manufacturing compared with twelve per cent in Germany and no more than six per cent in other European countries and the United States. The comparable figures for marketing were France four per cent, Italy thirty-nine per cent and UK twenty-two per cent (Brua 1969). These figures are difficult to interpret but they do suggest that there are great differences between European countries in opportunities for advancement from production into general management. But they may also indicate that the numbers suitable for promotion to top management positions, broadly reflecting their managerial and executive ability, varies widely.

One problem may be the poor 'image' and status accorded to production management in some countries; the UK and USA being typical examples. The majority of graduates entering the production function are trained in engineering and science. Yet, the orientation of most universities towards research has encouraged young graduates to regard production as a 'lower status' occupation than research and development. One of the largest engineering companies in the UK became so concerned by the low standards of its graduate entry into production that it initiated a unique graduate apprenticeship scheme. This was designed with the attraction of a proportion of the best recruits into production, away from their first preference of research and development, as its main objective. Initial indications are that this scheme met with only limited success.

Skinner (1966) writes of the USA

'We are not getting enough of the kind of men needed in manufacturing, either from the lower ranks of industry or from the graduate schools of business. A generation ago the men with ability but without the means for college became skilled mechanics and craftsmen; many moved up to become foremen and managers. Now there are far too few who train themselves for manufacturing management.

'For college men, the manufacturing life typically has had little appeal. From my talks with students it appears that factories still represent grease and sweat and unimportant trivia; the minutiae of small details; and the confrontation with rough, uneducated people and a militant union . . . 'Factories are for engineers' is the theme of most business school graduates.'

We seem to be caught in a vicious circle. The low status associated with production management, both within the company and to the outside world, discourages the entry of the right calibre of recruit to redress the balance. The problem begins in the board room with inadequate representation compounded by the inability of many production directors to embrace the broader executive responsibilities required of them. For example in Philips N.V. Eindhoven, one of the largest European international companies, emerging from a traditional production orientation there was only one representative of the manufacturing function on the board in 1971.

The picture is not, however, universally black. Many companies have overcome these difficulties and in such cases there is little to choose between their production and other executives. This is most evident in the younger growth companies and industries where the challenge of technological change tends to attract a higher calibre and younger production manager.

7.3 Management development

The need for continuous development

From the day the new recruit enters a production department until he retires there is a continuing need for the development of his abilities in order to fit him either for increased responsibilities or to meet the changed circumstances brought about by technological and industrial progress. This development is a continuous process of learning, a great deal of which will be derived from his experience 'on-the-job'. But increasingly, we are seeing an appreciation of the need for periodic inputs of more formal training either inside the company or on external courses. This training will take into account not only the requirements of his current job but also the need to prepare him for the future. It must not be overlooked, however, that each manager and his needs are different. It is therefore essential that the training he undergoes is matched not only to the tasks he will be performing but also to his own personal development needs.

We can identify two major milestones in the production manager's career when considerable care and time needs to be devoted to his development:

- firstly, when he makes the transition into management from being first and foremost a technologist
- secondly, when his management responsibilities demand an understanding of activities throughout the company rather than solely within the production department.

Technologist into manager

Production managers, who are graduates, usually have a degree in engineering or science. Their initial employment in industry will normally require the exercise of their technological training. Only a few move directly into a management post, although the majority can expect to spend a high proportion of their time on management tasks within ten years of entering industry. Most large companies will put their new entrants through some form of graduate apprenticeship scheme, perhaps supplemented by part-time courses containing a management element. The aim of such schemes is primarily aimed to re-orientate the new entrant so that he can bridge the gap between university and industry, rather than to prepare him for a subsequent career in management. At this stage he is both by training and inclination a 'technologist.' It is only after he has been in industry for several years that he will find himself increasingly occupied with activities which can be described as managerial. This change of emphasis from technology to management often occurs over a period of years and may not at the time be perceived clearly by the individual. Typically he will have little training or development to help him with the transition.

In the past the majority of production managers were non-graduates. They entered industry at an earlier age than the graduates and were generally better tuned to making an immediate contribution to industrial life. Their promotion in a competitive environment resulted from strength of character rather than intellectual ability. In many cases their abilities became less appropriate to the organisational needs the higher they rose. They gave rise to the archetype of the production manager as 'brawn not brain' which has done so much to discourage production as a worthy occupation in the eyes of the graduate.

Because of the increasing sophistication of both technological and management techniques, the non-graduate is likely to become the exception in senior production management. And yet, as we have seen, the technological graduate is also ill-prepared. Furthermore, the depth of managerial abilities needed for the task is such that its development cannot normally be left to chance or short courses. It requires a commitment of time and resources which are still the exception rather than the rule. In many ways this is a role admirably suited to the business school graduate particularly if his initial employment is in line management. Many industrial problems can be attributed to the remoteness of top management from the shop floor. The increasing influence of business graduates, who may rise to top management without ever gaining line management experience, could lead to a widening of this gap still further. And yet production management has little attraction for business graduates. Thus, although we can see the need to attract a higher proportion of business school graduates into production as a desirable part of their preparation for senior posts, any major improvement in production management standards is likely to come more from the development of the managerial capabilities of the technological graduate.

Departmental manager into general manager

The second major change in the production manager's outlook is required when he reaches a sufficiently senior position to be in daily contact with managers from other functions. The interactions between production decisions and other company functions have been a continuing theme throughout this book. We have observed a variety of decisions where the company's best interests may not be served when they are taken within a framework of narrowly drawn departmental objectives. At the same time he should become increasingly concerned with manufacturing policy, strategic considerations and planning for the long term. Both the breadth and the time scale of his decision making have increased.

This transition does not come easily. Failure to achieve it is evidenced by the common complaints of inability to delegate, concern with the minutiae of the job often leaving the major decisions to go by default, and sub-optimisation. Such a radical re-orientation of his attitudes and thinking will usually follow only from a major intellectual challenge and stimulus. This is the type of experience which can best be provided by one of the longer business school executive programmes during which he will have the opportunity of living in close contact with executives from other functions, companies and industries and working with them on common problems.

7.4 Analysis of management development needs

In order to analyse the manager's development needs in greater detail it is convenient now to consider the nature of the manager's role and its fulfilment under the headings of knowledge, skills and attitudes.

Knowledge

The last two decades have seen an explosive growth of the knowledge base in all technologies and in management. This has been accompanied by the growth of specialisations. Whereas we saw the application of the principle of division of labour applied to manual tasks in the first half of the century, it has been applied to mental activities in the second. Both movements have introduced new problems. In recent years we have seen attempts towards reversing the effects in manual labour through job enlargement and job enrichment. But the impact in technology and management raises a different type of problem the implications of which are equally important.

No longer is it possible for the production manager to be as knowledgeable as all his subordinates. Many of them have undergone long periods of training in specialised topics such as operations research, ergonomics and systems engineering. The specialist himself finds it increasingly difficult to keep up with the advances of knowledge in his own field. It is clearly impossible for his manager to hope to keep abreast of advances in a whole range of technologies. This he must accept. But his early training makes it extremely difficult for him to accept this. Courses in most universities are concerned almost exclusively with the acquisition of knowledge. He is thus inclined to equate his professional competence with the size of his knowledge base and will, consequently, suffer from a sense of frustration and inadequacy when he realises that there is hardly any topic upon which one of his subordinates is not more knowledgeable than he is.

He must learn to live with this situation and realise that his contribution is of a different order from that of his specialists. Where it is important for him to have knowledge it will be decreasingly within the production area and more in other fields such as accountancy where his specialists are likely to be largely ignorant. In general, the more senior he becomes the more important will become managerial skills and attitudes rather than specialist knowledge.

Skills

The skills required of the manager place upon him very heavy demands. Many of them are unlike the skills he was taught in his technical training. When we normally use the word skill we tend to associate it with the expertise which is gained from the repetition of a task which changes very little from one time of performance to the next. It represents training followed by cumulative experience. Each skill can be clearly identified. The manager on the other hand, will often have to draw upon a variety of his skills in any given situation and no two situations are ever likely to be exactly the same. Experience too may be as much a hindrance as a help for, in a rapidly changing environment, the experience gained in tackling past problems may have little relevance to the future but can easily cloud the manager's judgement.

The exercise of management skills draws upon the whole of the manager's faculties as a human being. Technical skills, judgement, human emotions, ethical standards, personality, political skills and many other attributes are involved. Although it might be possible to draw up a list of all the required skills for a manager, no one person is ever likely to reach the desired standard in all respects. This is specially so because the 'desired standard' is also changing all the time. Thus it can be argued that perhaps the most important skill of all is the ability of the manager to recognise where he is deficient so that others whose skills are complementary to his own can be drawn into the management team. Another important point for the manager to remember is that some of his personal characteristics are unchangeable. Similarly, it would be unrealistic for him to try to change some of the personal characteristics of other production managers or of other people with whom he works.

The production manager's earlier training will have introduced to him many technological skills the application of which will generally lead to a clear unambiguous solution to a problem. Consequently, he is inclined to think that all problems should have a unique 'right' solution provided that the problem definition is correct, the analysis is logical and the right data is used. This mechanistic approach can lead him into serious difficulties when he moves into management. There is rarely a 'right' solution; it is often difficult to establish what the real problem is, much of the information and data is either unobtainable or too expensive to obtain and often cannot be expressed in quantitative terms, and his effectiveness will depend to a great extent upon how he relates to other people. He must learn to live with uncertain information and develop a range of managerial skills new to him which in many cases may seem to him incompatible with the scientific tradition within which he has been educated.

We shall now examine some of these skills under the classification of:

1. technical
2. observation and problem finding
3. information and data selection
4. solution formulation
5. conceptualisation
6. human

Management technical skills

During the last thirty years a range of quantitative management techniques have been developed to tackle a wide variety of problems. It is becoming increasingly important that the manager becomes proficient in a number of these or at least is sufficiently aware of the contribution they can make to his decision making. They include such techniques as operations research, systems analysis, network analysis and decision trees. We may expect that in the future an increasing number of production managers are likely to be drawn from specialists in these areas.

These techniques are a valuable aid but no substitute for management. Their slow rate of acceptance in industry is probably due to two causes. Firstly, practitioners of the techniques have 'oversold' them but have been unable to convince or demonstrate effectively the contribution they can make. Secondly, managers who are not numerate have been unable to communicate properly with the specialists. We thus see that the management scientists moving into management need to develop their understanding of the importance of many other factors, often qualitative, which form part of a management problem. The non-management scientist on the other hand needs an understanding of the proper relationship of the skills of the specialist to his decision making.

Observation and problem finding

The average manager spends a considerable proportion of his time in 'trouble shooting', that is, dealing with operational problems which require remedial action. Control systems are designed so that he can 'manage by exception' when pre-set standards are not being attained. Although, it is important that adequate control systems are operated they tend to relegate the manager to a passive role. Control information is historical. It records what has happened in the past and enables comparisons to be made between actual and expected performance by bringing variances to the manager's attention. The good manager needs to go beyond this. He must be able to anticipate problems through his powers of observation and analysis so that he can take preventative action.

A scientific training provides the production manager with the facility to observe, analyse and hypothesise, although he is often unable to apply these skills to human behaviour. Unfortunately, because of the scale of managerial decisions, it is rarely possible for hypotheses to be tried out under laboratory conditions. He is thus faced with the need to take decisions without being able to determine their effect in advance. This requires the ability to take decisions under a degree of uncertainty which requires intellectual courage and may run counter to the precepts of his scientific training.

The uncertainties arise because in this active role the manager is making decisions which affect the future on the basis, partly of control information, partly by projecting past trends and partly by exercising his judgement on what changes are likely to occur in the future. He is anticipating rather than reacting. In a thought-provoking article Livingston (1971) writes:

> Managers need to be able not only to analyse data in financial statements and written reports but also to scan the business environment for less concrete clues that a problem exists. They must be able to 'read' meaning into changes in methods of doing business and into the actions of customers and competitors which may not show up in operating statements for months or even a year.
>
> 'But the skill they need cannot be developed merely by analysing problems discovered by someone else, rather it must be acquired by observing first hand what is taking place in business.'

Information and data selection

The manager's raw material is information and data gleaned from a variety of sources. Some will come from written records, some will arise from personal contact and may be first-hand or hearsay. He will receive it through all his senses for often what he is told is less important than the way in which it is told or even the demeanour of the person who is telling it to him.

Throughout his working day he will be receiving a mass of information consciously and sub-consciously. And it is the application of his managerial skills to this information which guides his actions. However, the 'raw' information needs to be 'processed' before he can use it effectively. Some of it needs to be discarded as irrelevant to the problem or situation with which he is dealing. Sometimes its significance only emerges when associated with another piece of information which may also appear to be irrelevant by itself.

Fact and opinion will be inter-mingled. Frequently managers fail to distinguish clearly between the two. Facts can be established and are incontrovertible. Opinion on the other hand is usually purely subjective but nonetheless is relevant. But opinion itself can be divided into two categories according to whether it is possible and worthwhile or not to establish the facts by further information research. This process is shown diagrammatically in Fig. 7.1. Most management decisions will be based upon this mixture of fact and opinion. What is important for the manager is to recognise this and to replace opinion by fact wherever it is feasible and economical to do so.

A further sub-division occurs between quantitative and qualitative information. The application of mathematical techniques, e.g. risk analysis, decision trees associated with subjective probabilities, enables a great deal of qualitative information to be operated upon as if it were quantitative factual data. This enables decisions to be taken which are consistent with the manager's judgement exercised on each of a number of related factors. These techniques will be used increasingly in the future and can be expected to form part of most managers' skill requirement.

Fig. 7.1 Categorisation of information

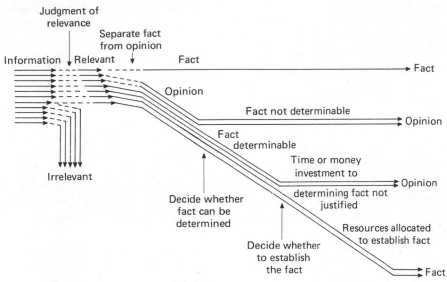

When he has been through the process described, the manager will have ordered the information he has selected as relevant to his problem. This can be represented by a simple matrix:

	Quantitative	Qualitative
Fact	1	2
Opinion	3	4

The technologist is primarily concerned with fact and with measurement. He is thus biased towards information in square 1 and to a lesser degree square 2. Consequently, when he becomes a manager he is inclined to undervalue information in squares 3 and 4, or alternatively, delay his decision making unduly until he has established all the facts he considers he needs before he can take his decision. It is of extreme importance for the production manager to realise that information in square 4 can influence the situation, the problem-solving and the whole decision-making process more than information included in the other squares.

Solution formulation
We have seen that only rarely do management problems have a clear cut solution. Consequently there is a range of alternative decisions that could be made in a given situation, the choice depending upon the relative importance attached to the information available.

Sometimes it may be that some considerations are so over-riding that there is little choice; but usually managers find that there are several alternatives which merit careful evaluation. However, he must first generate these alternatives. In many ways this is the most creative aspect of the manager's role. Only a small proportion of men are truly creative. Many competent managers make adequate decisions without being creative. Nevertheless a creative mind is capable of generating ideas for action and problem solving which by their ingenuity enable a major improvement in the quality of decision making.

There is evidence that a recognition of the need for more creativity in management is spreading. There are several possible explanations why this should be so. Creativity and the characteristics of the entrepreneur have a great deal in common. The company which has reached a stable formal organisation structure with highly sophisticated management techniques will not in general be inclined to foster the innovation which stems from creative thinking. There is thus a considerable danger that the creative manager will be frustrated in his desire to innovate or will move to another company. Yet, because of the rapidly changing nature of the business world there is an increasing need for original thinking applied to new problems.

During recent years a number of approaches to the development of creative problem solving have emerged. Syneitics (Gordon 1961) and lateral thinking (de Bono 1967, 1969) are among the best known and it is likely that we shall see a great deal more attention being paid to the development of creativity during the next few years. A parallel can be drawn with management development. It is not so long since the common attitude was that 'managers were born' and there was little that could be done to develop their potential. We no longer accept this in relation to management but the idea that creativity can be developed is still new.

We may thus infer that many production managers of the future will need to pay much more attention to creativity, not only in relation to their own thinking but also within their organisations. This will show itself particularly in the formulation of novel solutions to problems and thereby improve the general quality of decision making.

Decision taking

Faced with a range of alternatives and the information upon which to base his decision, the manager is in a position to make it. This calls for the exercise of his managerial judgement. The quantitative information he has may well point towards one alternative whereas the qualitative considerations may favour another. His decision will depend very much upon the interpretation he places on the latter. How should he weight the importance of a particular consideration? How reliable is a certain person's opinion? As we have mentioned earlier it is not easy for the technologist to take an objective view of opinion particularly when un-quantifiable.

Timing is also important, and introduces another dimension to be considered. For in an evolving situation decisions cannot be made in isolation from the present and future environment in which they take effect. Nor are they made for all time. As soon as a decision is taken new information may become available which makes it essential that it be modified or reversed. Thus we are not concerned with isolated decisions which follow from a cool analysis of unchanging information, but rather a web of interlocking decisions depending upon a constantly changing mass of information.

A further complication is introduced by the human factor, since a decision is nothing until translated into action. Thus what is a right decision for one manager may be wrong for another if not consistent with his management style and abilities. Furthermore effective implementation depends upon acceptance by those responsible for carrying it out.

The importance of decision-making is recognised as central to most business school courses. Those courses which place heavy emphasis on the case method accord the greatest priority to developing these decision-making skills. The behavioural scientists are also playing an increasing part in developing the human skills necessary for the implementation of management decisions.

Business school graduates entering production may, therefore, be expected to have undergone an intensive development of their decision-making faculties. This takes time and the majority of production managers follow a path into management which does not prepare them systematically for developing decision-making skills. If the development of these skills is as important as it is claimed to be by business schools, there seems a clear need either to, (*a*) attract more business school graduates into production, which seems unlikely in the short term, or (*b*) develop non-business school graduates, although, apart from a small number of executive programmes, the facilities for doing this do not exist.

Conceptualisation

We have said that no two decisions are identical and also that past experience is no sure guide for the future. Nevertheless, a given situation is not an isolated event in history. It relates to other on-going situations as well as to past decisions. Thus the manager is dealing not with a number of independent *ad hoc* decisions but a series of situations which form a pattern.

This pattern is not defined for him. He has to 'structure' his thinking so that he can perceive concepts which can guide his decision-making. He should be able to develop a series of mental models at a first degree of abstraction into which large number of problems fit. These concepts then provide a structural framework which helps to bring order and simplification to his problems.

The word 'model' appears frequently in management literature. At its simplest it is a conceptual model which enables problems to be structured. But it may also be a complex mathematical model embracing a wide range of parameters affecting the operation of a business. When sophisticated mathematical models exist for a company system or sub-system, the manager is at last approaching the laboratory conditions be desires. For the model is a mathematical representation of the inter-relations which exist in the real business. He is thus able to take an experimental approach to decision-making; by varying inputs he can establish the sensitivity of the outputs and the likely results which would be attained in practise.

The ability to conceptualise is an important attribute for every manager, tackling almost any problem. But we can also expect a rapid growth in mathematical modelling particularly when used for sensitivity analysis. Production managers may not be accustomed to think on these lines, but their technological training with its emphasis on bringing order into chaos fits them uniquely for being in the forefront in the introduction of systems thinking into business.

Skills in human relations

Previous chapters have stressed the importance of the production manager's skill in handling human relations. Industrial relations throughout Europe have been deteriorating in recent years. But an effective production system and good decision-making count for little if the products cease to flow due to poor industrial relations. We have also seen that in process industry human relations become more important in spite of the smaller number of people employed.

The technologist with his positive bias towards the rational, is often deficient in his handling of human relations. To quote Livingston (1971) again:

> Many men who have more than enough abstract intelligence to learn the methods and techniques of management fail because their affinity with other people is almost entirely intellectual or cognitive. They may have 'intellectual empathy' but may not be able to sense or identify the unverbalised emotional feelings which strongly influence human behaviour. They are emotion-blind just as some men are colour-blind.

Attitudes

Finally, we must turn our attention to attitudes. Schein (1961) writes '. . . adequate managerial performance at the higher levels is at least as much a matter of attitudes as it is a matter of knowledge and specific skills, and that the acquisition of such knowledge and skills is itself in part a function of attitudes.'

It is beyond the scope of this book to examine managerial attitudes in any depth, other than to underline their increasing importance as a person becomes more senior. The manager's success depends upon the effective translation of his decisions into action by others. How effective this is will depend to a high degree upon the manager's attitude both to his job and the people with whom he is associated and his ability to motivate them to carry out his wishes. The attitudes which determine his behaviour towards other people are thus central to his performance as a manager. The manager's commitment to succeed and his will to manage are also vital ingredients.

Two aspects of the production manager's job which are influenced significantly by his attitudes have been mentioned repeatedly:

- his relationships with other departments
- his role as an innovator.

Any individual is a member of a number of groups of people of varying size—his immediate colleagues, his department, his company, his profession etc. As his career progresses it becomes necessary for him to change the reference group with which he identifies closely. We have seen, for example, that the relationships between production and marketing departments are often strained. The conflict which arises may not be important at lower levels of responsibility; yet if these attitudes persist at departmental manager level the effectiveness of the organisation will suffer. Thus we may find that a person's identification with his working group evolves naturally up to departmental level, but that it becomes difficult to develop an identification with company objectives when this involves working with other departments often at the expense of making some compromises on the achievement of departmental objectives. For it must be remembered that the loyalty and commitment of his own subordinates depend upon him being seen as their champion in inter-departmental conflict. The resolution of the resulting dilemma places a heavy burden on his managerial skills.

We have seen earlier that the manager is frequently faced with introducing change into his organisation. In many ways this might be regarded as one of his most important roles. To do this requires the ability to identify the need for change and formulate the nature of the changes to be introduced as well as the exercise of skill and judgement in choosing the timing for change and obtaining its acceptance. But this does not follow unless the manager has a will to innovate. Yet timely and appropriate change is one of the most vital ingredients for survival and success in any organisation. This attitude of mind cannot be over-estimated for it is all too easy for the manager to appreciate intellectually the need for change without doing anything about it, either because he feels frustrated by the organisation's opposition to innovation or because he lacks the will and determination to introduce it.

7.5 Summary

There is strong evidence to support the claim that production management lacks appeal both to business school graduates and the better graduates in technology. Yet we have seen that the quality of production management is not only of vital importance to manufacturing companies but that management calls for the exercise of a whole range of skills and conceptual powers which provide a challenge worthy of the highest intellect entering business. If this is not generally recognised there is cause for concern since the future will place increasingly heavy demands upon manufacturing management.

Having accepted that, for the foreseeable future, production management is likely to be drawn largely from technologists, we compared the attributes required of the manager with those inculcated by technological training under the headings of knowledge, skills and attitudes. We noted that the needs of management and technology differ considerably. Many aspects were identified where the training of the technologist creates attitudes which may be detrimental to good managerial performance. In particular we noted possible difficulties in the field of human relations, with non-quantified information and with subjective opinion. On the other hand there are other areas where a scientific training provides a valuable preparation for applying the scientific method to management.

Since the application of management science techniques can be expected to become more widespread in the future we can hope that the scientifically trained production manager will take the initiative in introducing systems thinking into operational management. In general, however, we concluded that a major weakness was that many manufacturing managers were 'thing' orientated rather than 'people' orientated.

As he becomes more senior we see that he needs to adapt to a changed working environment calling for new skills and attitudes.

In conclusion, we would repeat that the demands of production management are frequently under-rated. There is a clear need for the attraction of high calibre men into production followed by a personal development programme matched to the needs at various stages in their careers. The challenges are great. The personal satisfactions to be gained are considerable, and the contribution to business success is vital.

The organisational problems we have mentioned in this book are universal wherever manufacturing organisations exist and develop technologically. They are, however, specially pertinent in the European scene where, it seems to us, organisational developments lag behind technological ones. This is primarily so, we believe, because of the cultural differences between European countries and their strong linkages to former dominating types of organisation such as the Church, the Army and Government, the functional requirements of which were, and are, much simpler than those of industrial organisations.

List of cases

Case 21
British Aircraft Corporation

'The firm was conscious that loss of employment, and the fear of such loss, constituted a very human problem. If they were ever put in a position where they had to deal with it, and they were doing all that was possible to avoid such a situation, they would do so in a human way'. These words were contained in the Memorandum of a Works Conference held at the Weybridge Division of the British Aircraft Corporation Ltd. on 22 February 1965. A few weeks later when it appeared likely that the Government would cancel one of B.A.C.'s major projects, the TSR 2, Mr Adrian Dent, Chief of Personnel Services for the B.A.C. Group, was sitting in his office overlooking Pall Mall. He was faced with the unenviable task of defining the B.A.C. redundancy policy to be adopted if the TSR 2 were cancelled; this would eventually be sent to the Managing Directors of the divisions concerned.

British Aircraft Corporation Ltd.

The formation of the British Aircraft Corporation had been completed in 1960, largely as a result of pressure from the Government of the day which maintained that the number of independent aircraft manufacturing companies in the UK was excessive in relation to the size of the industry as a whole. The Government had given a warning that combination into larger units was essential and that future Government Contracts would only be awarded to such groupings. Accordingly B.A.C. had been formed by the merger of the aircraft manufacturing interests of three major companies, Vickers Ltd., English Electric Ltd., and the Bristol Aeroplane Co. Ltd. (in the ratio of 2 : 2 : 1), together with a smaller company Hunting Aircraft Ltd. A similar amalgamation of most of the other major manufacturers led to the formation of the Hawker-Siddeley Group. After this extensive re-organisation, the British aircraft industry consisted of these two large competing groups, the engine groups, the Westland group which concentrated on helicopter production and a few independent companies such as Handley-Page and Short Bros. and Harland Ltd.

On the formation of B.A.C. the constituent companies failed to reach agreement regarding the complete merger of existing projects mainly because of difficulty in assessing future profits. It was only natural that a company with a highly profitable contract was unwilling to share the profits with its partners; on the other hand

Case material of the Management Case Research Unit, Cranfield, Bedford, England, and prepared as a basis for class discussion. This case was made possible through the generous cooperation of British Aircraft Corporation.

where a company had a project which was likely to make a loss, no other company wanted to share it. It was decided therefore that only new contracts would be treated as Group projects. In 1965 this separation of interests was still to be seen in both the divisions manufacturing the TSR 2. At Preston, manufacture of the Lightning fighter for the R.A.F. was still being carried on as an English Electric and not a B.A.C. activity and at Weybridge the VC 10 airliner was a Vickers Ltd. project.

TSR 2

The contract for the TSR 2 was the first to be placed with B.A.C. Indeed it was the prospect of gaining this contract which was largely instrumental in the Group's formation. This aircraft was to be the first supersonic bomber with a nuclear capability to see service with the R.A.F. Notable features were its high performance at low altitude with a navigational system claimed to be the most advanced in the world and its ability to operate from short runways. Work began in 1958, and the first prototype made a successful maiden flight on 17 September 1965.

In spite of mounting cost estimates the future of the TSR 2 seemed assured until the general election of October 1964. However, after the election the new government, which had been highly critical of the TSR 2 when in opposition, wasted no time in announcing that the future of a number of aircraft projects of advanced design would be the subject of a detailed re-appraisal. No final decision on the TSR 2 had been made by March 1965 although it was apparent that it could not be deferred much longer.

The B.A.C. interest in the TSR 2 amounted to 25% of the total cost, the remainder being accounted for by equipment and systems installed in the aircraft, e.g. engines and navigational equipment. By early 1965 the number of B.A.C. workers employed on the TSR 2 had risen to 6,000; 2,400 at Weybridge and 3,600 at Preston. These figures compared with a total labour force of 14,000 at Weybridge and 11,000 at Preston.

Aims of a redundancy policy

Immediately the Government announced the cancellation of the TSR 2 all the workers in the Preston and Weybridge divisions would feel their jobs threatened. Unless this uncertainty was quickly dispelled morale would suffer and labour troubles could easily follow. It was clear to Mr Dent that if this were to be avoided a statement of the Group redundancy policy must be made very shortly after the announcement; this should be followed as soon as practicable by the first redundancy notices. He felt that the success of the whole operation depended upon it being completed speedily. Nevertheless any premature release of plans before a final decision on the future of the aircraft would itself have a bad effect upon morale apart from being politically unwise. He realised that in preparing his plans for the approval of the Board of Directors discussion would have to be confined to a very limited circle.

Over the past few years an increasing proportion of TSR 2 work had been transferred to the Preston Division because of its facilities for the production of supersonic aircraft and the pressure of other work at Weybridge. It would probably be possible to transfer temporarily a number of TSR 2 workers at Weybridge on to the VC 10 and BAC 111, both of which were falling behind on their production programmes; this could delay the impact of the redundancies. However, the wisdom of such a delay could be questioned since it might be preferable to complete all the TSR 2 redundancies throughout the Group at the same time. It might also be difficult to convince the Government that the delayed redundancies were in fact attributable to the TSR 2, thereby qualifying for redundancy payments under the cancellation charges for that aircraft. The Weybridge division was employing approximately 400 contract workers from Vickers Ltd. at South Marston; these could be withdrawn at short notice thus reducing the number of B.A.C. employees to be made redundant. All in all it looked as if the impact of redundancy would be felt much more heavily at Preston.

The possibility of transferring work between divisions had to be rejected. This could not be effected easily and the delivery programmes for all types of aircraft were so tight that any temporary disruption could not be accepted. For the same reason it would not be possible to close one division completely even if agreement could be reached within the Group as to which division was to be closed.

Individual divisions had a great deal of autonomy and it would be the responsibility of their Managing Directors to make the final decisions of how many workers were to become redundant, who they were to be and also to a certain extent the timing of redundancies. However, the Group would retain responsibility for overall policy, redundancy payment, the timing and content of public announcements, and ensuring that differences did not occur in the treatment of workers in the two divisions. There were also a number of areas within the prerogative of the divisions which Mr Dent felt they should refer back to the Group before putting into effect; he made a note of some of these

All the companies within the B.A.C. Group had a long history of good labour relations. They felt they had a deservedly good reputation as employers and this they were determined to preserve. A well-handled redundancy programme might even enhance this reputation since it would be apparent to the workers that the cause of it was beyond the company's control; on the other hand any mishandling of this problem could leave wounds which might take years to heal. There was also a particular reason why an aircraft manufacturer should enjoy a good reputation with its workers, due to the sudden contractions and expansions to which the industry was prone. This made it necessary to preserve good relations not only with present employees but also with former workers who might well be required to work for the company again in the future.

Selection of redundant workers

Although the selection of the names of workers to receive redundancy notices was to be left largely in the hands of departmental managers, it was necessary for the

Group to establish criteria for their selection. This posed a number of difficult problems since it was here that there could well be disagreement between the Company and the Trade Unions. Although B.A.C. had a genuine desire to minimise hardship it must at the same time ensure that future productive efficiency would not be impaired.

It was decided that redundancy would be confined to workers who were employed on TSR 2 production rather than to consider the whole work force of the two divisions. A complete separation was not, however, possible in some departments where work for more than one type of aircraft was carried out. The redundancy plan would cater for all levels of employee although it was expected that hourly and weekly paid workers would be those most seriously affected.

It was thought from past experience that the manual workers' unions would initially propose that the remaining work should be shared by all employees and that there should be no redundancy. It was expected that this extreme position would not be maintained and that the Unions would agree to the principle of redundancy but would press for the following conditions:

(*a*) Last in, first out.
(*b*) Workers who had not served a recognised apprenticeship should be the first to go.
(*c*) An overtime ban should be imposed.
(*d*) Volunteers should be called for.

None of these conditions would be wholly acceptable to B.A.C. and some they would oppose strongly. The main objections would be on the grounds that they must try to retain the best workers and maintain a correct balance between skills and departments. Workers who had not served a recognised apprenticeship had in many cases been with the companies since the Second World War; they were often more loyal and skilled than some who had served apprenticeships, many of whom had only been with the companies a short time. A general overtime ban was also considered impractical since it was not always possible to transfer workers into departments working overtime due to the special skills involved.

It was, however, with the last condition that the major difference of principle lay. B.A.C. would object to calling for volunteers on two grounds. Firstly, the volunteers could well be the best workers whom they would wish to retain or from trades in which there would not be a surplus of labour. Secondly, there was likely to be a protracted period before the redundancy was completed since it was considered that volunteers would not come forward in the numbers required. They would therefore have to introduce a compulsory scheme at a later date to provide the balance. It was during such a period of continued uncertainty that labour troubles might well develop.

Some indication of other terms that the Unions might try to impose were given in the 'Proposed Redundancy Policy and Procedure' tabled by the Draughtsmen's and Allied Technicians Association at the Works Conference held at Weybridge on 22 February 1965 (See Exhibit 1). B.A.C. would agree to many of those conditions which were in line with Group policy but others were considered to be unacceptable.

Compensation payments

There had been a number of occasions in the past when changes of Government policy had caused redundancy in the aircraft industry. The scales of compensation had shown considerable variations although the trend in recent years had been for larger payments. It was also known that the Government was preparing a Redundancy Payments Bill which would impose minimum rates. In the case of the TSR 2 redundancies the payments would be chargeable to the Government as part of the cancellation charges for the project, so there was unlikely to be any objection from the shareholders if the terms were generous. Nor was the Government likely to object provided the terms did not appear excessive compared with what they were proposing in the Redundancy Payments Bill. However, B.A.C. must be careful not to establish a precedent with which they may have to live in the future when faced with a redundancy for which the company would have to pay itself. Nevertheless there were strong practical arguments for generous payments. During a period of continued uncertainty it would be easier to retain good workers if they thought they would be well compensated should they be declared redundant at a later date. Furthermore B.A.C.'s reputation as a good employer would be enhanced with the workers who remained and those leaving would not harbour a grudge which would prevent them returning to B.A.C. employment during a future period of greater prosperity.

Nevertheless it was not easy to fix a satisfactory rate. On a previous occasion B.A.C. has paid compensation at the rate of half a weeks pay for every year of service. Mr Dent prepared some comparative figures for two other redundancies (see Exhibit 2). The first of these followed the cancellation in 1962 of the Blue Water missile and the second related to payments by another company when it closed a factory. Mr Dent considered it was right that all workers declared redundant should receive some payment, however short a period they had been employed by B.A.C. There was also a case for making special provision for the older workers; although it was a period of full employment when most men would have little difficulty in finding new jobs, it was much harder for men over sixty particularly without a reduction in pay.

Week of decision

On 1st April, 1965 the Government published the Redundancy Payments Bill (see Exhibit 3 for extracts). A few days later on 6 April, in the course of his budget speech the Chancellor of the Exchequer announced the decision to cancel the TSR 2.

Exhibit 1. Draughtsmen's and Allied Technicians Association Proposed Redundancy Policy and Procedure Weekly and Monthly Staff Employees

1. Definitions
(*a*) The purpose of this memorandum is to provide a policy of procedure in the event of redundancy in the Company.

(*b*) The 'Company' means British Aircraft Corporation Ltd., Vickers-Armstrong (Aircraft) Ltd., and Vickers-Armstrongs Ltd., as applicable.

(*c*) Redundancy is defined as that situation in which Management and D.A.T.A. representatives agree that there is staff in a department or office surplus to the requirements of the Company.

(*d*) The procedure does not apply to the discharge of unsuitable or inefficient personnel, who will be dealt with in the normal manner.

2. *Preliminary action*

Before a decision is taken to make personnel redundant, the following action will be taken:

(*a*) The Employment Office will be closed and no further staff will be engaged.

(*b*) Sub-contract labour within the Company will be discharged.

(*c*) Work sub-contracted will be brought back to the Company.

(*d*) The working of overtime in all departments and offices covered by D.A.T.A. will cease immediately.

(*e*) Work sharing will be carried out without loss in salary, followed by shortening of the working week when necessary.

(*f*) Where the shortage of work is confined to one department or office, inter-departmental transfers, within the Company in the first instance, and the British Aircraft Corporation Ltd. in the second instance, will be made without loss in salary.

(*g*) D.A.T.A. representatives will be informed as soon as possible of an impending redundancy. An indication of the timing and an estimate of the numbers involved will be given to D.A.T.A. representatives at least one week before individual warnings of impending discharge are issued.

3. *General Policy*

(*a*) (i) In addition to the period of notice, employees will be given warning of impending discharge. This will not be less than one month.

(ii) In addition to the period of warning, notices will be two months plus one extra week for every year of service, with a minimum of three months.

(iii) Employees who are absent from work due to certified sickness will not be made redundant.

(iv) In the event of the Company's deciding to give payment in lieu of notice, the payment will be for the period of notice to which the individual is entitled.

(v) A weekly staff person leaving at own request during the *Period of Warning* or in the final week of notice will be paid up to the end of that week.

A weekly staff person leaving at own request during the *Period of Notice* before the final week will be paid for that week plus, in addition, one week's basic salary.

A monthly staff person, leaving at own request during the *Period of Notice* before the final month will be paid for that month plus, in addition, one month's salary.

(vi) Employees under warning or notice will be afforded reasonable time off with pay to attend for interview with potential employers.

(*b*) During a period of redundancy, employees over the normal retiring age of 65 (60 for women) will not be retained in employment.

(*c*) Full use will be made of the Ministry of Labour to assist those requiring alternative employment. Facilities will be provided for the relevant Officer of the Ministry of Labour to interview applicants for employment, on Company premises.

(*d*) Employees made redundant will be given preferential consideration for re-engagement if subsequent recruitment campaigns are carried out within six calendar months from date of discharge, and will not be deemed to have broken service with the Company upon such re-engagement.

(*e*) On receipt of notice of discharge, a note will be distributed to the employees affected, drawing their attention to the conditions set out in paragraph A, page 9 and paragraph C, page C, page 11 of the Pension and Life Assurance Plan for Staff Employees booklet.

(*f*) Length of continuous service with the Company will be the factor determining the order of discharge. Date of commencement of employment or apprenticeship with the Company determines length of service.

(*g*) The Management will notify D.A.T.A. representatives when the period of redundancy is ended and further when the Employment Office is re-opened.

(*h*) Facilities will be provided for the use of D.A.T.A. representatives to contact their members within the Company premises during a period of redundancy, preferably a room or office.

4. Procedure:

The following procedure will be applied:

(*a*) The Personnel Department will prepare a list giving the name, age, date of entry and nature of employment of all affected personnel for the Department or Office concerned. This list will be handed to the D.A.T.A. Representative as in 2(*g*).

(*b*) At least one week after the lists are agreed by the Management and D.A.T.A. representatives, all possible transfers having been effected, Departmental or Office Heads will inform employees of their impending discharge. Following the period of warning, Departmental or Office Heads will issue individual notices of discharge.

5. Compensation (*ex gratia payment*)

To compensate those made redundant an ex gratia payment will be made one month's basic salary for every year of service.

Exhibit 2. Payment details for two previous aircraft industry redundancies

Years of Service	Redundancy Payments Bill		Hourly Paid Employees		Weekly Paid Staff		Monthly Paid Staff	
	Service Under 41 years of age (Weeks Pay)	Service 41 years of age and over (Weeks Pay)	Blue Water Stevenage (Weeks Pay)	Company X (Weeks Pay)	Blue Water Stevenage (Weeks Pay)	Company X (Weeks Pay)	Blue Water Stevenage (Weeks Pay)	Company X (Weeks Pay)
Under 1				3·0		3	4·0	9
Over 1	2		0·3	3·0	1·2	3	4·4	9
Over 2	3	3	0·6	3·6	1·4	3	4·8	9
Over 3	4	4½	0·9	4·0	1·6	4	5·2	13
Over 4	5	6	1·2	4·6	1·8	4	5·6	13
Over 5	6	7½	1·5	5·0	2·0	4	6·0	13
Over 6	7	9	1·8	5·6	2·2	5	6·4	13
Over 7	8	10½	2·1	6·0	2·4	6	6·8	16
Over 8	9	12	2·4	6·6	2·6	7	7·2	16
Over 9	10	13½	2·7	7·0	2·8	8	7·6	16
Over 10	11	15	3·0	7·6	3·0	9	8·0	22
Over 11	12	16½	3·6	8·0	3·4	10	8·8	22
Over 12	13	18	4·2	8·6	3·8	11	9·6	22
Over 13	14	19½	4·8	9·0	4·2	12	10·4	26
Over 14	15	21	5·4	9·6	4·6	13	11·2	26
Over 15	16	22½	6·0	10·0	5·0	14	12·0	35
Over 16	17	24	6·6	10·6	5·4	15	12·8	35
Over 17	18	25½	7·2	11·0	5·8	16	13·6	35
Over 18	19	27	7·8	11·6	6·2	17	14·4	35
Over 19	20	28½	8·4	12·0	6·6	18	15·2	35
Over 20	20	30	9·0	12·6	7·0	20	16·0	48
Over 21	20	30	9·6	12·6	7·4	20	16·8	48
Over 22	20	30	10·2	12·6	7·8	20	17·6	48
Over 23	20	30	10·8	12·6	8·2	20	18·4	48
Over 24	20	30	11·4	12·6	8·6	20	19·2	48
Over 25	20	30	12·0	12·6	9·0	22	20·0	48

Note (1) Company X are permitting employees to take money in lieu of contractual notice in addition to the terminal payments outlined above.

(2) At Stevenage the above payments were increased by one week's pay for employees with more than 10 years service who were between 55 and 59 years of age, and two weeks pay for employees with more than 10 years service who were 60 years of age or over.

Exhibit 3. B.A.C. redundancy – extracts from Redundancy Payments Bill

1. Extracts from explanatory memorandum

1. The main objects of the Bill are to require employers to make payments to employees who become redundant and to establish a fund, under the management and control of the Minister of Labour and financed by employers' contributions, from which employers may recover a proportion of such payments.

2. Clause 1 requires employers to make payments to employees dismissed by reason of redundancy, or laid-off or put on short-time, and defines redundancy.

23. Clause 26 provides for the establishment of a fund under the control and management of the Minister of Labour, to be called 'the Redundancy Fund'.

24. Clause 27 prescribed the amount of employers' contributions to the Redundancy Fund and that these may be varied by order subject to affirmative approval by each House of Parliament. Contributions are to be levied by a surcharge of 5d. per week for men and 2d. for women on the employer's national insurance contributions and are estimated to yield about £18 million in a full year.

27. Clause 31 empowers the Minister to make payments from the Fund to employers liable to pay contributions in respect of certain classes of employees excluded under Clause 16 from the provisions of the Bill.

SCHEDULES

SCHEDULE 1

Calculation of redundancy payments

1. (1) The amount of a redundancy payment to which an employee is entitled in any case shall, subject to the following provisions of this Schedule, be calculated by reference to the period, ending with the relevant date, during which he has been continuously employed; and for the purposes of this Schedule that period shall be computed in accordance with Schedule 1 to the Contracts of Employment Act 1963, but as if:

    (*a*) any week which began before the employee attained the age of eighteen were excluded, and

    (*b*) the continuity of an employee's period of employment were not broken by a week which does not count under that Schedule, if the whole or part of that week falls within any such interval as is referred to in section 8(3) of this Act.

    (2) Where section 17 or section 24 of this Act applies, sub-paragraph (1) of this paragraph shall have effect subject to that section.

2. Subject to paragraph 3 and 4 of this Schedule, the amount of the redundancy payment shall be calculated by reference to the period specified in the preceding paragraph by starting at the end of that period and reckoning backwards the number of years of employment falling within that period, and allowing:

    (*a*) One and a half weeks' pay for each such year of employment which consists wholly of weeks in which the employee was not below the age of forty-one;

    (*b*) one week's pay for each such year of employment (not falling within the preceding sub-paragraph) which consists wholly of weeks in which the employee was not below the age of twenty-two; and

    (*c*) half a week's pay for each such year of employment not falling within either of the preceding sub-paragraphs.

3. Where, in reckoning the number of years of employment in accordance with paragraph 2 of this Schedule, twenty years of employment have been reckoned, no account shall be taken of any year of employment earlier than those twenty years.

4. (1) Where in the case of an employee the relevant date is after the specified anniversary, the amount of the redundancy payment, calculated in accordance with the preceding provisions of this Schedule, shall be reduced by the appropriate fraction.

(2) In this paragraph 'The specified anniversary' in relation to a man, means the sixty-fourth anniversary of the day of his birth, and, in relation to a women, means the fifty-ninth anniversary of the day of her birth, and 'the appropriate fraction' means the fraction of which:

(*a*) the numerator is the number of whole months, reckoned from the specified anniversary, in the period beginning with that anniversary and ending with the relevant date, and

(*b*) the denominator is twelve.

5. (1) For the purpose of this Schedule the amount of a week's pay shall, subject to the following provisions of this paragraph, and except as may be otherwise provided by regulations made by the Minister, be taken to be the minimum remuneration to which the employee would in the week ending with the relevant date have been entitled, under Schedule 2 to to the Contracts of Employment Act 1963, if the conditions in the next following sub-paragraph had been fulfilled (whether those conditions were in fact fulfilled or not).

(2) Those conditions are:

(*a*) That the contract of employment was terminable by notice, and was terminated by the employer by giving such notice as is required by section 1 (1) of the said Act of 1963;

(*b*) that, in a case falling within paragraph 2 of Schedule 2 to that Act, the employee was ready and willing to work during the week ending with the relevant date but no work was then provided for him;

(*c*) that, in a case falling within paragraph 3 of that Schedule, the employee was willing to do work of a reasonable nature and amount to earn remuneration at the rate mentioned in sub-paragraph (2) of that paragraph;

(*d*) that the employee was not absent from work with the leave of his employer;

(*e*) that Schedule 2 to that Act, if by virtue of section 6 of that Act it did not apply to the employee, applied to him notwithstanding that section.

(3) Notwithstanding anything in sub-paragraph (1) of this paragraph, but subject to the following provisions of this paragraph, the amount of a week's pay shall not in any case be taken for the purposes of this Schedule to exceed £40.

(4) The Minister may by order that, subject to such transitional provisions (if any) as may be contained in the order, the last preceding sub-paragraph shall have effect as if, for the sum of £40, there were substituted such larger sum as may be specified in the order.

(5) Any order under this paragraph may be varied or revoked by a subsequent order thereunder.

(6) Any power to make orders under this paragraph shall be exercisable by statutory instrument; but no such order shall be made unless a draft of the order has been laid before Parliament and approved by a resolution of each House of Parliament.

6. For the purpose of any provision contained in Part 1 of this Act whereby a tribunal may determine that an employer shall be liable to pay to an employee either:

(*a*) the whole of the redundancy payment to which the employee would have been entitled apart from another provision therein mentioned, or

(*b*) such part of that redundancy payment as the tribunal thinks fit, the preceding provisions of this Schedule shall apply as if in those provisions any reference to the amount of a redundancy payment were a reference to the amount of the redundancy payment to which the employee would have been so entitled.

7. The preceding provisions of this Schedule shall have effect without prejudice to the operation of any regulations made under section 14 of this Act whereby the amount of a redundancy payment, may be reduced.

8. Where the relevant date does not occur at the end of a week, any reference in the preceding provisions of this Schedule to the relevant date shall be construed as a reference to the end of the week in which that date falls.

9. In this Schedule 'week' means a week ending with Saturday, and 'year of employment' means fifty-two weeks (whether continuous or discontinuous) which, in accordance with Schedule 1 to the Contracts of Employment Act 1963, count in computing a period of employment'.

SCHEDULE 5

Calculation of rebates

PART 1

Rebates in respect of redundancy payments

2. Subject to sections 30(6) and 34 of this Act, and to the following provisions of this Part of this Schedule, the amount of any rebate payable in respect of a redundancy payment shall be calculated by taking the number of years of employment by reference to which the redundancy payment falls to be calculated in accordance with Schedule 1 to this Act, and allowing:

   (*a*) one and one-sixth weeks' pay for each year of employment falling within sub-paragraph (*a*) of paragraph 2 of that Schedule;

   (*b*) two-thirds of one week's pay for each year of employment falling within sub-paragraph (*b*) of that paragraph; and

   (*c*) one-third of one week's pay for each year of employment falling within sub-paragraph (*c*) of that paragraph.

Case 22
Sonning Mead Boilers Ltd.

It had been several weeks since Herbert Pressel had played golf. The incessant rain and fog had made conditions impossible. Besides, as Managing Director of Sonning Mead Boilers, Limited he had found himself regularly working at the weekends.

This Sunday, however, he hoped to combine a day of relaxation with a needed business discussion. The Sonning Board of Directors had called for a report on the company's plans for training management supervisory staff for the company's construction sites. Consequently, Mr Pressel invited Mr Seymour Glasser, a lecturer and consultant from a well-known Midlands Business School, as well as Mr Sydney Jordan, and Mr W. E. Culver, members of his own staff, for a day of golf and conversation.

As one of the principal water-tube boiler makers, Sonning Mead Limited was engaged in the construction of steam generating plants for the Central Electricity Generating Board (CEGB). Current projects included both conventional and nuclear powered generating stations.

In 1958 the typical boiler had a capacity of sixty megawatts. (It is normal to describe the size of a power station boiler in terms of the equivalent electrical power it is capable of generating). Today it was common to have a series of four 500 megawatt boilers constructed on one site.

This rapid growth had resulted in vast changes in the technology, logistics, and administration of each contract. The need for qualified staff to implement these changes had drawn Sonning's attention to the question of management education.

The Sonning Board of Directors had become increasingly aware of the implications of the Industrial Training Act. Under this Act, Industrial Training Boards had been established which were empowered to make substantial levies. The Engineering Industry Board had decided to make a $2\frac{1}{2}$% levy on the wage bills of companies (excluding firms with a wage bill less than £5,000 p.a.) This wage bill included executives as well as hourly paid personnel. For the Boilermakers the levy was $2\frac{1}{2}$% of total wages. The company could then claim grants in respect of any training of workers or management personnel employed by or intending to be employed by the firm.

The Industrial Training Act created a strong incentive for the companies to finance training up to the amount which had been levied by the government. Sonning Mead expected a levy of over £200,000 in 1966. Questions of how such a sum should be allocated had become a matter of some urgency.

After greeting his guests at the car park, Mr Pressel led the way to the clubhouse and suggested that before they changed they should have some coffee. The following conversation ensued:

Herbert Pressel (Managing Director)
'Gentlemen, I though that while we enjoyed our golf we might have a useful discussion on the company's plans so far as training is concerned. Why don't we start with the qualities we are looking for in future site supervision'.

W. E. Culver (Training Manager–Sonning Mead Ltd.)
'Existing site staff are, in many cases, die hards. They have their own ideas on construction and often are not amenable to modern techniques. They are generally capable but have difficulty imparting their wisdom to juniors.'

'My experience is that Resident Site Engineers have an excessively high opinion of their ability to improvise and consequently don't spend enough time planning at the start of a job.'

Sydney Jordan (Resident Site Engineer–Sonning Mead Ltd.)
'That which you call an excessively high opinion of themselves, Mr Culver, I'd call a reflection of the inadequacy of the juniors, section engineers, and labour that have to be supervised. Remember, the design of boilers has changed drastically in recent years. Most of our top site staff have come from the ranks. They were good foremen and have extremely strong personalities. The new systems needed to build a modern station are foreign to many of them.'

Herbert Pressel
'That's right. The older members of our site staff have not all had formal technical education. In one sense the influx of young people with such education is a threat to them and in itself builds resistance to new methods.'

Seymour Glasser (Lecturer)
'I've noticed that your section engineers are generally young men and that there is a fairly high rate of turnover. In particular I've notice a lack of understanding in labour relations and in handling of the men.'

Sydney Jordan
'Seymour, you can't teach your grandmother to suck eggs and similarly the only way you can learn labour relations is to spend years fighting these problems on the job.'

Seymour Glasser
'In one sense you are right but you must admit that living with a problem can develop a hard line orientation that results in a lack of perspective in a particular situation. Antagonism, even when it's a result of experience is not a healthy condition.'

Herbert Pressel
'I'm convinced that the administrative aspect of site supervision needs more emphasis. Work on site needs to be more sequential than work in the factory because of the heights involved, access problems and the close integration of one operation with another. In the factory they can more easily go back to things; on the site they can't because they'd be putting up cranes and derricks and involved in all kinds of erection equipment and plant.'

Sydney Jordan
'The quality of supervision is critical. Men have to respect the supervisor. The foreman is number one. A good foreman will make the job; not a good section engineer, not a good resident, but a good foreman.'

W. E. Culver
'So what you are saying is that the section engineer should be a planner and an administrator rather than a technical expert.'

Sydney Jordan
'Yes, but he must understand the technique and gain enough respect to be the leader. And the chief engineer must be a born organiser.'

Seymour Glasser
'The term "resident engineer" would seem to be a misnomer. On large CEGB contracts he is more of a general manager than an engineer. He controls a large labour force, consisting in the main of relatively unskilled labour. And he has to apply discipline in his organisation by negotiating from a position of strength. And today he oversees the planning, progress and budgetary control of the contract. All of this is much beyond the definition of "Resident Engineer".'

Herbert Pressel
'I agree. It's not enough to be a qualified engineer. He also needs a firm grounding in Trade Union Law, National agreements, Current Planning methods and Proper Site Organisation as well as the legal aspects of employment.'

Sydney Jordan
'The ideal site man should have a working knowledge of all the construction trades and have held direct responsibility for erection work himself, and a man needs at least five years as a section engineer before he is ready to become a resident. The important point is that a man should be fully educated and experienced before real site responsibility is given to him. Full practical experience is of much greater value than a ton of theory. You can't create the aggressiveness and enthusiasm it takes to be a leader by studying books. You can only find out who possesses the ingredients of leadership on the job itself.'

W. E. Culver
'Considering the complexity of today's site work, you need young people with National Certificate or HNC qualifications. They need lots of experience in the works and drawing office but formal management education is also necessary; particularly in human management, self expression, report writing, communication techniques, and work study methods. It's the lack of this formal education that needs our attention. No one will argue that experience is not vital. The point is that in today's world experience is not enough.'

'And as you know, formal education at the site is difficult. Men can't be spared for part-time courses. The location and working hours make it difficult particularly among juniors. And it's difficult to convince management of the value of formal training. They say that since they didn't have formal training and are successful why can't today's juniors manage without it.'

Herbert Pressel
'The fact that we are discussing this subject seems to contradict you doesn't it, Mr. Culver?'

W. E. Culver
'Yes Sir, it would appear to.'

As the group moved into the dressing room to change it began to rain so they agreed to continue their discussion in the bar.

Herbert Pressel
'Mr Glasser, would you review for us the kinds of formal training that are currently available.'

Seymour Glasser
'I brought along some pamphlets for you to inspect. Why not take a few minutes and we can talk around them.' (See Exhibits 1 to 4.)
   'What you are really looking for is the best way to spend your educational funds. Remember that very few programmes will satisfy every requirement unless they are specifically tailored for your company. Also a programme might include some subjects which seem to have no immediate relevance to your needs. Therefore your choices in formal education will be usual business decisions in that there will be a full measure of uncertainty involved.'

Herbert Pressel
'I understand management education to mean several things. It means developing the ability to make rational and informal decisions. It also means increasing a man's effectiveness in working with and through people as well as enlarging his capacity for taking responsibility.'

W. E. Culver
'What we want is a course that is valuable to men who have proved their effectiveness as junior managers, in a specialists role, and are considered ripe to take on greater responsibilities, either within their specialist function or by assuming a broader cross functional responsibility.'

Herbert Pressel
'We want our men to develop substantially in a variety of ways. They should increase their understanding of the business world and its environment and they should develop greater powers of analysis and decision-making. They should develop skills in human relations, both in relating themselves to others and predicting human reactions to change. They should develop a more conceptual framework in which to lead out their business lives. And finally, they should develop a greater perception of the interplay in different business functions.'

Sydney Jordan
'But do we want to prepare men for wider responsibility in the company? Or should they be more effective in discharging predefined responsibilities. It should

also be pointed out, that by being mistakenly prepared to take greater responsibility a man is likely to develop heightened expectations of the role he is able to play. Thus it is important that when a man is selected by his company to attend a programme, serious thought be given to the question of his future career, if the programme is apt to give him ideas of grandeur.'

Seymour Glasser

'The quality of a programme must depend in part on the quality of the participants. It is assumed that when a man is nominated for attendance, the company will have selected a man of genuine potential and demonstrated competence.'

Sydney Jordan

'Yes, but you are still assuming we are training potential Managing Directors.'

Seymour Glasser

'No, not really, but what I am saying is that business schools are not in the business of readjusting misfits. Good men can ill be spared. But the loss of such a man for a time must be weighed against the continuing benefit of a brighter, more knowledgeable manager over the many years of active life remaining to him in the service of the company. The new ideas and enthusiasms which such a man brings back with him do not remain locked within him, but are an injection into the company as a whole and spread to the man's associates in widening circles.'

W. E. Culver

'It seems to me that a smaller and smaller number of good young men for recruitment as managers will be available from non-university sources. And that to get the right men business will have to increase its intake of graduates. The graduates, while highly educated in their particular subjects, have in most cases acquired little familiarity with the business world and will be arriving three years older. All these factors will make them less suitable, less willing subjects for the historical training and indoctrination which they normally would have received.'

Sydney Jordan

'This sounds rather general to me. A man will never find out the proper way to rig a tackle except on a site. And what conceivable relevance does the determination of National Income have to building a boiler.'

Seymour Glasser

'It all depends on your goals Sydney, a manager must have broad perspectives. There are, however, special programmes arranged to suit particular needs. Such courses have been arranged for the services, technical college teachers, trade union officials, and nationalised industries.'

Herbert Pressel

'I can see that it is critical that we define specific goals for our training. There appears to be such a diversity of courses offered that unless we target our purposes we will go off in many directions at once.'

'We seem to be troubled by the question of the relevance of offering a broad spectrum of courses to a man who will be concerned essentially with production planning and human management. Perhaps management development cannot be a once-for-all exercise. In a world of cumulative change, ever more intricate complexity, expressively increasing knowledge and constantly widening horizons, what could suffice today would almost certainly be inadequate tomorrow.'

Seymour Glasser
'For the individual man, a single course, however, good, at any one stage in his life, will not be enough.'

W. E. Culver
'That is why there are series of general courses for trainees, younger managers, middle managers, senior managers and directors of companies, each complete in itself, but together providing a progressive system of courses available to the manager at the decisive levels throughout his career.'

Sydney Jordan
'If anything I prefer a large number of specialised courses, conferences and seminars in particular subjects or for particular types of managers.'

Seymour Glasser
'You can see, gentlemen, that many schools are active in the field of business education. There are many more than the programmes we have noted. However, these are representative and the number of business schools is growing rapidly. You will not lack in choices of direction. Fees, in each of these institutions, vary considerably, but in no sense will the fees be out of proportion, if you have chosen the right man, the right institution, for the right reason.'

W. E. Culver
'Of course, the least expensive means of training is within our own company.'

Herbert Pressel
'The difficulty is in achieving new perspectives in the individual man when he is taught generalist subjects on the job within the atmosphere of the company's existing value system. What we are really looking for is constructive change and there is a strong argument for injecting new thought, new ideas, new techniques, into the thinking of our younger men. These new ideas will then be modified by the facts of life within the company, when they return from a particular institution. Nevertheless, they will make their mark.'

W. E. Culver
'Should the method of instruction mean anything to us? There has been a good deal of controversy in this country over the best way to develop management skill in the classroom.'

Seymour Glasser
'At one extreme you have the pure lecture method in which the teacher imparts his knowledge directly to the students. At the other you have a pure participative scheme in which the students discuss the materials they have studied with only guidance and control supplied by the teacher.'

'The answer as to which is the best method depends on what is to be taught, the calibre of the students, and the aim of the particular course.

'For example, in your case, subjects such as labour relations might deserve a different approach from method study techniques.'

Sydney Jordan

'If we are going to have courses I think they should be individual company training schemes. I think formal training in things like labour relations would be next to useless. Practical on-site experience is what's required.'

Herbert Pressel

'We must ensure that we give special training only to men whom we expect to stay with the company. This raises the question of how early in a man's career we should spend money on his training. I feel initially direct site contact should be maintained to give a realistic basis for the labour relations education, and an awareness of site conditions and erection procedures. Perhaps by employment as an inspector, plant erection procedure can initially be studied. If possible employment as a section engineer should take place on a small job where every aspect can more easily be studied in detail. For erection procedures and heavy lifting, a transfer to a large project would be preferable. At that point perhaps, training and theoretical aspects of site work from organisation to planning to human relations could be phased into the training.'

Sydney Jordan

'There is no substitute for experience provided you are willing to learn from and by it. Thus the highly qualified man, academically speaking, generally does not make the best site man. He must above all be practical, and somewhat of a jack of all trades. Therefore I would recommend an apprenticeship period that would last four to five years that would be spent in the drawing office, works, design service, maintenance departments, and planning and estimating departments, as well as in periods of learning trades, such as welding, fitting, rigging, pipe fitting stores. I would also advocate periods of work in gangs or with gangs of men, perhaps as a foreman, then a period as a section engineer and within this period, perhaps a course of work study or method study. I frankly can see very little value in the company spending its money on broad academic courses.'

W. E. Culver

'My personal observation after twelve years in the business world, working for two different boilermakers, is that I have never known or heard exactly what a company's objectives were with regard to management training and I think it would probably be found that nobody else has heard either. One can only guess.'

Seymour Glasser

'I think this is the point of our discussion today.

'In terms of the basic value of formal education, it is interesting that those individuals who have had it are those that endorse it. And those individuals who haven't are those that decry it. There is a lesson in the examination of this fact as well.'

Herbert Pressel

'Gentlemen, thank you very much indeed. I think we have had a fair statement of the qualities we are looking for in future site supervision and a representative glance at the kind of formal education that is available. It is now up to us to equate the two.'

Exhibit 1. Programme A

This is a ten-week residential course taught by lectures and participative method. The programme is broadly divided in two phases, approximately equal length. In the first phase, the focus is on the development of background knowledge in three major areas; analysis and measurement, human behaviour, and the environment of business. Analysis and measurement is covered by problem-oriented instruction in quantitative methods, in financial and cost accounting, in the analysis and measurement of demand in costs, and in the economics of production.

The human behaviour course develops an understanding of the nature of the individual, group and intergroup behaviour as it occurs in a business setting, and draws creatively on the behavioural sciences to increase the individuals awareness of the nature of his own behaviour and his own attitude.

The study of environment concentrates on three major aspects. These are: (a) the overall workings and management of the British economy, including an introduction to national incomes accounts, balance of payments, and national planning. (b) social control of industry which covers problems of monopoly, competition, restrictive practices, and resale price maintenance. (c) the corporate legal environment which is studied through an introduction to the underlying principles of company law, and the law of contracts, sales payments and labour relations.

The second phase of the programme is directed toward the application of the knowledge acquired in the first phase to actual business situations. The programme is divided along the lines of the major functions of business, production, marketing, finance, industrial relations, personnel management. The work is largely based on actual situations drawn from business and effort is concentrated on the development of skill for dealing with particular problems. There is also a section in operations research methods which introduces many of the newer techniques and indicates both their potential and their limitation.

The last element in the second phase is a course in policy making which offers the opportunity to develop skill and the integration of functions through the concepts of setting objectives, and the development of coherent strategy with the subsequent formation of policies, and the organisation, development and motivation of people to achieve objectives.

Exhibit 2. Programme B

Instruction in techniques—a series of operating courses taught by lecture and laboratory work where appropriate.

Course number 1

A one week course in recent developments in management techniques.

A survey of contemporary management services with particular reference to management sciences. The course covers the modern scope of work study, ergonomics, cybernetics, operational research, industrial dynamics, linear programming, statistical methods for managers, control of stocks, investment policy making, distribution, modern organisation theories, organisation and methods of computer studies, the current economic background to management activities, and finally the integration of management services.

Course number 2: Network Analysis

This course consists of critical path planning, PERT and other related methods, and the general technique called network analysis. The course offers sufficient practical training in network analysis to enable those who successfully complete it to introduce the technique in their own organisation. Case studies from industry are worked through in considerable detail. The students are also required to complete a practical project. The application of electronic computers in this field is dealt with and a computer is used for a demonstration in critical path analysis.

Course number 3: Statistical Methods for Solving Industrial and Commerical Problems

The course aims to give a thorough but simplified instruction in a limited but powerful range of statistical techniques. Areas covered include the use of sampling procedures to give better control of quality, lower inspection costs in the office as well as the factory. The course includes the use of computers as an aid to statistical analysis, and the design of experiments and research to obtain the required information with a minimum of experimentation. The course provides a valuable introduction to statistics for managers and supervisors. A high level of mathematical ability is not required. Only elementary algebra is used in the course. The approach is essentially practical, formal theory being reduced to absolute minimum.

Course number 4: Materials Handling

A two week course with emphasis on the solution of problems by the use of critical analysis. The aim is to maximise utilisation of resources at least cost, an approach which is often absent in the field of management.

Course number 5: Data Processing and Computer Studies

This is a three week practical course in data processing for which no other knowledge of computers is required, and which develops a sound critical approach to the problems of electronic computers.

Course number 6: Method Study

This is a four week course which prepares individuals to return to their organisations capable of carrying out method study investigation under some guidance from management. The course therefore meets the need for sound basic training which few organisations are able to provide from their own resources.

Course number 7: Organisation and Methods

This is a course in administrative work study, and covers such subjects as analysis of procedures, office and work measurement, office equipment, organisation theory, management information analysis, and elementary statistical theory.

Course number 8: Production Planning and Stock Control

This two week course has been drawn from actual methods in current use, carefully selected so as to illustrate most modern principles in practice. It is essentially concerned with teaching practical techniques in production planning and stock control.

Exhibit 3. Programme C

Course number 1: Short lecture courses in specialised subjects

These short courses include balance sheets for the laymen, business tax, corporate taxation, cost and profit evaluation techniques, a profit planning seminar, production control, critical path analysis, value analysis seminar, work-study appreciation, organisation and methods appreciation, industrial marketing, new product development, market forecasting, capital expenditure decisions, interviewing skills for managers, systematic selection methods, management by objectives, and appraisal by results, the negotiation of productivity agreements, as well as others. These short courses run from one day to ten weeks and can be selected to the particular needs of an individual company or industry.

Exhibit 4. Programme D

Course number 1: Weekend residential lecture courses

These courses are held in both England and N. Ireland. They offer a series of elementary as well as advanced courses. The number of students accepted for each course is limited in order to give ample opportunity for discussion. The advance course includes job evaluation, incentives, increasing cost consciousness, organising for production, weighing up people and jobs, men, money and trade, and supervisory decision making.

Case 23
The Tetley Tea Co. Ltd.

In the Spring of 1964, Mr R. W. Parker, the factory manager of The Tetley Tea Co. Ltd., of Bletchley, Bucks, was searching for ways of increasing the production of tea bags for the domestic market. Recent sales promotion had reduced his stocks of tea bags and predictions of future sales were in excess of current output with his existing labour force.

Background

The Tetley Company was founded by the brothers Edward and Joseph Tetley. Formerly tea peddlers on the Yorkshire moors they had established offices in Huddersfield in 1837 to deal in tea. For over a century the business prospered both in the United Kingdom and later in the USA where they became established in 1921. In 1961 Tetley was bought by an American Company, Beechnut Chewing Gum, but since that time the United Kingdom operations had been allowed to function as an autonomous operation.

Production at Bletchley started in 1954, the move to a new location having been decided upon after the destruction of the previous factory by bombing during the war. Even as late as 1954, the country was divided into zones to conserve transport, and factories were limited to serving certain zones in their neighbourhood. The choice of Bletchley was largely influenced by the fact that five zones could be served from this central location. The factory was situated on an Industrial Estate containing a number of other companies.

With annual UK sales of 400 million tea bags, Tetley accounted for 90% of the total market although tea bags only comprised about $1\frac{1}{2}$% of British tea sales compared with upwards of 60% in the United States. Nevertheless tea bags had been gaining in popularity in the United Kingdom particularly in recent years since the introduction of bags made from long staple fibre paper which did not impart a flavour to the tea as had been the case with the muslin bags used before. Most of the increase in demand, which had been increasing at an annual rate of 30% for several years, had been from the domestic consumer, although the institutional trade had also been expanding concurrently.

By late 1963 it became apparent that current production schedules were not going to meet the growing home demand. On previous occasions temporary reductions of stocks had occurred following television campaigns or other special promotions. However, in the winter of 1963/4 stocks continued to diminish and forecasts indicated rising sales considerably in excess of existing production capacity.

© Cranfield Institute of Technology.

Production facilities and labour employed

Mr Parker's main problem lay with the first floor tea bags line which was producing for the home market. This line consisted of nine tea-bagging machines which formed the bags and filled them with a measured quantity of tea, two box machines and two cellophane packaging machines. The general layout of the production line is illustrated in Exhibit 1. Each bag machine required three operators to put the manufactured tea bags into the boxes; additional personnel operated the box and packaging machines.

At that time Mr Parker was running eight of the tea bagging machines, each of which had a production rate of 300 bags per minute, on a one-shift basis for a forty-two-hour week. He realised that if production were to be raised significantly, it would be necessary to institute two-shift working from which he could expect a total of seventy-five hours working per machine each week.

Sixty-seven men and 140 women are currently employed at Tetley. Over the coming two or three years the company hoped to expand production by bringing two lines of nine high speed tea bag machines into use on a two-shift operation, and running the individual packing machines on the ground floor at a similar rate of use. These changes would require a total staff of 300, and a further expansion contemplated by 1970 would require an additional 120 workers.

Both the UK and US factories employed a similar degree of atuomation. It was possible to have machines which would automatically pack the tea bags into a carton, but Tetley had not yet used them mainly because inspection was impossible.

Wages and conditions of employment

The tea bag production line at Tetley was staffed almost entirely with female labour—the majority were on shift work. Although a few of the girls were paid a basic wage of £8·45[1] a week, the average wage paid was £10·02½ made up of the basic union rate of £8·07½, plus 40p 'lieu' bonus, 55p machine money and £1 shift work premium; there were no incentive payments. This compared favourably with neighbouring factories, although it was possible for girls to earn with bonus payments as much as £13 at a cigarette components factory in the area. Mr Parker considered that most employees preferred the steady tempo of work at Tetley and security of employment, to the higher wages offered by the cigarette components factory.

There were a number of fringe benefits that Tetley Tea give their employees. These included free transport to work, sickness benefits and medical facilities, cheap uniforms, a Social Club and a canteen.

Availability of labour in the Bletchley area

Mr Parker knew that the increased number of workers required to operate a two-shift system might not be easy to obtain in the Bletchley area where

1. Figures throughout this case have been converted to British decimal currency.

unemployment was low and there were a number of unfilled vacancies. He decided therefore, to ask a firm of management consultants to undertake an investigation into labour availability.

This report, when submitted, began by quoting figures provided by the Ministry of Labour which confirmed the existing shortage of labour. The Bletchley Labour Exchange, covered an area well beyond the Bletchley Urban District Council, and on the rolls of the Labour Exchange there were only twelve men and thirty-five women registered as unemployed. These 'unemployed' were understood to be virtually unemployable. On the other hand there were recorded vacancies for 296 men and 174 women which could not be filled.

Bletchley urban area

The inadequate provision of housing was a main factor contributing to the labour shortage. A housing shortage existed and the report mentioned that some firms which had engaged employees by promising accommodation had later lost them due to the delay in housing availability.

The report also gave details of the growth of employment and housing over the last ten years together with an assessment of the likely trend for the next three years, based where possible on existing plans. These figures are included as Exhibit 2. A projection for 1967 was made of the growth of population compared with the labour requirement. This took into account the needs of new industry, expansion of existing industry, the natural growth of population, and the growth from new housing. These figures are given in Exhibit 3.

A further consideration was an agreement between Bletchley and London under the Town Development Act, for Bletchley to receive over 10,500 of the London 'overspill' population. By mid-1961, the population received by Bletchley under this scheme totalled 4,300, leaving a capacity of 6,200 still to be taken up.

Rural area

The situation in the rural area covered by the Bletchley Labour Exchange was found to be rather different from that in the urban area. None of the rural authorities had an agreement to provide housing for the London overspill population, no appreciable industrial expansion was visualised, and new housing was mostly confined to providing for natural population growth and slum clearance. Winslow Rural District Council, however, did propose to build thirty more units in the next two years.

In addition, approximately 400 privately built houses were projected. Newport Pagnell, where most of the expansion of the last ten years had taken place, expected a population increase of up to 1,000 persons per year for the next fifteen to twenty years.

Married women workers

The consultants also carried out a survey amongst women living in the housing estates lying to the South and West of Bletchley. The aim of this survey was to assess whether many married women not working at that time wished to work, and if so why they had not taken jobs. Exhibit 4 summarises the replies received from this survey.

Working conditions and pay

So far Mr Parker had only considered any additions to the working population. An alternative might be to attract a greater percentage of the existing labour force by offering better conditions of pay. Conditions at Tetley already compared favourably with other firms in the area, and the sole improvement consultants could suggest was the provision of free overalls. This suggestion was hardly likely to solve his recruitment problems! His thoughts next turned to pay. The report agreed that the machine and shift premiums raised the shift rate to £10·02½ which was greater than the minimum paid elsewhere. Nevertheless, in some other firms incentive payments and rates graduated for skill raised the top shift and day rates to more than £13 a week.

The long-term position of Tetley Tea

In addition to solving the short term labour problems facing Tetley Tea, Mr Parker was also concerned with the longer term position of the company, particularly in the light of the uncertainties arising from the recent publication of the Government's 'South East Study 1961-1981'. He felt that the part of the study dealing with the future of the Bletchley area was particularly relevant to the long-term position of Tetley Tea in the area.

The future of Bletchley

The authors of the Study were of the opinion that expansion of the existing town of Bletchley (pop. 16,900 in 1961), would not provide a sufficient base for building up the area, while the growth potential of the area's existing industry was only moderate. However, it was envisaged that the natural economic advantages of the location would ensure the success of a new town in the area. It was envisaged that the Bletchley area would be a particularly attractive location for industrialists with its close proximity to the main lines of communication, including the M.1 (the motorway connecting London with the Industrial Midlands and North) and the main railway line, and the immediate availability of abundant building space. The study continued, 'There should be no trouble in finding enough employment for a new town here, and a large and successful development should be possible . . . In the very long term, a new town of a quarter of a million might arise. By 1981 a growth of 75,000 might be achieved'. (See Appendix I table I).

Population growth in the South East Region

Mr Parker thought that, in the long run the large forecast increase in the population of the South East Region would only help to resolve the labour problems of firms such as Tetley Tea. However, he fully appreciated that the supply of labour was but one side of the equation. What was the demand for labour in the region likely to be over the long run? On referring to the South East Study he read:

'. . . more new jobs are being created in the South East than in other parts of the country . . . All the factors point towards the conclusion that there is unlikely to be a sudden decrease in the number of jobs being created in the South East'.

Referring to the tables of employment increase and growth given in Appendix I tables II and IV, he noted that the percentage increase was greater for the South-East than for any other region in England and Wales. Furthermore, he noted a statement in the study to the effect that if additional jobs were created in the South East at the same rate as they had been during the ten years 1952-62 (over 1m.), there would be 2 million extra workers by 1981, equivalent to a population increase of about 4m. However, if the rate of increase over the last three years (1959-62) were to be sustained, there would be three million extra workers, corresponding to a population increase of six million by 1981. (see Appendix I table V for changes in the distribution of employees for England and Wales).

Effects of Government action

In both the long run and the short run, the rate of growth of The Tetley Tea Co. Ltd., and of the South East region in particular, would be affected by Government actions, particularly in the form of direct control over the location of new industry and the measures to build up the economic strength and attractiveness of the less prosperous regions. Mr Parker thought that it was particularly relevant that the current employment increases in the South East had taken place in spite of determined efforts by the Government to locate manufacturing industry in other parts of the country. He wondered whether this meant that new industrial projects in the South East would be unlikely to receive industrial development certificates and furthermore that extensions to existing factories would be discouraged. Figure II in the Appendix shows the Industrial Development in England and Wales 1952-61.

Mr Parker slowly knocked the ashes out of his pipe as he reflected on the problems involved. What could he do in the short term and in the longer term and would these two objectives conflict?

Exhibit 1. Layout of first floor tea bag line

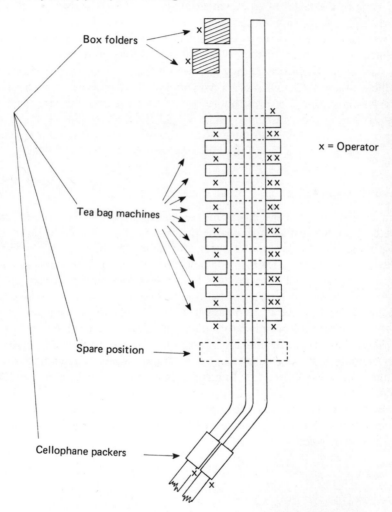

Exhibit 2. Expansion of housing and employment in Bletchley

	1954-1964 (Actual)		1964-1967 (Planned or estimated)	
	Total	*Average/ year*	*Total*	*Average/ year*
Factory developments–number	39	3·9	10 (by end 1965) 10/12 (by end 1967)	6·6
–total area (sq. ft)	850,000	85,000	400,000 (by end 1965). Not known (by end 1967)	–
Persons employed in above	2,500	250	1,250	416
Housing units				
(a) by council–built	2,250	225		
–under construction			170	177
			360*	
(b) Privately	850	85	500	166
(c) Total–(a) and (b)	3,100	310	1,030	343

* The Council has applied for permission to build a further 360 units. There is some doubt of the outcome and their construction can be considered only a possibility.

Note: Housing cannot be directly associated with employment due to the number of workers living in Bletchley who work outside the area.

Exhibit 3. Bletchley–growth of working population and labour requirement– projection for 1967

	Working population			Labour requirement		
	Men	*Women*	*Total*	*Men*	*Women*	*Total*
Estimated labour force, 1964	6,300	2,700	9,000	6,600	2,900	9,500
New industry need				875	375	1,250
Expansion of existing industry				330	145	475
Natural growth (school leavers– pensioners)	540	600	1,140			
Growth from new housing (Assuming maximum planned council building)–say	830	100	930			
Total	7,670	3,400	11,070	7,805	3,420	11,225

Exhibit 4. Summary of replies from 40 women interviewed in Bletchley housing estates

Q. Are you working now?
A. No—29.   Yes: Day work   1
                        Shift work   1
                        Part time   9

Q. What type of work do you do, or have you done previously?
A.

	Now	Previously	Total
Factory	3	10	13
Domestic and catering	6	2	8
Clerical	1	8	9
Shop	1	5	6
Police and forces	—	2	2
Tailoring	—	1	1

Q. Are you married?
A. Yes—38;No—1;   Widow—1.

Q. Have you children, if so, how many?
A. Yes—37 (average number 2·35 each)
    No—3 (two obviously about to have)

Q. What are their ages?
A. Analysis of answers showed that the majority of children were below the age of 5.
    , The youngest child exceeded 9 years in only 6 cases.

Q. Would you be prepared to work now?
A. Yes—15;   No—14 (three medically unfit)

Q. If not now, at some time later?
A. When children are all at school—3
    After next child is born—4

Q. What hours could you work?
A. Normal day work   7
    Shift work   2
    Part-time, day or evening   14
    6 a.m. to 2 p.m. shift only   4
    2 p.m. to 10 p.m. shift only   NIL

   Note: Replies included some already working who might change their work,
           also those covered by the previous question.

Q. What pay would you require for the work?
   The majority were unable to answer. Positive replies indicated:
       Day work   £7 to £10 per week
       Shift work   £11·50 per week
       Part time   Proportionately less than day work.

Q. How long have you lived in Bletchley?
A. Less than 5 years   17
    5-15 years   13
    Native born   10

Exhibit 5

New Cities ◆
Big New Expansions ○
Other Expansions ⬚
Symbols indicate only general locations
Metropolitan Region Boundary ——
Built-up areas 1958

0 10 20 30 40 50
miles

Areas suggested for expansion
The symbols are diagrammatic only and are not intended to represent the actual
location of any planned expansion

Appendix I. Statistical data from the South East Study 1961-1981

Table I. Area suggested for expansion

	Population 1961 (1)	Estimated natural change 1961-1981 (2)	Possible scale of increase (3)	Possible progress by 1981 (4)
A. New cities				
Southampton/ Portsmouth area	750,000	144,000	250,000	150,000
Bletchley area	17,000	4,000	150,000	75,000
Newbury area	20,000	3,000	150,000	75,000
B. Big new expansions				
Stansted (Essex)	–	–	100,000	75,000
Ashford (Kent)	28,000	3,000	100,000	75,000
Ipswich	120,000	19,000	60,000	60,000
Northampton	100,000	7,000	100,000	50,000
Peterborough	60,000	7,000	50,000	50,000
Swindon	90,000	14,000	50,000-75,000	50,000
C. Other expansions				
Aylesbury	27,000	6,000		
Banbury	21,000	3,000		
Bedford	65,000	8,000	All of these places seem	
Chelmsford	50,000	7,000	to offer scope for an	
Colchester	60,000	8,000	expansion of at least 30,000	
Hastings	65,000	–2,000	At some of them (e.g. Chelms-	
Maidstone	60,000	8,000	ford and Southend) considerably	
Medway Towns	170,000	24,000	more; though some of the growth	
Norwich	120,000	14,000	could not take place before	
Poole	90,000	9,000	1981.	
Reading	120,000	16,000		
Southend	165,000	8,000		

Notes

1. Targets for planned increase (columns 3 and 4) are additional to natural increase (column 2).

2. At some of the places mentioned town expansion (mainly on a small scale) is already proceeding. They are Ashford, Aylesbury, Bletchley and Swindon.

3. The estimates of natural change are provisional, and are made on the assumption that these places will continue to receive the same share of the total natural growth as they have received in recent years.

Table II. Population growth in England and Wales—Natural increase 1961-81

Northern England	1·8 m.
Wales	0·2 m.
Midlands	1·4 m.
South West England	0·3 m.
South East England	2·4 m.
Total England and Wales	6·1 m.

Table III. Employment and Migration

	Employment increase (per cent of employees) 1952-1962	Migration gain or loss (per cent of total population) 1951-1961
Northern England	4·0	−2·0
Wales	4·4	−2·0
Midlands	12·4	+1·7
South West England	13·3	+2·2
South East England	14·9	+2·5
Total England and Wales	10·3	+0·7

Table IV. Employment growth in the major divisions of the country 1952-62

	% increase employment growth
Northern England	+2·4
Wales	+3·1
Midlands	+7·4
S.W. England	+9·2
S.E. England	+10·1

Table V. Changes in the distribution of employees England and Wales and South East England 1955-62 (see also Fig. B)

Area	Distribution 1955		Change 1955-62		Distribution 1962	
	No.	Per cent	No.	Per cent	No.	Per cent
(1)	(2)	(3)	(4)	(5)	(6)	(7)
England and Wales	19,307	100·0	1,310	6·8	20,617	100·0
South East England	7,579	39·3	766	10·1	8,345	40·5
Metropolitan region	5,784	30·0	571	9·9	6,356	30·8
Midlands	3,595	18·6	266	7·4	3,861	18·7
South West England	1,113	5·7	102	9·1	1,215	5·9
Northern England	6,074	31·5	147	2·4	6,221	30·2
Wales	946	4·9	29	3·1	975	4·7
South East England	7,579	100·0	766	10·1	8,345	100·0
London conurbation	4,444	58·6	293	6·6	4,737	56·8
Outer metropolitan region	1,340	17·7	278	20·8	1,619	19·4
Inner country ring	677	8·9	168	24·7	845	10·1
Outer country ring	663	8·8	111	16·7	774	9·3
Rest of South East England	1,795	23·7	195	10·9	1,990	23·8

Note:
The estimates for sub-divisions of South East England, except the London conurbation, incorporate adjustments to cover employees (such as established civil servants not holding national insurance cards) who are excluded from the Ministry of Labour statistics for areas smaller than complete regions and the London conurbation. They are, therefore, less precise than the other estimates.

Table VI. Industrial development England and Wales and South-East England 1952-61 (see also Fig. C)

Area	Floor space completed (million sq. ft.)	Estimated employment (thousands)			Employment provided as a percentage of the total insured population June, 1952
		Total	Male	Female	
(1)	(2)	(3)	(4)	(5)	(6)
England and Wales	395·0	599·1	389·2	209·9	3·2
South East England	128·3	203·9	128·2	75·7	2·8
Metropolitan region	97·7	139·4	91·5	47·9	n.a.
Midlands	91·2	109·8	66·9	42·9	3·2
South West England	21·6	38·0	24·9	13·1	3·4
Northern England	128·8	202·7	136·7	66·0	3·4
Wales	25·1	44·7	32·5	12·2	4·8
South East England	128·3	203·9	128·2	75·7	2·8
London conurbation	44·5	44·2	27·4	16·8	1·0
Outer metropolitan region	53·2	95·2	64·1	31·1	n.a.
Rest of South East England	30·6	64·5	36·7	27·8	n.a.

Notes
1. In this table South-East England is defined in terms of Board of Trade (cols. 2-5) or Ministry of Labour (col. 6) and does not include Dorset.
2. The statistics of industrial building relate only to those new buildings and extensions for which Board of Trade locational approval has had to be obtained. In respect of such schemes approved up to 31 March 1960, only those completed projects which involved more than 5,000 sq. ft. of floor space and which were for applicants engaged in the manufacturing industries have been included. All completed projects for which approvals were given since that date are included. In these cases the figures cover only those parts of buildings for which an Industrial Development Certificate, as provided for in the Local Employment Act 1960, was required.

Fig. A Employment structure 1962
The total number of employees is represented by the area of each circle; the sectors indicate the proportions employed in primary, manufacturing and service industries

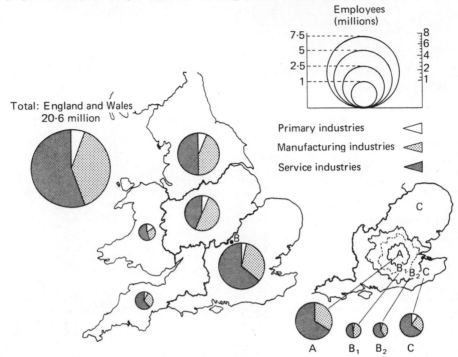

Fig. B Increases in employees 1955-62
Volume of employment growth is represented by the height of the columns; percentage increases are given in figures at the head of each column

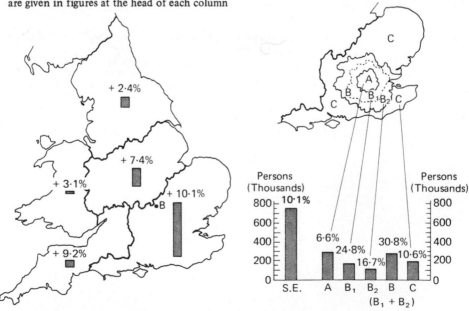

Fig. C Industrial development 1952-61

The estimated additional employment provided in new factories and extensions built in 1952-61 is represented by the area of the circles. The estimates relate only to buildings for which industrial development certificates were required.

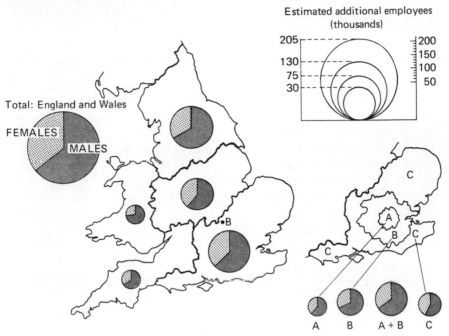

Case 24
Thamesport

In 1965 the management of the B.W. Ltd. neoprene plant at Thamesport, near Tilbury, England was concerned about the level of overtime being worked in the plant, the productivity of the plant labour and the changing pattern of management-union relationships.

The Thamesport management was responsible to the Board of B.W. Ltd. who were in turn responsible to the Board of Bremwohr (Bremerhaven), the holding company of which B.W. Ltd. was a wholly-owned subsidiary. The policy of the Bremerhaven Board, however, was to concern itself only with the appointment of top executives and with long-term capital budgeting, and to encourage subsidiaries to take all operating decisions themselves.

Union organisation in the refinery

In 1965 the Thamesport plant employed approximately 1,200 men, almost 900 of whom were hourly paid. Of the hourly-paid workers approximately 400 were employed on maintenance and construction; 200 were engaged in 'Process' work—the operation of the plant; and the remainder technical and miscellaneous. The maintenance and constructional workers were represented by six craft trade unions, which were in order of membership:

The Amalgamated Engineering Union (AEU)
The Plumbing Trades Union (PTU)
The Electrical Trades Union (ETU)
The Boilermakers' Society (BMS)
The Amalgamated Society of Woodworkers (ASW)
The Amalgamated Society of Building Trade Workers (ASBTW)

B.W. preferred, however, to negotiate with a body known as the Thamesport Craft Union Negotiating Committee rather than with the individual unions. All non-craft employees were represented by the Transport and General Workers Union (TGWU).

The Craft Union Negotiating Committee (CUNC) had declined in importance since the second World War, but still represented local craft unions in negotiations with a few firms in the area. Only the five members with membership at Thamesport participated in the discussion of B.W. business. Friction existed between some of the member-unions within the CUNC, principally arising from problems of overlapping areas of jurisdiction and of competition for members. The officers of the CUNC were full-time district officers of the constituent unions, one from each union concerned, and elected a chairman and a secretary. Similarly the officers of the TGWU were full-time union employees, appointed by the General Executive Council of that union. The Thamesport management negotiated variously with the district secretary or the regional trade group secretary of the TGWU. The full-time officials of both the TGWU and the CUNC were referred to at Thamesport as 'Union Delegates'.

There were, in addition to the Union Delegates, twenty-four shop stewards at Thamesport. Each craft union elected a senior shop steward: the TGWU elected 'shift branch secretaries' who had comparable status. There was no single overall 'convenor' in the plant.

The Unions operated a form of 'closed shop' amongst both the maintenance and process workers. No craft workers were employed unless they were union members, and the management accepted also that all chargehands in the maintenance area should be members of the union. In the process area, management retained the right to employ non-union members but did not make use of this right, and had adopted the practice of asking any new non-members, whom the shop-stewards had not been able to persuade to join the union, to do so. In all, rather more than 700 of the 900 hourly-paid workers were union members in 1965.

A Works Council had been in existence since 1961, and consisted in effect of a general council and two sub-committees, one dealing with maintenance and constructional matters and the other with operations. It was laid down that all workers' representatives on these councils were to be shop stewards elected by the unions concerned. The works council were not empowered to alter any agreement made between the Company and the union delegates, but could and did discuss any topic, including those which were the subject of union agreements, with the sole exception of wage rates.

The Thamesport management had adopted a policy of keeping management-union relationships as informal and flexible as possible. No clear distinction between the duties and prerogatives of the union delegates and those of the shop stewards had ever been made. Nor was there any formal arbitration procedure: it was laid down that

'Any dispute which may arise shall, in the first place, be referred to the management and representatives of the men, and failing a settlement, shall be referred to officials of the unions for them to take up with the company'.

No attempt was made to define the level of management or the 'representatives of the men', to include a timetable or to make any provision for arbitration.

In place of a formal negotiating procedure a system of un-written agreed practices had developed. It had been customary, for instance, to negotiate a wage increase annually, and the moves made each year in this negotiation had become established customs. The union delegates were, in fact, infrequently involved in any negotiations with management other than these annual wage increases.

Disputes other than wage increases tended to be taken up on the spot with the appropriate shop stewards, and the Thamesport management's insistence upon informal procedures intensified this tendency. Most demarcation agreements, for instance, were signed by senior shop stewards rather than by union delegates. Similarly men exercising their right of appeal to higher management against disciplinary measures were accompanied by their shop steward, never by the union delegate. Management found that by dealing with the stewards they avoided the more impersonal and formal manner of negotiation likely to be encountered outside the Company. Inevitably, however, this tendency to deal more with the shop stewards enhanced the authority of the stewards within the organisation.

The wage negotiations of 1964 and 1965

The 1964 wage negotiations were unusually protracted, largely because the B.W. Board responded to the Chancellor of the Exchequer's plea that wage increases should be limited to $3\frac{1}{2}\%$ unless they were coupled with an agreement to raise productivity. The Board ruled that only a 'non-inflationary wage increase' should be given at Thamesport, and after some study of wages in the area a figure of 3d. an hour was recommended. The Thamesport management argued that this figure would not be considered adequate by their workforce. The union delegates expected an increase of 5d. an hour for craftsmen and a proportionate increase at least for non-craft workers. The negotiations continued for four months, and the craft unions, with the support of the CUNC imposed an embargo on overtime. In July negotiations were resumed, the overtime ban lifted, and an offer of $3\frac{3}{4}$d. an hour made. Finally agreement was reached at a figure of $4\frac{1}{4}$d. an hour. One outcome of these negotiations, however, was that an informal shop stewards committee which had developed some years previously amongst the craft unions and had obtained the support of the TGWU in 1963, was able to strengthen its position considerably by making capital of the 'need for militancy' if the desired increases were to be achieved. One member of this committee is reported to have said at this time 'The day will come when you will have to negotiate with us'.

In 1965 the B.W. Board authorised an increase of 4d. an hour before any claim had been received from the unions, thus seizing the initiative from the shop stewards committee and offsetting, to some extent, the accusations of cheeseparing that had been made in 1964. Prior to the increase given in 1964 wage rates at Thamesport had been lower than those being paid by some comparable firms in the area. The wages which could be earned in the London docks, for instance, were higher than those in the neoprene plant, for both skilled and unskilled workers. Moreover, the neoprene plant employees earned substantially less than craftsmen employed by contractors working there (£17.14.3 average compared with £22.15.0d. for contractors during the six months ending in April 1964).

The fact that B.W. could continue to recruit an adequate workforce at Thamesport despite these wage differentials must be attributed to the security of employment offered and to the fringe benefits provided. These included sickness and accident pay, holiday pay and company pensions scheme. All plant employees, for instance, were entitled to twenty-six weeks full pay and twenty-six weeks half pay if absent through illness, after seven years service, with a further twenty-six weeks full pay for employees with twenty years service. In 1956 the provision of benefits accounted for 25% of the total wages and salaries bill. In 1963, when the working week was reduced from forty-four to forty-two hours this proportion increased to 29% of total wages and salaries.

The overtime problem

All work in the plant performed outside normal hours was classesd as overtime and was paid at a time-and-a-half, with double time on Sundays. It was an established precedent that all workers would do 'reasonable overtime' when called upon to do so.

Between 1957 and 1965 the overtime being worked increased steadily from 6% of total hours to no less than 16%. This latter figure was equivalent to an average of nearly seven hours overtime per man per week, and represented an average increase in weekly earnings of 30% of the basic wage.

The Thamesport management denied that the possibility of considerable overtime earnings had been used to attract new employees, or that overtime had been allowed to reach its existing level for this reason: of the 16% of total hours being worked as overtime, only 5% was said to be 'policy' overtime. Certainly there was little need to use such methods to attract labour: after 1962 the labour force at Thamesport was, in fact, being reduced.

A proportion of the overtime being worked arose from the technical characteristics of the plant. The need to shut down each item of equipment for overhaul and inspection produced periodic workload peaks which could best be accommodated by overtime rather than by 'hiring-and-firing' or permanent overstaffing, and it was this factor which had led to the 'reasonable overtime' requirement to which the unions had given their agreement.

During the early years of Thamesport's operations overtime levels were highest in the maintenance and construction activities. This was attributed partly to a severe cutback in the original capital budget which had eliminated many items of 'standby' equipment, thus producing a need in certain circumstances for crash action as well as making management unwilling to postpone any maintenance work, and partly prior to 1961 to a shortage of skilled craftsmen. The increase in the numbers of craftsmen employed after 1961 as a result of a special recruiting programme did little to reduce the overtime burden, however: between 1961 and 1962 a 10% increase in craftsmen employed resulted in only 3% reduction in average hours worked per craftsman. Management began to suspect that the practice of working as much overtime as required was in effect self-perpetuating in that work during the normal day was performed without any sense of urgency in the knowledge that any task not finished during the day could be completed by overtime working.

After 1962 the overtime being worked in the process activities also began to increase rapidly. This was attributable partly to the practice, introduced that year in agreement with the TGWU, of giving time off in lieu for working on public holidays instead of the previous system of bonus payments, and partly to the reduction of the working week from forty-four to forty-two hours. As a result operating manpower resources were stretched to the limit, and any loss of workers through holidays, sickness or training requirements automatically resulted in a need to work more overtime.

One further factor intensifying the growth of overtime working was the demand for 'fair shares' of extra time by different departments. Whereas most of the original increases in overtime had come about through good practical reasons, a secondary effect now becoming apparent was that employees in any one department felt that they were being unfairly treated if the overtime available to them was significantly less than that in other departments. This pressure was becoming a major factor in the increasing amount of overtime being worked.

The demand for overtime parity was also becoming one of the most time-consuming aspects of labour relations in the plant, and was tending to increase the authority of the shop stewards. The allocation of overtime, although nominally the responsibility of production supervision, was watched so closely by the shop stewards that it was virtually this latter group who controlled its distribution. Whereas in earlier years the pressure had been for equality of overtime opportunity between departments or working groups, after 1963 the shop stewards demanded that overtime being worked by individuals within each department should be substantially the same. The result of these tendencies was a shift of power away from the union delegates, who had no say in the determination of this increasing and substantial element in real wages, towards the shop stewards. The use of an overtime ban as a sanction by the shop stewards in 1964 has already been noted.

The plant management were, by 1965, seriously concerned about the growth in overtime working and the increasingly large proportion of the total wage bill this made up as well as the effects of virtually unlimited overtime on the general productivity of labour. The mounting cost of fringe benefits was also causing some alarm. These problems forced the Thamesport management to think very seriously about relations with the trade unions represented in the plant and about the whole question of labour relations at Thamesport.

The Water-Tube Boilermakers' Association

Incentive schemes on steam generating plant construction sites

Mr Harold Dimond, an official of the Water-Tube Boilermakers' Association (WTBA) was preparing for a discussion with Mr C. S. Taylor, Managing Director of Brooks-Watkins Engineering Ltd., Mr Marshall Smith, Chief Resident Site Engineer of Cornwall-Devon Engineering Ltd. and Mr Dominick Reddi of the Engineering Employers Federation (EEF). All the major boilermakers were Federation members and not all negotiations with trade unions were conducted through the EEF. Brooks Watkins Ltd. and Cornwall-Devon Ltd. were two of the leading Water-Tube Boilermakers in the country.

Mr Dimond reflected upon the changes that have occurred in his industry over the past few years ... In recent years the time required for the construction of steam generating plants had been greatly reduced. Seven years previously, twenty-two months was allocated for the erection of a boiler of 60 megawatt capacity. (It was normal to refer to the size of the associated electrical generating unit when quoting the capacity of boilers). Because of early delays in site preparation and other problems, the time available to the boilermakers was often less than this but the final commissioning date was usually achieved. Largely because of such successes the Central Electricity Generating Board (CEGB) currently required boilermakers to construct a boiler of 500 megawatt capacity in seventeen months.

In the case of 60 megawatt units each boiler employed upwards of 100 men at the site. The corresponding wage bill in 1959 for an hour amounted to about £35. On the 2,000 megawatt capacity stations under construction eight years later manpower was often four to five times as great and the wage bill eight to ten times the 1959 figure.

The Water-Tube Boilermakers was one of several industries involved in the on-site construction of generating plants for the CEGB. Current projects included both conventional and nuclear powered plants. Other major constructors at each site included steam turbine manufacturers, as well as structural steel and steel plate companies. In addition, the presence of many other contractors was required at various stages of the construction, among these were electrical, civil engineering and pipe manufacturing concerns.

Mr Diamond had noted four main causes of delay over which the erection departments had little control. These were: site labour disputes; adverse weather

© Cranfield Institute of Technology.

conditions; late or lack of proper access to the site; and late or out of sequence delivery. There were many other minor causes which contributed to appreciable direct and indirect losses but the four mentioned were the chief sources of trouble.

Another type of delay on most construction sites was the incidence of works or drawing office errors which prevented erection in the proper sequence of materials as delivered. Occasionally these modifications demanded the taking down and subsequent re-erection of a large fabricated section.

Another delay was in the double handling of materials. Provision of storage facilities for materials delivered out of sequence could involve considerable extra cost. Stockpiling could also be a result of lack of proper access to working places. In fact, many of the most serious problems stemmed from contractors starting to work on site before the infra-structure of roads, storage areas, lighting, power, and water supplies, were adequately provided. These problems resulted in large losses of man hours during the early stages of a contract and affected the men's spirit of enthusiasm and keenness to get on with the job.

The employers had no recourse to legislation when dealing with unconstitutional action by site labour. Such action could take the form of a ban on overtime, working to rule, go slow tactics and so forth. These situations, with the possible exception of an overtime ban, resulted in an almost complete cessation of work. In such circumstances the employers generally refused to negotiate until normal working had been resumed, but a clear definition of 'normal working' was usually lacking.

There was little flexibility in the rate of labour build-up on site. It could not be significantly increased or decreased or varied from week to week or even month to month. Therefore, unless planned progress was maintained throughout each period of site construction the labour force could not be fully utilised, and progress was made at a very high price.

Most employers had accepted critical path planning, network analysis, computers and planning committees as essential to the speedy and correct appraisal of difficulties as they arose on a site. Their application, however, suffered from the inherent weakness that these techniques depended on the accuracy of the original planning information. Time estimates were by far the most important of these.

Within the Engineering Employers Federation, there were a number of National Technical Committees covering different sections of the industry and a Liaison Committee at which joint problems on site construction were discussed. Represented on this last committee were all the National Technical Committees, the structural steel, steel plate, pipework and electrical generating sections as well as the Boilermakers. The purpose of the Liaison Committee was to consider on the broadest basis the whole field of site construction.

Joint planning and problems on individual sites were frequently discussed by erection managers meeting together in an informal setting at fairly frequent intervals during the early stages of construction; this practice was continued at longer intervals for the duration of the contract. These meetings attempted to establish similar standards of working conditions and strived to maintain a policy of no concessions to labour without prior consultation. Occasionally these discussions could, if not carefully controlled, become progress meetings or planning committees.

The primary object of the National Technical Committees was to negotiate wages and conditions on a nationwide basis. The Liaison Committee established communications between sections and endeavoured to create comparable conditions in each.

The Boilermakers site labour was recruited largely from members of the Constructional Engineering Union (CEU), the Transport and General Workers' Union (TGWU), the National Union of General and Municipal Workers (NUGMW) and the Boilermaker's Society.

At the meeting the following conversation took place:

H. Dimond (WTBA):
'One of our major problems is that the quality of labour on construction sites varies throughout the country. These differences stem from the fact that employers have little choice because of severe labour shortage particularly among skilled workers. We have, however, alleviated to some extent problems with undesirable labour by a probationary period which, though not written into the labour contract, is generally applied'.

C. S. Taylor (Brooks-Watkins, Ltd.):
'We find that the quality of our labour relations varies from site to site as well. Often we have communication problems between foremen, charge hands and men. Attempts by charge hands or foremen to settle minor disputes out of hand, sometimes result in major site disputes.'

D. Reddi (Employers' Federation):
'Site discipline, poor in some areas at all times, is made more difficult by the present conditions of full employment. Losses in time and money arise on some of the larger sites through bad timekeeping, wasted time at meal breaks, starting work late and finishing work early. Some contractors believe these losses to be of the order of 15-20% of total time.

'The problem of tea breaks is well known by all of you. It is not so much the act of drinking a cup of tea and eating a bun as the time wastage factor in getting to a point and back again. Another source of lost time occurs at statutory holidays when the fixed holiday period is disregarded on the merest pretext and the economic progress of the contract is severely hampered.'

H. Dimond
'I am troubled by the system of hiring unskilled and semi-skilled labour on a casual basis. The "travelling employee" as he has been known in the past is slowly disappearing and there is a growing problem in retaining regular employees. This is largely because they can obtain suitable work within reasonable distances of their homes. Of course this does mean that the boilermakers can recruit almost equivalent labour within a reasonable distance of most new sites. Nevertheless, labour turnover and its attendant troubles is often related to difficulties in

persuading men to move from site to site and in maintaining company loyalty during times of stress and troubles. Towards the end of a contract men are motivated to move on to new long term jobs before the current one is completed. This is reinforced when they see old friends leave as the contract runs down and others systematically laid off by the contractors'.

C. S. Taylor
'The impact of incentive schemes has not been felt on steam generating sites until fairly recent years and, perhaps because of lack of experience in such schemes, there have been signal failures.'

H. Dimond
'I think it is generally accepted that there is a need for plus payment in one form or another. It is necessary to improve and increase productivity. Also, we need to attract and retain good labour to meet the heavy programme we have ahead of us. An incentive scheme is not just a means by which we can pay men more money just to keep them sweet.'

C. S. Taylor
'In the first place I feel that a bonus scheme is only helping to put more on the man's rate and in effect to increase his take home pay. Nobody works any harder in a day. You might get a day's work for a day's pay but you are not gaining any more for the incentive. Shouldn't the emphasis be placed on control, and measurement of progress and not merely on another hidden method of payment to give the men more money? Shouldn't we adopt a more positive approach to bonus schemes? I believe we should first ensure that the employees produce a normal days work for the established rates; we should then remove all excuses which the employees may have for a strike before putting forward the planning of the bonus with management. We must also decide whether it is right to consult the union on these problems. Surely management should exercise its own prerogatives?'

D. Reddi
'Is the time right for a unified approach to this within our industry? It is only natural for the unions to take our differences and play them off against each employer. I must admit, however, that this is difficult when some of you have been operating targetted incentive schemes. With the backing of the Unions on a unified approach it might be possible to avoid some of the troubles we have now.

'I think the real aim is to try to agree on a common form of incentive scheme. It is in reaching this idea that we seem to be having trouble. No one would contradict when you say it would be a good thing, yet it is very difficult to persuade someone that his existing scheme which has worked well for a long time is not any good and that he must adopt another sort of scheme. It is no use saying that he must remove incentive from his scheme and perhaps adopt a scheme involving cost control when his existing schemes are bringing good results.'

Harold Dimond
'I do not think it is true to say that up and down the country incentive schemes have been a failure. Some have failed but I think that we are more or less agreed

that we should try to eliminate the section which gives the greatest troubles; this is man hour targets for squads of men that cannot easily be accurately assessed. The overall progress on a contract is a definite thing, easier for unions to assess themselves. They may argue about it but there is only 100% in the total work to be done.'

C. S. Taylor
'I do not fancy the overall bonus scheme as I always feel one is paying a bonus to a lazy devil on the site who's not pulling his weight and also it does not give the incentive to a man who is prepared to work twice as hard, but doesn't because he knows he has a bonus coming if he just works at a low level instead of a high level.'

D. Reddi
'The purpose of all schemes in operation is to get something more than a reasonable day's work from men working in arduous and often unpleasant conditions; no more, no less. As these conditions are so different from those existing in a workshop or factory, there is a strong argument for a supplementary rate, or a national or industry construction bonus dependent on reasonable overall work effort and general progress at the site. The payment of this would be subject to a monthly review and would, of course, be withdrawn immediately on the occurrence of a site disruption such as a "go-slow" or similar but less insidious tactic. A dispute regarding this nationally or industrially agreed payment of 30% or 50% would not be subject to negotiation at site level, but could only be considered at national or industry level.'

'It was mentioned that 50% of the disputes that came to the London level of negotiations were associated with bonus schemes up and down the country. I suggest that 90% of the disputes on the site never get as far as London and these are associated with bonus schemes as well.'

'You cannot work an incentive scheme on the same basis for a long time unless your men have confidence in it. If a body of men has been working happily for ten years or more they no longer query your time estimates. The fact remains that some companies have successful bonus schemes; it's saved them money and they've achieved their targets 'on the dot.' The lesson that can be drawn from this is that everything else in the wage packet is more or less fixed within limits, so that the only way of obtaining more money is by presenting claims for improvement in the bonus figure. Hence, I am not surprised that over 50% of the disputes were over bonus payments.'

C. S. Taylor
' I will agree that an incentive bonus scheme is an incentive to management to plan in greater detail and this may be one of its biggest virtues, but if it is just a question of improving management, then maybe one can achieve this in other ways. The type of union man one has to negotiate with seems to be the same type who has been in this country for the last half century. One visits a large boiler site today and sees an entirely different contractor's man from the old time bowler-hatted chap we

used to know. But the district union organiser is often the same old type. When one endeavours to put over to that gentleman what we think in terms of effort man hours and graphs it is quite impossible; and he is the man who has to put these ideas over to the men.'

D. Reddi

'The question of putting it over to the union is extremely difficult. We find it hard to understand one another. If you subject a union executive, never mind an organiser or shop steward, to the detailed planning and five figures of decimals used in our estimates and costing, both sides feel a little empty.'

H. Dimond

'This is why I think the payment in relation to progress is a simple one. Let's face it, it is a simple sum. We have to complete 100% and we have 100,000 man hours to do it in twenty weeks; so we're coming down to 5,000 man hours per week, which is 100 men for fifty hours. Thus we want 5% progress per week, and if they achieve this in the first week they will do it the next and next.'

D. Reddi

'The thing that struck me about the successful jobs we hear about was the sincerity that is expressed. The accuracy does not matter so much as the sincerity of the people putting the scheme through. I have been to meetings on a problem where I sounded insincere even to myself, and the meeting went extremely badly. Then a chap behind me came in and said the same thing but he rang with sincerity. Even though you are, in fact, honest you will achieve exactly nothing if they think you are insincere.'

C. S. Taylor

'Instead of dwelling upon incentives I believe that basic rates of pay should be increased because we are meeting so many extras that are additional to the basic rate that it is right and proper that some of these extras should be transferred to the rate so that you can recover some of the cost from the client.'

'I agree with Reddi about sincerity. However, I think one should also refer to firmness of purpose. Explain and negotiate at all times but I am afraid regretfully there always comes a time in site affairs when the last word has been said and then firmness of purpose is essential. Once the processes of "give" are started they are extraordinarily difficult to stop.'

Marshall Smith (Cornwall-Devon Engineering): commented

'My company has operated a scheme which has shown real results. We have two contracts; one nuclear, one conventional. The conventional is a 550 mw. unit and they're ahead of programme. In the nuclear contract we lost ten weeks from strikes. That has been more than recovered and we are now ahead on that programme too. This is the result of our financial control, planning, and control of progress. That is the answer. We believe we are running ahead of programme because we are running the correct type of incentive scheme. Do not make a mistake about this planning. It is no easy job. When we analyse our job we are considering about 6,000 activities.

We cannot do this in five minutes; and you cannot get progress by giving the workers a couple of bob an hour.'

'We have two incentive schemes; one is on overall progress and the other is on small targets. We have operated both these schemes very successfully and would not like to change them unless someone can prove to us that he has a better one.'

C. S. Taylor

'On a recent contract we have tried a new approach. We talked to the men, on and off, for about three weeks to gain their confidence and they agreed to do the job on contract. The contract that we gave them was a complete price for the job when it was finished and instead of talking man hours we talked pounds. This is the only thing the men understand. The job was completed three months before time. These men cut out all demarcations and most of the mates. We had less than half the number of men than there would have been if we had done it any other way. We made money and the men made money. Our other scheme was a small target scheme and I am pleased to say, that it is also working satisfactorily.'

D. Reddi

'I welcome such success stories but without a unified approach we are still faced with the big pipe manufacturers and big steel manufacturers, as well as the mechanical draught plant people and all the other engineering companies at the site who give us cause for trouble. As you know this starts in a small way in their own particular contract or subcontract and grows and spreads throughout the whole site. And the pipe makers themselves have said the boilermakers are usually established when they arrive on the job and are paying bonus and other incentive rates. The pipe men are met with stories from their men about high rates of pay which are beyond their ability to meet.'

H. Dimond commented:

'During the past year there has indeed been a tendency towards the adoption of incentive schemes which cover all the employees on a contract. There are the so-called overall schemes as against the schemes which select squads of men and give them a measured task to carry out in a certain time and pays incentive bonus according to that. I stress the word tendency. It is not entirely universal or unanimous. These incentives, of course, are to be distinguished from merit awards, qualification allowances, overtime, etc. They are schemes to increase productivity or to ensure that progress to a goal is made.

'In the case of pressure welders whose work can be accurately measured, target incentive schemes seem to be working very well indeed, but this is perhaps the only task in which work can be so precisely measured, and in which times can be so accurately targetted. The bulk of our troubles in the field of incentives on site has been with the targetting of tasks for squads engaged in many types of job. We cannot estimate man hours with enough accuracy to eliminate all cause for argument.'

D. Reddi

'If, in fact, incentive schemes are not at the moment bringing about their results and achieving their real purpose, any payment which we make is no more than a gift bonus scheme and if we accept this, perhaps the most practical step is a monthly profit-sharing scheme where you know exactly how much has been saved and how much each man has earned on the whole contract. Firms have also in the past period applied merit awards to their men, and this is another way in which individual earnings could be increased.'

H. Dimond
'Another alternative would be to adopt staff status and weekly wage structure for the men. In fact, I believe this applies to quite a number of the bigger oil refineries in the country. It results in a pretty high wage but the refinery people believe it produces the best possible work from the men because it offers them security for the future. I believe there are many other big companies which are considering this way out of the difficulty. It assumes however, that a company has the right to dismiss or downgrade labour if it is unsatisfactory and that there is more labour available if this has to happen.

'However, there are differences between our type of worker and the sort of labour I have just been talking about which is largely contained in one place under one control with a prospect of continuous employment ahead.'

Marshall Smith
'Another alternative might be along the lines of the Severn Bridge Agreement between the union executive and the main contractors. It was based on a forty-two hour week and a comprehensive form of payment which included all conditions of work. This comprehensive payment covered all abnormal conditions as well as including the effects of weather and the fact that the bridge was being built over water.

The scheme consisted of a comprehensive or consolidated payment comprising a basic rate, site condition money plus an incentive bonus payment. Money for working at heights was paid under the terms of a national agreement as conditions arose. The agreement listed a number of conditions which the employers insisted on and included stopping the payment if proper progress was not made. In periods of consistent below-standard work, it was anticipated that progress would have to be boosted and after consultation it could be agreed that the level of incentive could be raised for a period of time. The whole idea was to try to remove the causes of disputes, e.g. because one man is being paid on a higher wage than another man.'

H. Dimond
'If I were forced to generalise I would say that incentive schemes bring good results if accompanied by proper planning, good supervision, an amenable labour force, punctual and reasonable access, good site conditions and prompt deliveries of materials in proper sequence. If any one of these requirements is lacking for very long results can range from merely an unhappy site to complete and utter chaos. Good labour relations must persist in order that planned progress can be maintained.' (Laughter)

D. Reddi

'I think we have to look at some of the other things which motivate people in their behaviour at work. We have mentioned the question of security, and I think apart from a good wage they want some sort of security of employment. Without doubt many of our troubles stem from insecurity arising from CEGB policies. Fluctuations of CEGB policy regarding orders for power stations have been a major factor in the insecurity of your employees.'

H. Dimond

'Another question is that of satisfaction in work. I think we must create the feeling in a man that his job is important so that he gains satisfaction from his particular work. We must also look at the question of status, and some sort of recognition. We tend to treat site labour as being rather low grade. When we treat people like this the probability is that they will react in the same manner.'

C. S. Taylor

'Marshall has made a case for early and careful planning. Realistically, however, there is a multitude of reasons why complete information cannot be made available at an early stage. There are doubtless, many reasons also why site conditions, amenities, and access dates, vital to main contractors programmes cannot be accurately forecast at the time of the tender. Information concerning local labour potential, transport facilities and the like is often misleading and sometimes incorrect.'

H. Dimond

'No one can disagree with that.'

C. S. Taylor

'Both "overall" and "target" schemes are open to one main criticism. How do you negotiate with these union people to decide what the man hours should be? If you say "I'm going to give 1,000 man hours" do they accept it? I cannot find a way out when I tell the men they have 1,000 hours to do a particular job; and they say, "OH, I think the job is worth 1,500 hours." If you offer them 1,500 hours then they want 2,000. That is where the difficulty comes in.'

D. Reddi

'You could possibly persuade the unions to adopt a flat rate of bonus. This would certainly help to control your costs and curtail the high rates which now sometimes emerge from a site. However, it would create a new platform and it would only be a matter of time before they wanted an incentive bonus on top of that.'

H. Dimond

'Yes, but the multitude of bonus schemes being applied by various firms in the construction industry is creating ideal conditions for industrial strife. The unions, and particular individuals within the unions, are being provided with such a varied selection of ammunition that they can pick the best features of one scheme to play off against the other at will.'

Marshall Smith

'You must admit that although in theory an incentive scheme should pay for itself in terms of increased production, in practice a contractor has to carry the cost of subsidising earnings to preserve good labour relations and to retain his workers.

H. Dimond

'It still seems to me that we have to stick together on first principles. We all know that lieu payments for wating time or idle time will bring chaos to the best of incentive schemes, and with the best will in the world, waiting time will never be entirely eliminated. We also know the trouble that can be caused by our differing definitions of productive versus non-productive labour. How does each of us decide what contribution the various classes of non-productive man make. And the question of whether to pay a bonus on the basic rate or on the rate including qualification allowances is still with each of us.'

D. Reddi commenting:

'If I were a union man I would want to know what a bonus scheme was all about. I would want to know how it worked, how much take home pay I was going to get, how you set your targets and what I am expected to do for the money I am to receive. The unions claim that the basic rates of pay in this industry are inadequate. They allege that our rates are inadequate for people having to work under such conditions as prevail on the sites. Site men are said to be earning only as much as bus drivers and underground workers but they are specialists in their own way. The union is not interested in our conversations about maintaining balance in the economy. They want what *they think* they deserve.

'In fact, the unions have proposed that we abandon incentive schemes entirely and put the rates up to time and a third or time and a half and from then on forget all our troubles.'

Case 26
Dupont-Maynard Ltd.

Dupont-Maynard Ltd. was an electrical equipment manufacturer, which experienced a fairly rapid growth after the end of the war, following the development of market and import restrictions.

Its turnover, which rose to 60,000,000 new francs, divided more or less equally between high tension electrical equipment, produced on order for government concerns: (e.g. Electricité de France) and low tension electrical equipment, sold to the public and above all to contractors.

The firm consisted of a factory of 1,500 employees and a Head Office of 300, where the Commercial Departments were situated.

Although the Management had for some years followed a coherent policy for salaries and social benefits which were comparable to the best in their region, the firm saw the social climate deteriorating since the adoption of incentive bonuses. The operation of the bonus system was introduced by specialists; these were engineers recruited to form 'company experts'.

The system functioned satisfactorily for a time, but then, during two years, workshop stoppages, general strike threats and a variety of difficulties multiplied rapidly.

After numerous discussions with the workers' representatives, the Personnel Department put the entire blame for this state of affairs on the time study method. Workers complained of 'infernal rhythms,' declaring that allotted times were changed as soon as they were agreed.

The General Management had its timings evaluated by an expert, who also verified the work-methods used. According to the expert, all was in order. But the difficulties continued. Heads of departments tended to consider that the bonus system was entirely responsible for their difficulties and maintained that its continuation was not an economic proposition.

The General Management hesitated to reverse their policy, and called in, as a last resort, an outside consultant who undertook a study among staff and workers, using opinion polls.

This enquiry showed that the timing system was really at the root of the trouble, for the following reasons:

1. The members of staff, to whom the Efficiency Drive Programme tried to give a sense of responsibility, were unwilling to accept the intervention of specialists from the Industrial Organisation Department. They resented and expressed their disagreement with the policy of the General Management exercised

Copyright INSEAD. This case was prepared by the European Institute of Business Administration to act as a basis for discussion in its educational programme.

through the Training Department, and the introduction of timekeepers. Therefore, they had a tendency to lean towards the workers when the latter complained and, at best, not to support decisions of the Industrial Organisation Department.

2. The workers representatives seemed to find a relatively sympathetic ear for their complaints about timings in the Personnel Department. The Personnel Department tended, in fact, not to concern itself with these matters, in order to concentrate on problems which directly affected it: selection procedures, sackings etc.

3. When workers believed that they had been unjustly treated in the calculation of their individual bonuses they did not know if they should go—

to the Central Salary Office which does the calculations, or

to the Industrial Organisation Department which determines the standards.

4. In case of complaint the staff declared itself powerless, and the workers therefore went to their shop-stewards.

In concluding his report, the investigator indicated that the solution of the problem of Dupont-Maynard Ltd. lay, in his opinion, in a structural reform.

Exhibit I presents the organisation chart of Dupont-Maynard at the time.

Exhibit 1

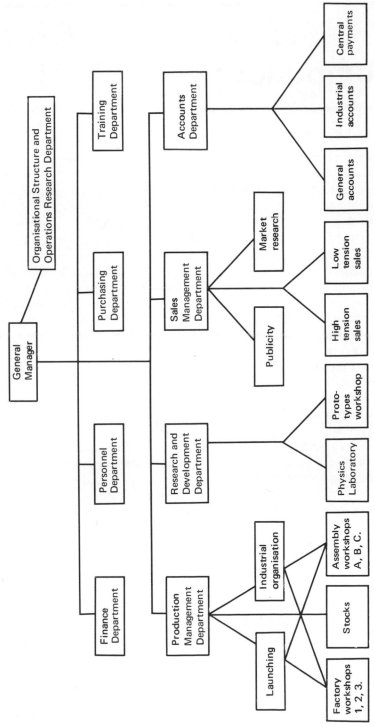

Pompadour Steel Mills[1]

Foreign Labour Relations Problems

Economic expansion since the creation of the European Common Market produced increasing labour shortages for the industries of some member countries. Many firms like Pompadour Steel Mills attempt to meet this shortage by importing foreign workers.

The Pompadour Steel Mills, a medium-size company in Lorraine, the north-eastern section of France, specialises in high-grade steel alloys and sells to a world-wide market. The company employs over 5,000 workers, about 6% of which are foreign labourers from seventeen nations, employed in various skilled, semi-skilled, and unskilled occupations (see Table I). Thirty-six per cent of the aliens have been employed at the steel mills less than three years; 24% between three and five years; 12% between five and ten years; 17% between ten and fifteen years; and 11% of the aliens have been employed more than fifteen years. Almost three-quarters of the foreign labour force are twenty to forty years of age.

The Personnel Department considered the native labour market insufficient to supply the number of workers needed, particularly for its rolling mills and unskilled jobs. Most native workers, who were in great demand by many firms, could bargain for more desirable and better-paying jobs. Therefore French workers were unlikely to accept these types of job while there were more favourable ones on offer.

After the signing of the Treaty of Rome, which among other things decreed a gradual increase of labour mobility in the European Economic Community, the member countries began to relax their entry restrictions, both because of the new law and in response to the dire need of many industries for more workers. As a result of these developments, the director of the Pompadour Steel Mills Personnel Department, M. Flintstone, decided to hire two groups of Italian Labourers who were migrating to the Lorraine area in hopes of finding employment.

The first group, Group A (about fifty people) of diverse semiskilled and unskilled workers, came from various small steel centres near Turin, Monza, Trieste, and primarily from the Mezzogiorno near Naples and Genoa. Almost all of these workers arrived individually. The second group, Group B, consisting of about twenty men, had migrated together from two neighbouring villages in Southern Italy. Except for six who had previously been employed in the Naples shipyards,

---

1. Company name and personal names are ficticious.

This case was prepared by Leo Spier for the University of California at Berkeley as a basis for class discussion. It is not designed to present either a correct or incorrect illustration of the handling of administrative problems. Reproduced by permission.

they all came from agricultural areas and were generally unskilled. Only a half dozen of the Italians were able to converse in French; most of the others relied mainly on a combination of pantomime and similarities between the French and Italian languages.

Unlike many situations in Germany, where industries often provide or at least help secure some living quarters, the Pompadour Steel Mills did not concern itself with the alien labourers beyond the confines of the plant. The chronic housing shortage in the surrounding areas complicated the immigrant workers' assimilation, since they had to compete for space with native rentees, and had to communicate in an unfamiliar language. Consequently, a large number of alien workers ended up paying exorbitant rents for inadequate living quarters. Almost all workers attempted to split costs by lodging together, sometimes three and four per room.

Inasmuch as the employment of these Italian groups was the first such major venture into the hiring of aliens on a large scale by Pompadour Steel Mills (most prior foreign employees had been hired individually for special jobs in the firm), Mr Flintstone thought it best to secure the services of an interpreter, and to put the new Italian labourers through a brief training programme in the anticipated work areas. This method he hoped would assist him to become familiar with the behavioural pattern of the foreigners.

Since the laws of the E.E.C. under which aliens may be hired do not permit discrimination in treatment between foreign and native employees, the pay scales had to be the same for a particular job. To circumvent this legislation and to take advantage of 'inexpensive' alien labour, the firm decided to establish new job categories under which the foreign workers would receive less pay while essentially working on the same jobs as their higher paid native fellow workers.

At the end of the training period, fifteen men of Group B were assigned as helpers to furnace operations, loading of materials, and other unskilled work. Most of the semiskilled workers from Group A and the rest of Group B were assigned to the rolling mill. Because of language difficulties, it was thought best to group the Italians together on the job as much as possible, rather than to disperse them among native workers. M. Flintstone furthermore felt that intermingling of foreign and native labour might result in animosities between them, due to the indirect discrimination through wage differentials in job categories.

About three months passed fairly uneventfully; the newly hired Italians appeared not only to have adapted themselves to the new jobs, but also to the new environmental conditions. The work performance, according to the Personnel Manager, was better than expected. The language difficulties declined as the Italians learned to communicate in a sort of broken patois.

Soon, however, the first complaints began to filter in to M. Flintstone. In the beginning, he paid little attention to them because they seemed rather minor and were unrelated to company activity. They were stories of several noisy fights in the flats in town among the Italians, allegedly those from the rolling mills (Group A). Then the first arrests of the same Italians began to worry the Personnel Department of Pompadour Steel Mills. The police had been called in when eight of the semiskilled Italians started a brawl among themselves in a tavern. The fight

Table 1. Number of workers by nationality and occupation at Pompadour Steel Mills

	Furnace	Steel Manufacturing	Rolling Mills	Foundry	Heat Treating	Research & Development	Maintenance	Machine Operators	Plant Transport	Expediters	Helpers	Other	TOTAL
German	1	—	6	1	1	2	2	—	—	—	1	—	14
American	1	—	—	—	—	—	—	—	—	—	—	—	1
Belgian	—	—	1	—	—	—	1	—	1	—	—	—	3
Canadian	—	—	—	—	—	1	—	—	—	—	—	—	1
Spanish	1	4	1	2	—	—	4	—	1	1	2	—	16
Greek	—	1	—	—	—	—	—	—	—	—	—	—	1
Hungarian	1	—	3	1	—	—	1	—	2	—	3	—	11
Italian	10	16	32	11	—	2	30	3	15	4	33	1	157
Luxemburgian	—	—	—	—	—	—	—	—	—	—	—	—	0
Algerian	—	1	—	—	—	—	—	—	—	—	—	—	1
Portuguese	1	—	—	—	—	1	1	1	—	—	—	—	4
Polish	14	3	15	—	—	—	2	1	8	5	1	5	54
Rumanian	—	—	1	—	—	—	—	—	—	—	—	—	1
Russian	—	1	1	—	—	1	—	—	—	—	—	—	3
Swiss	1	—	—	1	—	—	—	—	—	—	—	—	2
Czech	—	1	1	—	—	—	—	—	—	—	—	—	2
Tunisian	—	—	1	—	—	—	—	—	—	—	—	—	1
Ukrainian	—	2	1	—	—	1	—	—	—	—	—	—	4
Yugoslavian	5	2	—	3	—	—	4	1	2	1	4	1	23
TOTALS:	35	31	63	19	1	8	45	6	29	11	44	7	299

reportedly grew from an argument among them questioning each other's 'professional' capabilities on the basis of the pay they received.

After assurances that the Personnel Department would look into the matter, the eight men were released into the custody of the firm. M. Flintstone called the infractors to his office and warned them that they might have to be released with unfavorable records if such fights continued. Tempers had had some time to cool off, the occasion appeared to have been forgotten, and soon everything became routine again.

Only a few weeks later, the very same aliens of Group A from the various areas in Italy had their first fight in the rolling mills. Oddly enough, the aliens from the two neighboring villages, Group B, while they kept more secluded, had encountered no problems, either among themselves or with the native population. Following a relatively quick breakup of the fight, with the help of other Italian and French workers, the fighters were again summoned to M. Flintstone. The matter was now far more serious, because it directly affected the productive output of the firm.

After a severe reprimand, the Personnel Manager sent the Italians back to work. He promised to study the situation further, and to find a possible solution to the problem. While M. Flintstone conducted his human relations research, the Italians had split into two distinct groups, not by type of skill or by the job held in the plant, but by the geographical area from which they had migrated.

This *modus incommunicato* soon showed up as a drop in the rate of productivity. As a result, M. Flinstone received a summons from the President of the firm to present immediately his solutions to the problem before the Board of directors, which was faced with an increasing backlog of demand for steel, and competition from other firms. There was also the problem of unrest caused among the workers and the town community.

Table 1 presents the number of workers at the Pompadour Steel Mills, broken up by country of origin and industrial unit.

Questions:
1. What are the problems facing M. Flintstone?
2. Why doesn't there appear to be any difficulty with the other Italian group, or for that matter with other nationalities?
3. What actually led to these problems?
4. What courses of action are now open to M. Flintstone?
5. What should M. Flintstone do to prevent similar recurrences in the future hiring of foreign employees?

Case 28
Technikon-Larue S.A.

The Company Technikon-Larue S.A. is a French company manufacturing chemical products. The registered office and the main factory are in the North, although a secondary factory is in the Paris region. From 1949 to 1958 production increased more than five-fold and the work force of the factory had grown from 900 in 1950 to 3,500 in 1958.

The very rapid development of the company's activities had given rise to very serious personnel problems and in March, 1959, the head of personnel called together the members of his department to review the promotion programme which Technikon had undertaken in 1955.

Two principal trends, acutely felt, had characterised their personnel problems. The first was the result of ever-growing mechanisation, which required technical and psychological re-adaptation by the skilled workers. The second was the employment of a greatly increasing number of technicians and research workers. As a result, the management of the company feared that the impracticability of promoting technicians to the higher ranks would risk harming the quality of the technicians recruited as well as morale in the works. Thus, a programme of development for all the personnel of Technikon was initiated.

After many discussions and studies, it was decided to launch a programme aimed both at developing the existing 'skilled workers' and at the same time educating suitable men to reach the grade of skilled worker. In order to implement this programme it was necessary to estimate (a) the increase of production and of personnel and (b) the existing skilled workers who would be pensioned off during the period under consideration. It was thus possible by including an estimate for 'unforseeable losses' to set up a schematic picture of the needs for the ten years from the beginning of the improvement programme.

Then, the head of personnel was called upon to create a new service, whose principal function would be to coordinate this development programme. His responsibilities were as follows:

1. The selection of candidates for the improvement programme;
2. To assure liaison with the heads of departments before, during and after the programmes directed at their subordinates;
3. The preparation and administration of the programmes, and at the same time, the recruitment and education of the promoters of the programmes;
4. The preparation and the diffusion of information.

In liaising with the personnel service, the director of the new service 'Promotion and Information', M. Georges, first set up an evaluation system for candidates likely to pursue the stages of improvement. Each candidate was interviewed several times by M. Georges, as well as by a psychologist, to ensure the appropriateness of the stages of training. The psycho-technical tests and the group tests (discussion of a previously chosen subject) rapidly showed up a number of promising candidates from amongst the existing skilled workers.

This was followed by a meeting between M. Georges, his collaborators, and the head of the department to which the selected worker belonged, to obtain approval of his head of department, who had the right to reject the candidates nominated by M. Georges. If M. Georges and the head of department were not in agreement, it became obvious that the candidate must undergo several additional evaluations.

The improvement programme for the skilled workers was launched in October 1955 and extended over a period of two years at the rate of three hours per week. During the first year the study was aimed particularly at the development of technical knowledge; rudiments of physics, chemistry, mathematics, as well as the products of the factory and their application. The object of this course was to give the participants the means of understanding the evolution of technical progress, especially that which applied specifically to Technikon. Also, the first phase permitted the elimination of those who did not seem suitable for the teaching which was to follow. Then, during the summer holidays, each participant was allocated a duty different from his normal one. This permitted the head of department to gain an appreciation of the worker's ability to adapt himself to new circumstances. The second year was devoted to the problems of authority, human relations and work simplification. Training sessions in oral and written expression completed this programme.

Since October, 1957, when the first promotion cycle for skilled workers was successfully completed, the development programme for about a third of the skilled workers in the company was gradually integrated into the workshops. The management of the company believed that the success of this first experience justified the development of the system, aimed at both improving the general vitality of the organisation and achieving work improvements.

In the meantime, a second programme for the skilled workers was about to finish its cycle in October, 1958.

According to M. Georges, two supplementary activities were envisaged. The first consisted of choosing from amongst the available workforce, those suitable of becoming skilled workers after a period of education. The second was the aim of promoting skilled workers to the post of production engineers. At the same time certain engineers,* who were then holding jobs involving a certain degree of routine, could give their positions to educated skilled workers, in order to release them for positions calling for a higher degree of technical or administrative competence. He would be meeting the need expressed by the Managing Director, by giving greater flexibility to promotion from within the company.

* The term 'engineer' is used in this case in its British context, where 'engineers' are not necessarily university graduates.

The meeting to which M. Georges was called, together with three of his collaborators/group tutors, took place in the office of the head of personnel and his assistant. The agenda was to review the detailed study for a development cycle for engineers.

M. Georges opened the discussion by presenting his scheme:

The aims of the cycle were to offer the selected skilled workers a complete programme, which would allow them to be promoted to the position of engineer. The contents of the programme had to take into account the fact that the new responsibilities of a skilled worker promoted engineer were not only of a technical nature. M. Georges thought it was at least as important to incorporate elements of general culture, since an engineer often had administrative and human responsibilities which extended far beyond simple technical competence. M. Georges was convinced that it was more important to give the future engineers principles which would allow them to learn gradually from their experience, than to give them the total sum of knowledge. This need was great because the variations from post to post were often considerable. It was quite possible, for instance, for a former foreman to be called upon to perform the duties of production engineer, while a colleague had the abilities of a commercial engineer. In order to avoid a programme 'directif' risking pleasing no-one, M. Georges had set out an outline for the programme as shown in Exhibit 1.

The director of personnel raised the question of recruitment. According to his experience he was convinced that a programme such as that outlined by M. Georges, could only be aimed at the relatively young workers. This stemmed from the argument that the ages of maximum intellectual flexibility were between twelve and twenty-four, and so one could not expect skilled workers, whose average age was forty, to reach a standard comparable to that of an engineer leaving college. This was more true, it seemed to him, because the psychological attitudes of a skilled worker would be fundamentally influenced by his primary education. Thus, every skilled worker over the age of thirty-five, for example, tended to have an inferiority complex towards the engineers.

M. Georges was not of this opinion. According to him, age did not constitute a fundamental factor for recruitment. It was perfectly possible that a skilled worker aged forty, would be more open-minded in his interests and capabilities than another aged thirty. On the contrary, the problem involved obtaining a representative cross section of the heterogeneous elements of the existing workforce, in order to permit an exchange of viewpoints between the participants during the programme.

The director of personnel raised an objection to this last criterion for recruitment. It seemed to him that insofar as it was desirable to confront different educations and points of view, it would be better to create an inter-company centre, in cooperation with two or three other companies. This would also have the advantage of supporting the considerable cost of the programme by involving other companies. Thus the viability of the programme would not depend on a minimum number of participants provided by Technikon.

The assistant director of personnel asked why technicians were not considered as candidates for the programme. M. Georges replied that the programme did not exclude the participation of technicians. In fact, the average age of the technicians was twenty-eight to thirty and they usually held diplomas from a school of chemistry or possessed at least two baccalaureats.* In this sense they constituted a group, which was intellectually more suited to rise to the position of engineer than the skilled workers. Their problem was however different, since the technicians already had an open door to the position of engineer and there was a danger of discouraging the skilled workers.

In conclusion M. Georges used the argument that a promotion programme must consider the bridges to be crossed between different levels; it must knock down the barriers which have been set up by force of circumstances. Thus, whereas the technicians already had the road to high positions open to them, there was nothing for the skilled workers. Once the programme was in operation, it would be possible to envisage a special programme for the technicans.

The director of personnel then asked if it would not be better to review the whole policy within the framework of a programme aimed at the unskilled workers enabling them to rise to skilled positions. To sum up, it needed a chequer board permitting the evaluation of:

1. The number of engineering positions available,
2. The number of workmen following a programme in preparation for the available skilled postiions,

They had also to review the possibility of:

1. Passing the technicians on to positions of engineer and
2. Passing the skilled workers on to the intermediate stage of technician before becoming engineers.

M. Georges agreed to present a complete report on the various aspects of the promotion programme, taking into account the questions which were raised in discussion during the meeting.

Exhibit 1.

An improvement programme should have as its aims:

Economic and technical objectives
To put the personnel it needs at the disposal of the enterprise.

Psychological objectives
To influence individual behaviour in order to make for easier relationships.

Sociological objective
To increase awareness of the need for flexibility in the organisation.

---

* The 'bac' (baccalaureat) is a state high school certificate which would be taken in one or more fields (e.g. philosophy, natural sciences etc.)

Cultural objective

To make the personnel of the company participate in education for improvement. The programme would be devised in four parts:

1. *The technical rudiments*
   mathematics
   physics
   chemistry
   electrics/electronics

2. *Industrial organisation*
   social rights
   work rights
   administrative structures
   techniques of organisation

3. *General education*
   foreign language
   French language
   human, social and professional relations
   elements of political economy

4. *The means to be used*
   reports
   discussions
   practical work
   travel
   study

Goehrstahlwerken

The Goehrstahlwerken was a major manufacturer of heavy machinery located in the Ruhr, Germany. Some four thousand men were employed at two plants, both situated in the same city. The main buildings included what was referred to as the machine-tools department, a large workshop employing some 350 men (see Exhibit 1 for plant-layout.) The workshop contained a wide variety of machine-tools, ranging from gigantic carrousel lathes to hand-operated drilling machines. The machine-tool department performed most of the machining operations on small lot orders, which included drive shafts, mining equipment, marine engine crankshafts, railroad materials, cones, turrets, spindles, piston rods of unusual dimensions, etc. A large percentage of the work performed involved cast-iron objects weighing anywhere from one half to thirty tons. All of the 350 men employed were skilled mechanics earning some of the highest wages paid in the Ruhr; some thirty per cent had been with the company since the war; the average age of this group was fifty-five. Twenty per cent had joined the company since the war but all had substantial experience previously; the average age of this group was thirty-eight. The remainder were young men, most of whom had been apprentices at the plant before being assigned to a job in the machine-tools department.

Normally each man was regularly assigned to the same machine, thus becoming a specialist in certain well-defined tasks. The plant was operated on a two shift basis; the first shift came in at 6 a.m. and was relieved by the second at 2 p.m. Occasionally men were detailed to work overtime after the end of the second shift at 10 p.m. Infrequently special orders called for skeleton third shifts which were generally manned by a rotation system of those having already worked on the first shift. Overtime and night-work both gave rise to substantial wage premiums. There had been no strike in the department since 1952; general labour unrest in the steel trades in 1954 had not provoked any noticeable perturbations at Goehrstahlwerken, although the machinists had participated in an official petition for increased wages. In January 1955 human relations in the plant could have been described as middling; many workers privately expressed the feeling that management was 'remote'. Whenever company executives toured the plant machinists were distinctly uneasy. Part of this uneasiness could be ascribed to the fact that many workers felt insecure in their jobs; the continuous flow of refugees from East Germany provided business with a plentiful source of skilled labour, and on occasion some of the foremen in the plant had pointed out to a troublesome worker that there were plenty of men waiting outside the plant gates ready to take over his job.

A small section of the machine-tools workshop housed the plant's maintenance department. Although maintenance men kept their tools in this section, most of their time was spent in other parts of the plant on some repair job. The foreman in charge of the maintenance crew, Friedrich Muller, forty-seven years old, was notorious for being the most unpopular as well as the most competent individual in the whole company. A self-educated man, he had risen to this position of great prestige by dint of hard work and relentless driving of subordinates. His personal relations with his men were particularly frigid, although he was honestly admired and respected for his enormous capacity to solve difficult problems. He invariably was the first to arrive and the last to leave, he had no friends within the company and was considered by all to be a very lonely man.

On the morning of 23 January 1955, Mr Hans Schmitt, assistant plant manager of the Goehrstahlwerken, arrived at the main buildings to find the plant in an uproar. He was told that a serious accident had occurred in the machine-tool department; two men had been injured and removed to the hospital. The following is an account of the preliminary investigation carried out by Mr Schmitt.

The accident had occurred in the east section of the machine tools workshop. The overhead crane had been run over the end of the rails and had fallen injuring the two men in the crane's cabin. Mr Schmitt walked over to the scene of the accident. The normal path of the crane's travel, which ran down the length of the workshop, had been curtailed some two weeks previously. Part of the outer wall of the workshop was being torn down for the construction of an annex, and consequently the pillars supporting the crane rails had been removed, as far as the X on Exhibit 1. Mr Schmitt interviewed Mr Muller, the maintenance department foreman, who told the following story:

'Soon after the beginning of the first shift this morning at 6 a.m., a heavy spindle had to be removed from the floor as it was obstructing the passageway. Some of my men had to haul a piece of equipment through this passageway. I looked for the crane operator. He was not in his cabin, so I sent one of the boys to look for him. Now that the use of the crane had been curtailed the operator often leaves it to go and chat with a friend of his. My boy did not find him. I walked along the A alley thinking he might be hidden behind some machine. He could have been anywhere, and this job was urgent. I then detailed one of my men, who had had, last summer, some two-weeks experience operating the crane, to go up into the cabin and to remove the obstruction. I walked off and a few minutes later I heard the crash. Apparently he had taken young Ritholt, another maintenance man, up there with him, why I don't know.'

Schmitt: 'Meissen knew about the rail being cut up there?'
Muller: 'I had expressly instructed him to take care.'
Schmitt: 'How is it that no precautions had been taken to prevent the crane from going too far on the rail?'
Muller: 'The builders who are constructing the annex always place dynamite crackers on the rail whenever they have to take the rails down. The crackers are

placed about four feet from the end of the rail. Since the crane moves less than a foot per second., it gives the operator plenty of time to stop the crane as soon as he runs over the crackers.'

Schmitt: 'How come your man paid no attention to the cracker?'

Muller: 'Most of the men who were right here say that they never heard the crackers go off. We have found both crackers on the floor. One went off, it seems, but the other is a dud.'

Schmitt: 'Which one of the two men up there was driving?'

Muller: 'Nobody knows. Rithold's presence up there was unauthorized.'

Workman: (interrupting) 'It serves those young cowboys right; they were playing around up there like they always do.'

Schmitt: 'Where is the crane operator?'

Crane operator: 'You can't expect someone with no experience to go up there and drive that thing safely.'

Schmitt: 'Where were you when this happened?'

Crane operator: 'I was over in row four talking to a buddy. I don't have a thing to do, what with the rails being cut. I came in this morning, and seeing there was no work to do I just took a walk like I always do. They can find me easily enough if they want to. I always stay in the machine-tools department.'

Mr Schmitt walked over to the ladder leading up to the crane cabin level; a notice on a metal plaque warned:

'ACCESS TO THE CRANE IS FORBIDDEN TO ALL UNAUTHORISED PERSONS'

Mr Schmitt then drove over to the hospital; Meissen had two broken legs, Ritholt had a fractured skull. Meissen was conscious but apparently refused to talk. Both Meissen and Rithold had been with the company for less than a year; they were both twenty-six years old.

Back at the plant, Mr Schmitt talked to the superintendent of the builders firm in charge. The superintendent stated that for the last ten years the same procedure had always been adopted; as soon as the rails were cut during a construction job, crackers were placed on the rails. The crackers were supplied by a reputable manufacturer. The builder's firm had handled all construction jobs for the company since 1945 and there had never been any complaints.

Exhibit 1. Plant layout—machine tool department

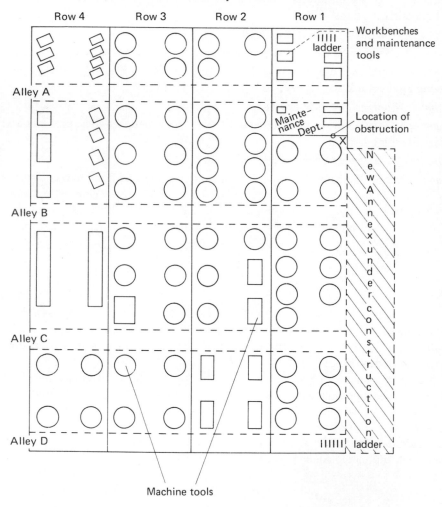

Machine tools

Conflict on board the frigate *Samson**

'He is not going to tell me what to do . . . Who does he think he is . . .' Those were the words of the worker involved in a dispute that arose early in the first week of 1960 in the Navy's shipyards.

The incident occurred as the frigate *Samson* was berthed at the shipyard for a general reconditioning. The frigate had been dismantled for the purpose, so that parts could be replaced and overhauled. To do so, the various installations had been taken apart. Jonathan, the electrical engineer of the frigate, together with his team, were posted at the shipyard for the operation. He was working on the frigate together with a team of electricians from the shipyard's workshop.

As he was inspecting the site, Jonathan saw one of the workers take apart an electrical circuit without marking the ends of the cables as he disconnected them. Jonathan pointed this out to the worker and Shlomo, that was his name, hastened to reply, 'I don't know you, get out of here . . .'

Jonathan got annoyed. He instructed the worker to do the marking in accordance with the professional instructions. Shlomo refused to do so and again used insulting language, including curses in Arabic, of Jonathan's mother, father and sister. When he had finished cursing, he added, 'Who gave you permission to talk to me like that and tell me what to do?'

Jonathan ordered the duty officer on board the *Samson* to have Shlomo taken off the boat. Since the frigate's Commanding Officer was not available at the time, Jonathan reported the incident to the Deputy OC and then left the frigate and went over to the shipyard to inform the officer in charge of the electrical workshop of the shipyard of the reasons for removing Shlomo from the boat. Later, it transpired that Shlomo was a member of the workers' council (see Exhibit 1, organisation chart of the shipyard).

The Navy's shipyards were used for its vessels, and one of its chief problems was the joint employment of both naval personnel and civilians within a setting which was, basically, a repair workshop for overhauling, reconditioning and maintenance of vessels.

The shipyard had both civilian workers and navy/army personnel. The civilian workers made up the main and permanent skilled and trade-school trained personnel. Soldiers doing their national service made up an alternating work-force at the skilled and trade levels, while officers were chiefly in the regular army. These officers were in charge of the shipyards and the civilian labour came under their

* All rights reserved to T. D. Weinshall. This case was prepared in the Technion—Israel Institute of Technology, Department of Industrial and Engineering Management.

command. From time to time, other officers took their place, according to the rotation practice of the IDF (Israeli Defence Forces).

Unlike the national service soldiers, who stayed on their jobs for about two years, the civilian worker remained indefinitely in his place of work, gaining both experience and seniority. Of the skilled workers at the yards, 85% were civilians, whereas 65% of the administrative staff were army/navy personnel (see Exhibit 1).

The relationships between civilians and armed forces personnel constituted a constant problem at the shipyards. Each side considered it had more rights than the other. The civilian skilled veteran or foreman felt himself sandwiched between two layers of forces personnel, officers from above and national servicemen from below. The servicemen considered the civilians privileged by virtue of being permanent, experienced and possessing seniority. Thus, each side felt underprivileged in relation to the other.

The Ministry of Defence and the General Federation of Labour (Histadrut) had come to an agreement establishing the rights of the employees and the employer in the various defence force units. The civilian worker was a wage earner who had to do his job, and that was that. But if he committed a security offence, the civilian became subject to military law. This meant that a civilian labourer could be brought before a disciplinary court, although such a procedure invariably ran into fierce opposition on the part of the civilian labour, for they considered that this constituted a conflict between the labour agreement and the jurisdiction of military law. Civilians generally objected to being brought before a disciplinary court, before a single judge not bound by the 'Rules of Evidence.'

Speaking about this practice, Mr Abramowitz, a member of the workers' committee, stated: 'There were instances where an OC, sitting as a judge, sentenced a civilian worker unjustly, merely in order to achieve a certain end.'

The civilian labourers objected to military enquiry commissions and to officers conducting investigations, because they did not see why the prosecution, the investigator and the judge should be representatives of one and the same side. There had been the case of a foreman who had come before a disciplinary court following which all the other foremen threatened to resign.

In Mr Abramowitz's opinion, the underlying causes for the disputes and misunderstandings were the following:

1. Deduction of income-tax from overtime, which does not make working overtime worthwhile. The worker feels himself discriminated against, especially in comparison with his counterpart in civilian enterprises.
2. No chance of advancement in the absence of the necessary establishment for civilian managerial employees.
3. Instances where civilian workers turned servicemen, thereby becoming master of their former civilian colleagues, despite their lower skills.
4. The frequent change in commanding officers who are not familiar with working conditions and the work force.
5. Outside the defence forces, a worker of comparable skills and qualifications could make much more money, in addition to having greater chances for

advancement. At the shipyards, the middle echelon worker made more than he would have outside. But, as soon as the quality of his work improved, he could not advance because of the low ceiling provided for, and thus his salary remains unchanged. This, in turn, led to tension.

6. Despite all this, the civilian worker had the feeling that servicemen looked on him as one who would shirk work whenever he could; as one who demanded a high wage in exchange for minimum effort. In the eyes of the serviceman, the civilian was protected, enjoyed privileges, and represented a stratum out to 'exploit' his employers.

Nissim, the current OC shipyards, stated in retrospect:[1]

'In the past, there were many conflicts at the shipyards and tension ran high between management and employees. The previous commanding officer had all the makings of a Prussian soldier and displayed a considerable lack of flexibility. If he had been more flexible, a lot of trouble could have been averted. Since then, we have tried to instil in the seamen a sense of the value and standing of the civilian worker. This was done by propaganda and through special projects and ceremonies, as I have already explained. For example, on the occasion of the thirteenth anniversary of the Navy, a special pin was issued to all those workers who had been at the shipyards for thirteen years, and a number of them together with their wives, were taken on a short cruise in one of the vessels they had helped to recondition.

'Today, we try to have civilian workers join in trips abroad; CO's of other boats are invited to visit the shipyards and, at joint meetings of ships' officers, we try to explain more fully and go into the problem of the civilian workers' status. In the past, naval personnel had no idea or comprehension of the civilian worker's status. They looked upon him as someone appointed to serve them, to fulfil a given task, carry it out and then "go home". This meant a slight on the worker's status, or rather, of the purpose he served. The workers were given the impression that they were simply "natives". This was especially true in the case of junior officers who previously had had no direct contact with civilian labour and simply did not know how to behave towards them.'

Referring to the conflict which had occurred on the *Samson* previous to his appointment as the Commanding Officer of the Naval Shipyards, the new OC, Nissim, said:

'As for the specific incident, it is inconceivable that the officer in charge of electrical circuits should tell a worker of the shipyards what to do. So long as the shipyard employee comes under our jurisdiction, he must also come under our authority in regard to instructions and discipline, even if the job is executed on board a ship at anchor. Therefore, Jonathan was at fault, although, of course, insulting language had been used. This really should not have happened . . .'

Following the clash between the Officer, Jonathan, and the civilian worker, Shlomo, which resulted in the removal of the latter from the ship, the workers went out on strike. After a few hours of strike an inquiry committee was appointed,

1. Relatively new, he had been at his job only a year. When the above incident occurred, he **had been** in another staff job, but not OC.

whose duty it was to investigate the circumstances of the case, and report its findings to the OC Navy.

In conclusion, Mr Abramowitz, the member of the workers' committee, noted: 'They may yet end up believing that all this happened because Shlomo is the only "Mapamnik" (member of Mapam party)[2] on the committee. We tried to get Jonathan to apologise to Shlomo, so that the matter might rest there, but he flatly refused to do so.'

Exhibit 1

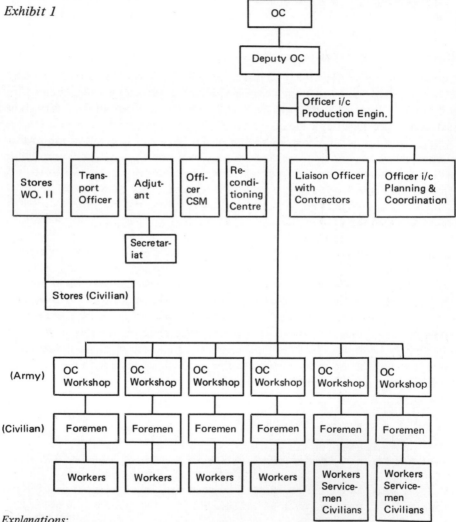

Explanations:

All foremen are civilians, but their number differs in each workshop.

Both servicemen and civilians work under civilian foremen.

As elsewhere, the Naval Shipyards has a workers' committee elected biannually.

The Shipyards operate under orders from an officer and as directed by the Operations Branch.

The OC Shipyards is directly responsible to the OC Navy.

2. Mapan—United Workers Party—was an extreme leftist labour party, Marxist, but Zionist.

Case 31
Kav-Kav Shoe Factory

'If you want us to work to premiums, we are under no circumstances prepared to do it in the same production groups with members of the Kibbutz,' warned Shlomo, a member of the hired labourers' committee at the Kav-Kav shoe factory at Kibbutz Givat Hatapuhim in the Upper Galilee, turning to Dr Arthur Levy and Mr Dov Landau of Hevrat Yeoul Hatassiya. 'You can forget all about our working with them on the basis of premiums in the same production groups,' he stated emphatically and walked from the room.

In 1969 a number of American professors expressed their impression of the Kibbutz in Israel in the following terms[1]:

'The kibbutz is a voluntary socio-economic community, an egalitarian society which provides complete economic, social, and cultural services for its members.

'There are no police in any kibbutz. Crime and delinquency are very rare in the usual meaning of those terms. Instead, social control of deviant behavior is exercised through standards of self-discipline. Its members obey its unwritten laws which embody the opinion of the majority. Moral compulsion and appeal to the force of conscience have largely replaced material incentives and coercion.

'There is less formal stratification and privilege, and life is based upon direct democracy. The kibbutz is a unique, small-scale social system. Solidarity and informality are the expected bases of member-to-member relationships. It is a system viewed by its members as morally right and bound together as a big family is bound together by ties of common values, common experience, common past, common fate, and mutual aid.

'The kibbutz community is a family-oriented society. The family has an important role in shaping public opinion of the community and in the socialisation of the children.

'The kibbutz always provides the economic needs of aged members. There is a system of gradual retirement of aged members: a decreasing number of hours worked per day according to age and sex. Every member when he reaches this age may have the right to work less. However, some members prefer to continue working to give more meaning to their lives and they, of course, may do so.

'The kibbutz community structure integrates two sub-systems: the *economic*,

1. From: A Report to the American Council for the Behavioral Sciences in the Kibbutz Management and Social Research Centre.

consisting of farming, manufacturing and services; and the *social*, consisting of education, health, culture, defence, etc.

'The General Assembly, consisting of adult members, is the supreme authority in the kibbutz. It enables the individual member to express his opinions and cast his vote. It provides a platform on which public opinion can make itself felt on all issues.

'Below the General Assembly there is a network of functional and coordinating committees. The coordinating committees are the policy making bodies. They integrate the system by deciding on crucial and boundary issues between and above functional committees. The coordinating committees are: The Executive Committee which is at the top of the social sub-system, and the Management Committee which is at the top of the economic sub-system (see Exhibit 1). Within the coordinating committees are located the four key office holders in the system structure: 1. the *General Secretary* is the chief executive coordinator of the social sub-system and the chairman of the executive committee; 2. The *Top Manager* is the chief coordinator of the kibbutz economic sub-system and the chairman of the Management Committee; 3. The *Treasurer* is responsible for the finances of the kibbutz and a member of the Management Committee; 4. the *Manpower Manager* is in charge of the allocation of manpower.

'These four key office holders occupy complementary roles which coordinate the kibbutz system as a whole. Their role definition is very diffused, thus giving every key leader a chance to maximise his contribution in those specific situations where he is most competent.

'The economic sub-system is organised into branches which carry out the work of the community. Members are allocated as workers to teams in branches in farming, industry, and services. They have maximum autonomy with decision-making involving their work situation. The branch teams are the foundation blocks of the economic sub-system of the kibbutz and they utilise group processes to increase performance. Every team elects its branch coordinator (supervisor) who plays a major leadership role in his team's performance. He serves as a link between the branch team and kibbutz committees and key office holders.

'The kibbutz system is based on planned rotation of office holders. Between one half and one third of the kibbutz members serve on committees. They are elected and about half of them are rotated every year. Key office holders and branch coordinators are elected for one to four years and then rotated. The kibbutz uses a system of planned rotation in order to be consistent with its democratic values, to maximise members involvement in the system, and to minimise stratification.

'The kibbutzim comprise 4% of the population of Israel. The number of members per kibbutz ranges from 100 to 1000 (average about 200), and the total population including children is from 200 to 2000 (average about 400). There is an annual growth of about 3% in the population of the kibbutzim.'

Until the end of the Second World War the Kibbutzim in Israel had been based entirely on agriculture. Subsequently some members in various Kibbutzim made the point that it was necessary to introduce industrial enterprises into the Kibbutzim in order to solve the following two problems which had been troubling them:

1. Finding useful employment for the elderly, the handicapped and the infirm who could not be absorbed in the various branches of agriculture. This was based on the assumption that in an industrial enterprise it would be possible to find suitable employment for handicapped members or elderly parents;
2. Creating a regulating factor to cope with the seasonal fluctuations, especially in respect of manpower, in the various branches of farming. Those advocating the introduction of industry into Kibbutzim assumed that such industrial enterprises would be able to absorb members who had temporarily become redundant in agriculture by reason of seasonal fluctuations or other factors. These members could, they believed, be transferred back from industry when agricultural demand rose again.

The early 1950s saw the introduction of industrial engineering, or as it was then called, production engineering, through the setting up of consulting management companies. This came in the wake of industrial engineers who had commenced work in industrial enterprises in Israel towards the end of the 1940s. One of the first firms in this field was Hevra le-Yeoul Hataassiya Ltd., founded in Haifa in 1950. In setting up this firm, Dr Authur Levy—an industrial engineer and a well-known expert on organisation who had emigrated from Switzerland two years previously—was joined by two young men who were to cooperate with him in the fields of management efficiency and industrial consultancy. The first of these was Dr Yaaqov Meiri—an economist who had gained prior experience in auditing work in Israel after emigrating from Switzerland. The other young man was Mr Dov Landau, a graduate in mechanical engineering from the Technion, who had gained experience in metal plants both in Holland and in England.

One day in 1952, Moshe, the manager of the shoe factory of Kibbutz Givat Hatapuhim in Upper Galilee, called at Dr Levy's office. He told Dr Levy that the factory he managed manufactured sandals and children's shoes and could be regarded as a medium-sized company in this industry; it employed abort forty people. Moshe complained to Dr Levy that in spite of all efforts on the part of the management, they had been unable to reduce the cost of production of sandals and children's shoes to a sufficient extent. He went on to say that his company was unable to meet the increasing competition from manufacturers in Tel-Aviv who had the natural advantage of being near the main consumer markets. Moshe further made the point that other Kibbutz members had complained to him and to those in favour of the factory, that its profitability was lower than the profitability of the agricultural branches of the Kibbutz. He also told Dr Levy that his Kibbutz, in setting up the shoe factory, had been one of the pioneers in the introduction of industries into the Kibbutz sector in Israel.

In 1969, as a result of their visits to Kibbutzim and their talks with members of the Kibbutzim, the American Professors recorded the following impressions of industries in Kibbutzim:[1]

'Since they were founded the chief economic basis of the kibbutzim has been farming. Communal settlement stemmed—in addition to the desire for cooperative

1. A Report of the American Council for the Behavioral Sciences

communities—also from the influence of socialist ideology, and perhaps more than any other, from a drive to work the land. There can be no doubt-that the kibbutzim have done extremely well and have a major share in the development and improvement of the different branches of farming in Israel.

'In the last few years there has been a shift towards industrialisation. The strong forces behind this industrialisation stem from:

(*a*) the limited natural resources in Israel (land and water);
(*b*) surplus of farm products in the local market;
(*c*) the increasing productivity per work day on the farm, 10% yearly;
(*d*) the increasing population of every kibbutz by birth and immigration;
(*e*) rising standards of living through more profitable occupations in industry as compared to farming;
(*f*) the need to add new occupations in order to attract the young generation and to open for them more paths to promotion, and, for the older generation, to find it employment in its old age.'

After an initial visit by Dr Arthur Levy and Mr Dav Landau to Givat Hatapuhim it was agreed that the latter should spend several days a week there for some weeks in order to carry out a comprehensive survey of existing work methods with a view to their improvement.

On his first visits Mr Landau noticed that occasionally members of the management could be found operating some of the manufacturing machinery. Thus, for example, Moshe himself would work a four-hour shift at one of the factory's machines. When asked by Mr Landau why the manager of the factory was himself working on the factory floor, Moshe retorted, 'I want to be close to the hub of things and want to go on being a worker, even if only a part-time one.'

In the same context another member of the Kibbutz with a university education, stated:

'I decided to give up being a "jobnik" (holder of a cushy office job) and asked for a transfer to field work. Of course it was difficult at first, I won't deny that, but I made up my mind the time had come to practise what I preach. And so I got back again to work in the fields. It certainly was no picnic, my back ached, my hands got swollen, and the worst of it was I dared not complain.'

One day, during one of the breaks, this same young man was sitting in a corner of the field with a group of hired labourers from a neighbouring development village. This is what he related:

'It was a hot day, I was thirsty but I felt I was achieving something. And then one of the labourers, illiterate but wise, said to me, 'What are you doing this for? You could do an equally worthwhile job at the office, not like me, labourer of his daily bread. If you weren't here the labour exchange would have sent an additional man.'

The Kav-Kav factory was a kibbutz enterprise manufacturing the simpler type of men's sandals as well as children's shoes and sandals. It was set up at Kibbutz Hatapuhim and was far removed from any urban centre. This in turn led to communications problems with potential clients. The Management members had difficulty in establishing direct contact with wholesalers and footwear distributors in the larger cities.

As a result of its remoteness, the higher costs of transport, as well as of the organisational problems at the factory, Kav-Kav found itself unable to match the current prices on the footwear market.

The factory was housed in an old building not suited for a plant. The machines were placed in such a way as to cause needless movement by the workers. Not even the floor was right for a factory. Production teams were mixed, i.e. made up of both kibbutz members and hired labourers from the neighbouring development village. The factory manager himself took a direct part in the production process, devoting about half a day's work to machine operating. As he put it in his statement above, this gave him the feeling of actively participating in the work process. Mr Landau, the production engineer who surveyed the factory, put it in the following terms:[1]

'The factory's chief problems were, (*a*) faulty management; (*b*) short production lines, each line constituting a stage of the manufacturing process with storage in between. Within each production line the workers were linked to each other, and the pace was set by the slowest member of the team. This in turn made the introduction of individual incentive wages even more difficult; (*c*) joint use of both members of the kibbutz and hired labourers from outside.'

In connection with the problem of hired labour at the Kav-Kav plant, it may be of interest to quote from the book by Aliza Levenberg[2] on hired labour problems in Kibbutzim in the Kiryat Shmone region, where Kibbutz Givat Tapuhim is located. Mrs Levenberg's description refers to the period during which the events set out in this case study took place:

'Despite the closeness of communal settlements and development villages within the same area, neighbourhood relations between the two are extremely complex. "If we did not have hired labour", one of the members of a settlement told me after having given the matter some thought, "everything would be quite different. We would be better neighbours, better friends, and our mutual relationship would be on a footing of equality. But as things have turned out we have stepped into the role, albeit reluctantly, of employers and supervisors. You know we had a considerable share in the establishment of these villages. However, after they had come about we found ourselves in an unexpected situation. New immigrants had moved into them who had no means of any livelihood. We had no choice but to employ them in the Kibbutzim if they were not to go hungry. That is how hired labour came about with which we have not been able to come to grips and which has undermined the very foundations of the Kibbutz movement. I know this sounds a paradox, and people prefer not to mention it, but whether we like it or not, we have become the symbol of capitalism." '

'And in fact when the Kibbutzim began to make more widespread use of hired labour it was done to a certain extent under pressure from the authorities. They

---

1. Mr Landau's statements were made fifteen years after the event described herein took place.
2. Aliza Levenberg, *Pirkei Kiryat Shmoneh* (Kiryat Shmoneh Chronicles), Schocken Publishing House, 1965, pp. 10-11; ibid. pp. 140-141.

were told by the government that unless they found employment for these new immigrants, the latter would die of hunger. When this process of hired labour got under way there was not a single Kibbutz who did it willingly. But the Government was adamant, as it lacked the means to provide other sources of livelihood. Before the new towns and villages were set up, many had believed that they were destined to turn into urban centres, providing services and shopping facilities for the surrounding kibbutzim and cooperative villages. However, they soon found out they had been mistaken. The immigrants from the Islamic countries lacked the necessary qualifications and means to meet the demands of the old settlers in these fields.'

'The Kibbutzim came to the rescue of the state's coffers, sensing that they were indeed offering a sacrifice. To some extent the feeling was justified, for hired labour did in fact undermine the Kibbutzim's standing in the eyes of the public and taint the esteem in which they had been held for so long, an esteem which to them was like the very air they breathed. The full implications of what was happening did not sink in until some time later. Meanwhile hired labour has become part and parcel of the Kibbutz' economy. Some of them would certainly founder were it not for the outside labour they employ unless, of course, their entire set-up were to undergo a revolutionary turn.'

In 1952 the manager of the factory called in the industrial consultants from Haifa, partly, as Mr Landau was to state later:
'because the idea of efficiency experts seemed to appeal to him (i.e. the manager), and partly from a desire to be competitive. There may also have been pressure put on him by the hired labourers to introduce premiums, for meanwhile workers in other plants in Israel were beginning to get wage incentives such as premiums as a result of work improvements.'

The consultancy work was carried out in stages, the first stage lasting from August 1952 until February 1953. To enable him to carry out his investigations which were to serve as basis for the survey, Mr Landau, as mentioned earlier, spent several days a week for a number of weeks at the Kibbutz. His investigations comprised time studies, systems analyses and their breakdown into elements, as well as coordination of teamwork systems. He was given a hand in the different time studies and investigations by Joseph, a kibbutz member working in the factory. Each month a report was submitted by the Haifa firm of consultants which in the first stage included suggestions for improvements in the production process itself, for clearance of needlessly used factory space, etc.

In the first stage the consultants saw their chief tasks as:

1. Standardisation of the work process at the factory
    (*a*) Clearing the plant of equipment, materials and tools not in use.
    (*b*) Slight changes in lay-out.
    (*c*) Effective means for moving materials and parts.
    (*d*) General improvement of work methods.

2. Establishment of norms for children's shoes with a view to:
   (*a*) Introduction of a wage system of piecework premiums based on time standards.
   (*b*) Procuring the necessary data for expansion of the factory (additional equipment, changes in machinery lay-out).

'In the first stage we set ourselves as target an output increase from 100 or 150 pairs of children's shoes daily to 250-300,' the consultants report for February 1953 read. Work teams at the factory were mixed and composed of both members of the settlement and outside labourers. Similarly, most of the administrative jobs were held by Kibbutz members. In all, however, only eight of a total workforce of forty were members of the Kibbutz.

Upon completion of the survey at the factory Dov Landau, the industrial engineer, realised that an incentive wage system could be introduced, based on group standards and group premiums. In other words, its yardstick was to be the output per group and not per individual member of the group. Each group was to be attached to a short line which in itself constituted one stage in the production process.

From his own experience Mr Landau knew that before an incentive wage system could be instituted, the workers had to be consulted. To do so, the industrial engineer called a meeting of all hired labourers at the factory, for he had found that in spite of the work teams being mixed, there were in fact two separate groups each with expectations of its own.

And so it was decided to introduce at the plant a system of group premiums, seeing that the technological structure did not permit institution of individual norms. However, in the wake of the premium idea fresh problems cropped up. During his talk with the hired workers in which Mr Landau explained the idea of group premiums, the workers claimed that the main problem was not the incentive wage method but rather continued teaming up with the kibbutz members for whom incentive wages provided no motivation. The hired labourers, on the other hand, were all in favour of the introduction of premiums, the more so since about that time premium systems had become common practice in other companies in the country.

'It was then that we thought of some other way of compensating the kibbutz member' Mr Landau went on. 'We proposed to let them have time off instead of sums of money. In other words, each week we would calculate how much was coming to them, and the following week they would be given a certain number of hours off as per the premium due to them. But when we submitted this proposal to the Kibbutz members, they argued, 'We can't agree to this, as those in the fields, for example, work much harder than we at the factory. Why then should we be given a day off?'

'And so back we went to the hired workers and told them there was no way in which we could pay the settlement members (neither in terms of money nor in terms of time); and that their sole motivation was owning the plant and seeing that it succeeded.'

The wage-earners went on to claim that the kibbutz members' behaviour did not seem to bear out this contention, and pointed to several among the latter who were in the habit of leaving their work at the factory for some hours every day in order to visit their children. This, in the opinion of the hired labourers, adversely affected their team work. Finally, they stated that they would agree to incentive wage methods if kibbutz members were taken out of the teams so that the groups would be made up of wage-earners only. To this, in turn, the settlers did not agree since, in their view, it put them in the wrong light in their relationship with the hired labour. Moreover, it would also affect the importance which they attached to work on the factory floor by their own members. Their fear was that this would lead to the creation of a class of bureaucrats and managers, exclusively made up of kibbutz members, while the actual operation of the factory would be in the hands of outside labour.

Exhibit 1. Structure of the kibbutz system

Social sub-structure		*Economic sub-structure*
Executive Committee	Key Coordinating Team Officers:	*Management Committee*
Education Committee	1. General Secretary	Reports by:
Cultural Committee	2. Top Manager	Dairy Team
Health Committee	3. Treasurer	Poultry Team
Defence Committee	4. Manpower Manager	Cash-crops Team
Young Generation Committee		Plantation Team
Consumption Committee		Factory Team
Social & Personal Committee		Maintenance Team
		Dining Hall Team
		Clothing Team

Filfort S.A. (A)

One morning in January, 1970 Mr Tuset, a management consultant, was visited in his Barcelona office by his friend Mr Puigrodo. He knew that Mr Puigrodo, now aged thirty, was a manager of Filfort S.A., the company he had joined immediately after graduating as a textile engineer. The salary he received from Filfort was his only source of income from which he supported his wife and five children.

Seeing that Mr Puigrodo appeared nervous and worried Mr Tuset offered him a cigarette and asked:
'Well Jaime, what brings you here? Although you did not tell me so on the telephone, I imagine it must be something to do with the company'.

Mr Puigrodo:
'Yes—the company and also my own future. My salary of 30,000 pesetas a month, plus something that old Mas gives me at the end of the year, enables me to live but not to save anything. If the company failed or I were to lose my job I don't know what would become of me or my family.'

Mr Tuset:
'Jaime, don't be so gloomy! You are young, competent and active. You are not likely to be out of a job. Also I understand Filfort is prospering, largely through your efforts, and now you are a senior manager I see no reason for you to worry.'

Mr Puigrodo:
'What you say is true. But I am conscious of personal conflicts in the factory which may have serious consequences. There are also indications of even more serious potential conflicts in the main office. These may not be apparent to the outsider in Barcelona, but please don't think I am exaggerating. These problems will not disappear by themselves. Of course, it is true that I could leave the company without any trouble, although it would involve a certain amount of personal disturbance. But I have been at Filfort for quite some time. We produce much more now than we used to, largely as a result of important changes I introduced in manufacturing and distribution. I have become fond of the company and regard it almost as if it were my own. I should be very sorry if Filfort did not prosper or I had to leave.

'Besides, I believe that with good management the company has a great future and could be the leader in the spinning of cotton and some synthetic fibres. It would be a pity if we failed through personal conflicts, lack of understanding and poor organisation.'

Reproduced by permission of Instituto des Estudios Superiores de la Empresa (IESE) Barcelona, Spain.

Mr Tuset:
'I can see you are very worried. How can I help you?'

Mr Puigrodo:
'A great deal. I see you as our salvation. I have come today with the authorisation of the "old ones" to ask you to undertake a formal consultancy assignment. It has taken me six months to get it approved but I have now succeeded by means of a subterfuge.'

Mr Tuset: . . . . ?

Mr Puigrodo:
'Yes. They don't even suspect the main problem as I see it. But there is another problem,–for me of much less importance–which they have agreed to your looking at.

'Five years ago, when I first joined Filfort, I engaged a foreign firm of consultants, specialists in the textile industry, to undertake a modernisation programme. They also carried out studies into production planning and control, incentive schemes and cost control. As a consequence we were able to reduce our labour force by fifty in spite of a factory expansion. This was done by a policy of voluntary early retirement. Later we had to recruit again to meet the demands of increased production. Within three years of the modernisation there were considerable improvements in both the quantity and quality of our output. By 1968 sales reached 150 million pesetas.

'Please don't take any notes, Jorge, I just wanted to give you the background which enabled me to obtain their agreement to asking for your help. Athough you are a specialist in human behaviour and organisation you are still a business consultant. As it is the cost control system and the incentive scheme recommended by the foreign consultants which are not working well, I have used this as an opportunity to convince them of the need for a business consultant to investigate out cost control.'

Mr Tuset:
'But you know I am not a specialist in quantitative analysis.'

Mr Puigrodo:
'Never mind; that is just an excuse for your intervention. You are always saying that a company is a system of interdependent parts. To fix the costing system you must know the people who work on it. This will lead to other human and organisational problems which will make the "old ones" think when it is presented to them by you.'

Mr Tuset:
'You refer to the "old ones". I suppose you mean the top management. Perhaps you can tell me something about them as I don't know them personally. Nor do I know anything of the conflicts in the factory you talk about.'

Mr Puigrodo:

'The trouble is I'm all confused. I see the conflicts but not their cause. I am incapable of telling who is speaking the truth or who is to blame for what is happening.'

Mr Tuset:

'Ignore your worries! Don't try to allocate blame, for it is not for us to judge others. What concerns us is the efficiency of the company. If there is anything dis-functional we shall try to correct it by concentration on the circumstances which bring it about. First, tell me how you see the existing conflicts. Then we can turn to analysis, to find their causes.'

Mr Puigrodo:

'Alright. As you know, Filfort S.A. is a major company engaged in spinning cotton, synthetic fibres and mixtures. The main offices in Barcelona are 100 km from the factory in the Pyrenean village of High Llobregat. The majority of the 500 workers are women.

'The shareholders are scattered all over Europe and, apart from some of the top managers, none owns more than 10% of the shares. Most of the shareholders have permanently nominated the top managers to represent them at meetings.

'The company's management is in the hands of seven men—those I call the "old ones". The majority have other businesses or professions and are well off financially, and socially prominent. Since the Shareholders General Meeting never intervenes, their appointment is virtually secure for life. When a vacancy occurs the place is filled with their unanimous support. Although the new man need not necessarily be a shareholder at least four of the seven must be. Each of them receives 2% of the profit for his services. Two of them—Mr Mas and Mr Poch—also act as sub-managers and are directly in charge of the company's operations. They live in the city and rarely go to the factory.

'When I first started working in the factory I was assistant to the then sub-manager although my position was never formalised or officially made known to the employees. On the death of this sub-manager Mr Mas accepted the post at the insistence of the others, but asked that someone else should share it with him because of his other heavy commitments. Thus Mr Poch was also appointed. D. Gerado Mas and I knew each other previously through family connections.

'After these changes my position remained unaltered officially, although I had a little more informal authority. Since he never visits the factory I act in his place but I have no established position to support my actions. I instigated the modernisation programme I mentioned earlier with the agreement of Mr Mas. Mr Poch is about fifty-four years old. He is an official in the Public Administration and gives half of his time to the company. Mr Mas, who is sixty-five, manages important businesses of his own and only goes to Filfort's offices once a week, although he does visit the factory occasionally. Mr Poch is really responsible for administration whereas Mr Mas is responsible technically and for manufacture.

'I visit the factory for two to three days every week. You will understand that it is difficult for me to give orders or interfere with the factory's human or technological problems without an acknowledged position. The employees used to call me "Jaimito" behind my back, but this nickname slowly disappeared as they saw the results of my decisions and the modernisation programme.

'Two years before my appointment Isidro Boix took over as factory manager. He lives in the village. Before joining Filfort he was manager of another textile factory. In the eyes of the top managers his practical experience makes him admirably suited to manage a factory, because of the machinery. To the "old ones" practice counts a great deal, whereas theory can be a drawback.

'Mr Boix is forty-five years old and has authority for all factory activities and operations. He reports to Mr Mas and indirectly to me as Mr Mas's assistant. I must acknowledge that I had to rely on Mr Boix's experience a great deal when I started at Filfort.

'Also, he was, and is, the factory manager and although I am a step higher in the hierarchy I have no authority in the factory. I act as the liaison between the main office and the factory when at High Llorbregat. I have no alternative but to get on with Mr Boix. Nevertheless as time went on I realised that he lacked both technical and interpersonal judgement. After all his qualification, Industrial Master, is not a great thing and anyway he obtained it by a correspondence course.

'Recently I have observed that the atmosphere between management and workers leaves a great deal to be desired. New employees were not always accepted by their fellow workers. There are constant complaints about the arbitrary way incentive rates and overtime are arranged. Boix is accused of allowing personal preferences to guide his judgement.

'Two foremen and fifteen charge hands report to Mr Boix. One of the foremen has been with the company for forty years and was brought up on single shift working, at a time when little attention was paid to costs, quality, personnel, maintenance and planning. With the introduction of three-shift working a new foreman was appointed, a young man and friend of Mr Boix. He quickly clashed with the old foreman. This situation is made worse by the shift time table since they both work two shifts and are together half the day.

'Mr Boix holds periodic factory meetings. But since it is difficult for his subordinates to voice their opinions he does most of the talking.

'Other people reporting to Boix are:

the chief mechanic, an efficient young man who does not get along with him very well.

Mr Puig, a young man introduced by Mr Boix to take charge of quality control and planning. At first Mr Puig clashed with the old foreman who believed he was interferring in his own area of responsibility.

Mr Moret, in charge of factory administration. He is forty-eight years old and has worked for the company since he was twenty.

'We now come to one of the problems which worry me most. Before the arrival of Mr Boix, Mr Moret was the backbone of the factory administration. While the sub-manager who died and the foreman ran the technical side Mr Moret never took a holiday, worked long hours and even went to the factory on Sunday. He is intelligent, though not well educated formally, and his long experience has made him really efficient. But he has always been an introvert and not very communicative. A very good worker and with a great sense of responsibility he is nevertheless excessively pusillanimous and punctilious. Rarely does he have any confidence in others and he likes to do things personally. He is well respected in the village where he is regarded as the live incarnation of the factory.

'The seven employees in the administrative office collect and despatch to Barcelona data on production, costs, deliveries etc. They also calculate the incentives. Before the arrival of Mr Boix they transmitted Main Office manufacturing orders to the factory. The office was also responsible for relations with outsiders, official organisations etc. and for personnel matters. After his arrival—I am now talking about the period before my appointment—Mr Boix made it known that as factory manager he should receive all the orders from Barcelona and would take charge of all matters concerning personnel. I think this was very reasonable since he was factory manager. But it led to contradictory orders and confrontations between Boix and Moret, sometimes in front of the administrative employees. Moret, used to another system, had been offended by all this, particularly as Mr Boix used his position as factory manager to ensure that differences were always resolved in his favour.

'I am worried by the consequences of all this. It is widely known that Moret has recently lost the interest he felt for the Company. He has gone quiet. His hands shake and I know he suffers from insomnia. Several times he has come to me crying and everyone knows he has started psychiatric treatment. I would like to solve this situation but I cannot see it clearly. Who is right? Moret is nowadays a cause of trouble to everyone in the factory. He is aloof and doesn't listen to anyone. In any case how can I interfere without a clear and definite position? I achieved modernisation because Mr Mas saw the need and gave me his backing. But in this affair Mr Mas is totally disinterested. He says it is just human behaviour which happens everywhere and the best thing to do is not to interfere. I have a fear that no good will come of it in the long run. But what can I do?

'The factory people know that every week I come from Barcelona with orders and go back with despatch notes, problems and various information. They know I talk to Mr Boix, but what do they know of my function? They see me as a link with the management; but officially no one has ever told them what my position is—I don't even know it myself. It is true that I am now respected but this does not enable me to act with a free hand.

'Although the situation in Barcelona is not so serious, don't think you can envy me. I suffer from the same lack of official recognition. Generally the employees are not satisfied. So you can see, Jorge, that I find myself in a mess. I fear the situation may degenerate and become insupportable. This would be a pity since we have such strengths besides being in an economic position which allows us to act freely'.

Mr Tuset:

'I appreciate the confidence you have in me and I shall try not to disappoint you.

But I feel it won't be easy. I must decide how best to start.'

Mr Puigrodo:
'First of all I think you should meet Mr Mas and Mr Poch.'

Mr Tuset:
'Certainly, let us fix a meeting with them.'

A few days after this interview Mr Tuset met Mr Poch and Mr Mas.

Mr Poch struck Mr Tuset as being a calm man and showed himself to be extraordinarily courteous. Yet he gained the impression that Mr Poch was accepting his interference only because of Mr Puigrodo's insistence. He also felt in him a lack of dynamic and grasp when management problems were discussed. Maybe it was because Mr Poch thought the company was doing allright and didn't have any problems. He only showed interest when Mr Tuset talked about production costs:

'We are actually in the dark about the costs of several types of thread', said Mr Poch, ' and it would be very useful if we could know them accurately. I trust you will help us with this problem.'

In contrast Mr Mas seemed a very active man with an intense desire to develop the company.

At one point in the conversation Mr Tuset asked who was in charge of production costs. Mr Poch answered: 'We put Mr Moret in charge after the reorganisation by the foreign consultant. We thought he was the ideal person to carry it out because of his experience of the company and his personal qualities. Nevertheless, it has not worked out and we don't know why.'

Mr Mas added that he personally believed it was because of Mr Moret's psychological disturbance. He also referred to the Boix-Moret conflict but did not associate it with the state of Moret's health. He made it clear that Moret was now a problem although he had been a very good worker in the past.

During the interview Mr Tuset felt that Mr Mas had great confidence in Mr Puigrodo's technical competence. He sensed that Mr Mas was attracted by techniques and that he looked to Jaime Puigrodo for agreement when they talked about machinery or industrial organisation.

Both Mr Mas and Mr Poch gave Mr Tuset a free hand for his assignment in the main office and the factory.

After the conversation Mr Tuset reviewed what he knew of the situation. It was obvious that something was wrong. He must diagnose the problems and prepare a plan of action; but he needed more facts. What steps should he take? In what order? What alternatives were there?

He felt responsible for the company's future.

Filfort S.A. (B)

Mr Jorge Tuset was a management consultant and a friend of Mr Jaime Puigrodo, an executive of Filfort S.A. Mr Tuset was asked by Mr Puigrodo to study Filfort and recommend what should be done. The conclusions reached by Jorge Tuset after his talk with Jaime Puigrodo and his brief interview with Mr Juan Poch and Mr Gerardo Mas[1] were as follows:

1. Something was deficient in the Filfort company regarding the relations between the men who occupied the positions of departmental executives.

2. It was possible that such deficiencies derived from the personal disposition of the individuals who composed the structure or may have occurred because the actual organization favoured conflictive situations. It was also possible that both causes coexisted and were reinforcing each other.

3. Top managers did not realise the importance of the human element in the progress of an enterprise. One of them, Mr Mas, attached a great importance to the industry's technological aspect; while the other, Mr Poch, considered of great value the application of an administrative technique enabling the calculation of costs with a maximum of accuracy.

4. Mr Puigrodo on the other hand, perceived the importance of human relations and considered that the human climate at Filport was not adequate to enable progress without difficulties. Nevertheless, because of his position, knowledge and experience, Jaime Puigrodo could not clearly diagnose the situation, nor decisively influence it.

5. He, Mr Tuset, needed more facts to be able to better diagnose the situation. It was clear to him that it would be impossible to obtain these additional data from the three persons he knew in Filfort. He could acquire the extra information from the persons implicated directly in the situation in Filfort's factory. It was evident to him that information given by each individual had various degrees of the subjective. Each person perceives a situation according to his personal characteristics, motivations, feelings, affections, etc. Nevertheless, Jorge Tuset's knowledge of people, his experience and professional abilities together with the great variety of facts and details supplied by different people, could represent a set of valuable facts to evaluate objectively the situation and to lessen the risk of error in diagnosing the problems.

He therefore decided to go to the factory and to contact its managers. At the end of January, 1970, Jorge Tuset and Jaime Puigrodo went to the factory. Mr

1. These conversations are described in the Filfort S.A. (A) case study.

Puigrodo suggested that Mr Tuset should first talk with Mr Boix, the Factory Manager. Thus, as soon as they arrived, Mr Tuset was presented to Mr Boix as the company's adviser on matters of organisation. Mr Puigrodo explained that one of Mr Tuset's first objectives was to study the newly established cost control system, for which it would be interesting for him to talk with him and with Mr Moret as well as with other persons who could inform him of the existing difficulties with its application.

Subsequently, Mr Puigrodo and Mr Tuset made a thorough tour of the factory together with Mr Boix, who was all along very helpful. While they went through the different sections, Mr Puigrodo introduced Mr Tuset to the managers in charge.

The factory was located near the river from where they took the water for their own uses. There were two main buildings, an old one and a new one. The equipment had been extensively modernized and expanded, but there was some equipment which had still to be renewed. The factory made, on the whole, a pleasant and tidy impression. The illumination was good and likewise the air conditioning. Once the tour was over, Mr Tuset settled in an office which had been prepared for him and started interviewing Mr Boix.

Interview with Mr Boix

Mr Boix was forty-five years old and a bit fat. Although he was quite courteous in his way of acting and looking at Mr Tuset, it seemed he was rather suspicious. While going over his 'curriculum vitae', he emphasized he had a masters degree in industrial engineering but did not mention the fact that he had obtained this degree through correspondence. He also emphasised the fact that he had occupied the post of factory manager in two other factories before coming to Filfort S.A.

Mr Boix began his work as Factory Manager by eliminating the situation in which every section had two persons in charge. He tried to appoint as section head the most competent person in the section so as to increase efficiency. He realized immediately that the factory had to be reorganized. When Mr Puigrodo entered the company, Mr Boix talked with him about this matter and convinced him of the need for reorganization.

Mr Puigrodo and Mr Mas were responsible for selecting the management consultants who advised them on this matter. As a consequence of the reorganization, many people had to be dismissed. Everything worked out without any problems. According to Mr Boix, the morale of the factory's personnel was high, thanks to the fact that he handled them well. He said: 'You must talk and have contact with people. Nevertheless you must bear in mind the worker's mentality. Although the morale is good, they lack enthusiasm. As you know these people always think that they are being exploited.'

Mr Boix explained that he had encouraged the establishment of a technical trade school in the area and that he encouraged the factory maintenance personnel to participate in night classes, studying mechanical engineering subjects. He talked about the Laboratory as a section practically created by him. He said that the

Laboratory, headed by Mr Puig, included eight girls and two boys and he was mainly occupied in quality tests and controlling the production.

When Mr Tuset asked Mr Boix about the progress of the introduction of cost control in production, Mr Boix said:

'Look, this matter was entrusted to Mr Moret and he has obstructed it. I don't know if you know that Mr Moret is a man full of ghosts. He sees enemies everywhere, he thinks that everyone is trying to attack him and is always on guard. He treats his subordinates badly and does not trust any of them. He is of the opinion that none of them is worth anything. Mr Moret's main function is the coordination between the factory's warehouse and the sales section in Barcelona.'

First interview with Mr Moret

Following the interview with Mr Boix, Mr Tuset asked to speak with Mr Moret in private. Mr Moret was forty-eight years old, of normal height, thin and with very sharp features. He entered the room occupied by Mr Jorge Tuset, to whom he had been previously introduced by Mr Puigrodo during the tour of the factory when they had visited the Administrative Section. Mr Moret greeted him very shyly and sat on the chair offered to him by Mr Tuset. Mr Moret did not look directly at Mr Tuset and his eyes wandered about the room. One could observe him slightly trembling. Mr Tuset started the interview by explaining the role which he was supposed to perform in the company and the need for the interviewees to speak sincerely and openly to him about the problems which they thought Filfort had, as well as of their own private problems which could be in some way related to the general ones. Mr Tuset specified:

'When a person doesn't feel well, he goes to the doctor and tells him sincerely what is the matter with him so that he is able to diagnose and advise a treatment. If the person is not sincere, the doctor has very little chance of succeeding. But it is not necessary to be ill to go to the doctor. It is good to have a check-up once in a while, even when we are feeling well, for, as the saying goes, it is better to prevent the illness than to cure it. On the other hand, none of us has perfect health. The enterprise, as an existing dynamic organism, is capable of growing or of getting old, it passes through times of crisis or of disturbances which can be attributed to a great many causes. Thus, in a similar way to the person who does not feel well, it is advisable for him to see an expert. All enterprises can be bettered in some way and none of them is free from some defect. But of course, the enterprise is not a person, but a human system composed of many individuals. The expert must talk to them so that they can give him more information. Of course, they must be sincere and outspoken if they want to collaborate in the bettering of the system. As in the doctor's case, the expert is unable to help if the information he receives is insufficient or wrong. The accuracy of the diagnosis and the efficiency of the plan of action will depend greatly on the truth of the information. On the other hand, the expert will not use the information to tell it to other people, but only to know the situation and act for the good of the company and of its components.

'Mr Moret, I believe you are one of the persons who can give me more information. I would like you to trust me. Tell me the company's problems and your own connection with them as you see them. I want you to talk freely. Maybe you could begin by telling me about your former experience, your life, the posts which you have occupied here, your past functions and your actual ones and the barriers, if there are any, which according to your judgement, hinder the company's and your own development.'

Mr Moret absorbed Mr Tuset's words in a sort of sad and distracted mood. It seemed as if he were partly interested and yet as if he would like to escape a nightmare. Following a short silence, Mr Moret said:

'Mr Tuset, I suppose that they have talked to you about me as a problem in the company. I admit that I am. When I was three years old my father died. My mother had to carry the family through. I studied high school, while working as a printer. When I was twenty years old I entered Filfort as an administrator. We had at that time 200 workers and a manager who lived in Barcelona and came over once a week until he died several years ago. In the factory, Mr Noguera, the foreman, was in charge of all the work under the manager's orders. Mr Noguera is still here. We all got along very well together, and the enterprise progressed.

'Today everything has changed. I feel very bitter and I don't know what to do anymore. The growth of the enterprise gave place to the nomination of Mr Boix as Factory Manager, while the manager's many activities led to the coming of Mr Puigrodo as his assistant. Some time after the previous manager died we were launched into a technical reorganisation which caused the dismissal of a large part of the personnel. Dissatisfaction spread in the factory and the malaise spread to the rest of the village. My position and my long service in the company, as well as the image which the village had of me, turned me into the target of all the disgruntled people, although I had nothing to do with that reorganisation. I had to calm the spirits and reassure the people as well as I could. We advanced the pension date of those who were nearing it and likewise offered the employees other advantages. These were done together with Mr Mas, when he detected the malaise.

'A notice of suspension of work was presented by Filfort to the regional trade union, which formed a committee to deal with the case summoning involved employees to report to the committee. This was the first news that the personnel had of a sizeable reduction. No one had informed them before. I had to explain everything and resolve the situation. It was very unpleasant. Please, don't believe that I am contrary or against the organization. I think that technically many things have been improved but many others have been neglected. The company is in great need of reorganization. There exists a big gap between the factory and the main office. Many projects are planned but very few are carried out. As for myself, this has affected me enormously. I have two daughters in Barcelona, one is studying medicine and the other one is finishing high school, they are both brilliant students.'

Mr Tuset ended the interview because of the late hour and he asked Mr Moret to come back and continue their conversation on another occasion.

Meeting of the employee-representatives

A week later a meeting of employee-representatives with Mr Boix took place. Mr Tuset returned to the factory to participate in it and observe the atmosphere and the proceedings of the session. Mr Boix opened the meeting by talking about a series of technical problems which were observed in several sections and explaining how they should be resolved. After talking for half an hour he invited the people in charge to give some suggestions. Most of them were silent. Only one or two of them spoke of some difficulties in implementing Mr Boix's solutions. Mr Boix refuted what they said without, as it seemed to Mr Tuset, reasoning sufficiently with the opinions expressed.

When the session ended, Mr Boix invited Mr Tuset to say something. Mr Tuset congratulated Mr Boix and the people responsible for arranging such meetings. He said that the most important part of the enterprise were the people composing it and that in reality they were the enterprise. It comprised everyone from the shareholders, through the executives, to the last day labourer. The good of the enterprise must be the good of its people and its main objective service to them and to society.

However, in order to achieve it, the free cooperation of everyone was necessary. Mr Tuset then added:

'Nevertheless, I have observed that you have talked very little. Each person has his individuality, his mentality and his opinion. Every person is free. You have the right to express your opinion; but I would even say more. You have the obligation of doing it; by forming part of the company you have the obligation of procuring its welfare, as it has the obligation of seeking your own good. If you think that something can be done to improve it you must say so, without feeling a grievance if those in authority and with a higher responsibility, decide against it after they have heard and listened to your reasons.'

Second interview with Mr Moret

When the meeting with the employee-representatives was over, Mr Tuset again asked Mr Moret to come to see him. Mr Moret entered the room even more nervous than he had been during their meeting a week before. The following conversation took place between the two.

Mr Moret:

'I believe you have goodwill and I thank you for the interest you show in wanting to know my opinion; but you must convince yourself that there is nothing that we can do. This is a lost case for the company and for myself. Do you like this landscape of mountains and forests?

Mr Tuset:

'I love it, I have always been very fond of mountains and besides, I know this region very well; but, why do you ask me?

Mr Moret:

'I guessed your answer. I also like the mountains; but after what has happened here, this landscape, these forests, just the silhouette of these mountains weigh over me like a grave. They oppress me. I have loved this company like a daughter, I have dedicated the best years of my life to it. I have wanted to see it powerful, a model. And for what? There is no planning. Everything is done crazily. There is a lack of information! Today I don't anymore.

Mr Boix and Mr Puigrodo were brought in before the former manager died. What have they done? Created conflicts. They badly managed technical innovations. The wage incentives are paid in accordance with the arbitrary judgment of Mr Boix. The management consultants who introduced the wage incentive scheme, invented such a complicated system that you would need a mathematical genius and a regiment of employees to calculate them each week. You cannot have a method which takes into account all the details of work.'

Mr Tuset:

'Don't you consider it practical to have to take into account all the details of raw materials?'

Mr Moret:

'Precisely, I have always liked to do everything in as much detail as possible. I admit that it has been one of my many defects. Experience has shown me that too much detail makes you end up in confusion. Well, the end of the wage incentive calculations has been the stroke of the pencil, arbitrarily, causing discontent.

'At the beginning Mr Boix backed me and we understood each other. Later, because of the reduction of personnel and of the consequent attitudes in the village, I protested about how things had been carried out. Since then Mr Boix has had resentment towards me. Our relationship has not been cordial any longer. Frequently Mr Boix gives orders to my employees which are contrary to the ones given by me. I certainly believe that I am stubborn; but he is twisted. He has a tendency to monopolize all authority.'

Mr Tuset:

'How are your subordinates, Mr Moret?'

Mr Moret:

'Not very good; but apart from some old ones, they have all been imposed on me and I have had no opportunity to participate in their selection.'

Mr Tuset:

'I believe that the management consultants have tried to introduce not only a wage incentives scheme, but cost control as well, for which you are personally responsible. What are your difficulties in implementing this system?'

Mr Moret:

'The way we are trying to implement this system makes it unattainable. In the first place I must say that the system was presented to me in writing, leaving various details without any further explanation. The consultants then left. I have never had the opportunity of expressing any doubt or raising any questions.

'The plan divides the factory into cost centres and pretends to attribute to each cost centre all its cost to the last detail. To calculate the detailed cost of each type of yarn is enormous work. Let me add to this, our lack of organization. Not even the warehouse possesses a minimum of organization. Nobody knows exactly what is stored in the warehouse. Most of the materials are old and will never be used. Accessories, spare parts and auxiliary materials are all mixed up. The people in charge just go there and take whatever they want without anybody saying anything, or finding out about it. I must say, that in spite of Mr Boix's great centralizing tendencies, he never finds out about 90% of the things that happen. Would you like to have a look at the cost control system that the management consultants left behind.

Mr Tuset:
'Yes, sure, please show it to me.'

Mr Moret went to his working desk and came back with a batch of papers which Mr Tuset subsequently examined. The plan seemed complicated to Mr Tuset. Mr Tuset asked Mr Moret if he had ever tried to calculate the production costs of the various products. Mr Moret answered that he had once worked on it very intensively. He showed Mr. Tuset another collection of papers including a system which would enable one to determine the cost of each type of yarn. Jorge Tuset had the impression, that Mr Moret's system was much more realistic, simple and effective, than the system proposed by the management consultants.

Nevertheless he thought Mr Moret's system could be improved technically. The following conversation subsequently took place between the two:

Mr Tuset:
'Well, Mr Moret, why don't you improve and apply your system?'

Mr Moret:
'It is not possible anymore. In the first place the management paid good money for the plan of the consultants and they want to profit from it and use it. In the second place I am unable to cope with technical problems of accounting, which I cannot overcome for lack of knowledge or of capacity.'

Mr Tuset:
'I can see that you have not had technical training in this area, but I cannot accept your saying that you lack the capacity.'

Mr Moret:
'I thank you for your words. However in addition to knowledge and capacity there is a third difficulty. Mr Tuset, it is too late. I am a finished man. Do you know? Every morning, when I see the sun, I think to myself: "I wish I would never see it coming out anymore".'

Mr Tuset:
'Please Mr Moret, don't say such a thing. The three difficulties could be removed and they will be. Have confidence.'

Mr Moret:

'I wish God would hear you; but it can't be, it is too late, too late.'

After the interview Mr Puigrodo and Mr Tuset returned to Barcelona. They had a general conversation. Mr Puigrodo informed Jorge that Filfort was thinking of purchasing a small spinning mill near Barcelona, for the manufacture of standard thick yarn. Talking about Mr Moret, Mr Puigrodo said:

'I am very worried about Moret. I met his wife yesterday in the street and she came crying, asking me to transfer her husband to Barcelona. I evaded answering her. Imagine what an absurd situation. I am worried that if she gets it into her head, the matter will become a very difficult one. I shall have to avoid such meetings in the future.'

Mr Tuset told Mr Puigrodo that he considered Mr Moret competent and active, but with strong feelings of frustration. He said that at certain points of the interview Moret had seemed to be very interested. His interest, however, suddenly dropped, giving place to profound anguish, bringing him back to the world of his actual situation. It seemed as if at times he would forget a nightmare in which he ordinarily lived. Mr Tuset thought, nevertheless, that Mr Moret could be rehabilitated.

Mr Tuset continued to visit the Filfort S.A. factory at Highllobregat every week in order to complete his information. His next interviewee was Mr Planas, one of the top employees of the factory's administrative office.

Mr Planas, who reported to Mr Moret, prepared payrolls, maintained the relationship with the trade unions, worker delegations, Social Security, etc. According to Mr Puigrodo, Mr Planas was intelligent and a hard worker but an intriguer. Mr Puigrodo's opinions were very valuable for Mr Tuset as a starting point. He wanted, however, to compare them with his own impressions. He therefore interviewed Mr Planas personally.

Interview with Mr Planas

Mr Planas was forty-nine years old, rather short, healthy looking and with a red face. He talked freely without any fear or restriction. During the course of the conversation Mr Planas commented:

'Before Mr Boix came, the company was ruled patriarchally. Everybody here praised the former manager. The people in charge knew that he did not want to see any machines idle and, therefore when he visited the factory all of them were working. As for Mr Boix, I believe that he considers himself too self-sufficient. Furthermore, he is spiteful. I cannot express an opinion about his technical capacity, but I consider his organizing capability to be very poor. The people in charge are displeased with Mr Boix for several reasons. He does not accept any suggestions. There are, however, suggestions which he likes, but which he has turned down; he applies such suggestions several days later, explaining to Mr Puigrodo that such an improvement had just occurred to him.

'If he gives someone advice, the one who gets it knows that he must carry it out, otherwise he exposes himself to Mr Boix's reprisals. The sanctions are generally very strong. A factory woman worker who disobeyed him but later apologized, lost her additional extra-activity pay for a whole year. If someone refuses to work on a Sunday when Mr Boix asks him to, he knows that he may be transferred to a more unpleasant working place. He does not permit anyone to interfere with what he considers to be within his own jurisdiction. Once, when one of the women was ill and had to be sent to Barcelona for an operation, I myself made out the necessary documents. He caught me doing it and said that I should have asked him about it. He then delayed the proceedings, until they learned about this case in Barcelona and asked for the woman to be sent immediately.

'As for Mr Moret, I must tell you that I have great esteem for him, but people do not trust him any more as they used to. Moret was the soul of the company, now he is not very important. He is a very good worker: but he has very little confidence in others and he neglects their training. He does not delegate functions. Everybody respects him very much. Sometimes we would like to make some suggestions to him but we don't because of the respect we have for him. Anyway he does not accept other people's opinion easily. He is very undecided. Before he was introverted and quiet, now he is pessimistic and reserved. He never laughs and he doesn't like others to do so. He never comments on anything and does not permit any conversation among the people other than that related to work.

'Boix and Moret do not get along and this creates bad feelings. I consider Moret to be better qualified in administrative matters than Boix. When they discuss something Moret argues, but Boix imposes his own opinion by virtue of his superior position. Boix sometimes gives orders to Moret's employees without telling him anything about it. Many times these orders contradict those given by Moret previously. Several violent scenes occurred among the employees, myself being one of them.

'I believe that Mr Puigrodo is technically very competent but he does not have enough contact with the personnel. He represented management on one occasion we had a strike. His involvement on that occasion made the people dislike him. The factory's organization is far from being perfect.

'The night shift personnel do not rotate. There are some jobs done in the Administrative Section which in my opinion should be done in the technical section. Job definition is lacking. As it happens the administrative personnel's tasks are so specific that when one of them is ill we must go to his house to find out about his task.

'The introduction of clocking in and out cards for personnel has improved punctuality. You only clock in when you arrive in the morning and back from lunch in the afternoon. We do not have to clock out, to prevent the queues. If an employee has to leave earlier he must hand in a note signed by the person in charge. You clock out only when you have worked overtime.

'I think that too much overtime is worked at Filfort. Personally, I consider overtime to be anti-social. When people get used to overtime it is difficult to abolish it. Furthermore, the workers start to wonder why the company can afford to pay twenty for some hours and only ten for the rest of the time. Their conclusion is that they are being cheated during the normal hours. I believe that overtime lowers efficiency, because people are fatigued. There are people who work overtime systematically. This arouses envies and grudges. Mr Boix is the one who decides who will work overtime.

'When it comes to wages, the workers never know what to expect. Mr Boix fixes the wages according to his judgement. There is the case of two woman workers, doing the same work on similar machines, producing approximately the same but who get different pay. One gets 50 Pesetas a week and the other 100. When the one who gets 50 protested, Mr Boix screamed at her; 'I have already told you that the other one gets what is due to her and you get what is due to you. Her pay is 100 and your's 50. This is the way it is and there is nothing more to say about it.' There is tenseness among the women. When one of them comes protesting that she has earned low weekly pay, she is really protesting more against the existence of higher wages than hers.

'Transfers of personnel from one section to another take place all the time. Let it be known that the people at Filfort are good and have good faith. They have never gone to the union to protest.

'The dissatisfaction among the managers is strong. When we expanded the factory and had to increase the number of managers, new managers were brought in from the outside by Mr Boix. Many of the junior managers over here believed that they were capable of occupying the new posts and felt they had more right to do so than those who were brought in. The salaries of managers are also in disparity with each other. There is one manager, who gets a much lower salary than another. He asked Mr Boix for an explanation but never received one.

'The two foremen, Noguera and Feliu, can't stand each other. Feliu was brought in by Mr Boix and gets on very well with him. Both foremen work together half a day. During this time the situation is a constant conflict. Frequently, when one orders something, the other one orders exactly the contrary. Noguera can't stand Mr Boix, something which he tells everyone.

'I believe that there is much wasted potential in the people we have; but no one worries about their training or about promoting them. The managers ask themselves how it is possible that Mr Puigrodo does not see what is going on.'

Mr Tuset thought that many of the observations made by Mr Planas made a lot of sense and showed a good deal of sensitivity on his part. He asked him if he was interested in human and personal matters. The subsequent conversation then took place.

Mr Planas:
'I have always liked human problems, but I don't want to interfere and intrude into other people's domains. Although today there is no formal head of personnel, I believe that these matters belong to Mr Boix.'

Mr Tuset:
'Do you believe that there could be a way of integrating the company's personnel, so that they would feel as if the company's objectives were their own?'

Mr Planas:

'Not with the existing policy; however, it could be done with another policy, more satisfactory to the employees, encouraging comradeship instead of discord. I must add that managers frequently consult me concerning their problems. I know they trust me.'

Following his interview with Mr Planas, Mr Tuset interviewed Mr Noguera, one of the two foremen.

Interview with Mr Noguera

Mr Noguera was sixty-one years old and had been with the company for forty years. When he was fourteen he learned the trade of locksmith in his home town. He then worked as a mechanic in another company and later on started as a manager in Filfort, where he became a foreman. He had not received formal education since leaving grammar school. His lack of education was clear in the conversation, which he tended to monopolize. Mr Tuset observed that Mr Noguera almost never listened to what the other had to say. Mr Tuset was continuously being interrupted when explaining to Mr Noguera his role as the company's adviser. He repeatedly interrupted to say that everything went on very badly at Filfort. Following is part of the conversation between the two.

Mr Noguera:

'When the former manager was here I did everything in the factory and we were alright. Now we are two foremen but as things are we are two too many. Mr Boix behaves very badly to me. He seems like a dictator, he wants to do everything himself. When he makes someone change a screw in a machine, he publishes it in the newspaper, but when it is someone else who has done it, he doesn't give it the least importance, unless he says that he is the one who did it. All the good things are done by him, and bad ones by others. He has brought in a foreman, whom he likes to ignore me. He has also banished many managers in order to put his own people in their places. When I tell somebody to do something, very frequently he doesn't obey saying that someone else with more power than me will be opposed to my orders. I once asked Mr Puigrodo what was my mission in the factory and he answered by giving me a very complicated paper which I don't understand.'

Mr Tuset:

'What is your impression of the managers who participate in the meetings which Mr Boix convenes?'

Mr Noguera:

'During such meetings the managers are very careful not to open their mouths to express an opinion which may be contrary to Mr Boix. They know that they may be transferred to some punishment section.'

Mr Tuset:

'There are punishment sections?'

Mr Noguera:
'There are sections where managers don't like to be.'

Mr Tuset:
'But, don't the managers ever specialize in some section?'

Mr Noguera:
'They don't have time, they are being constantly transferred. Sometimes the punishment is even worse. A manager who dared say that the introduction of wage incentives in the women's section was badly done, was dismissed several weeks later. I am just wondering if it is possible that Mr Puigrodo does not see the factory's disorder. I once went to complain to Mr Mas. He was very sincere, and amiable to me. He said: "Noguera, do you trust me?"—I answered: "Oh, of course." Fifteen days later he called me and said that if I had worked in his private business I would have been dismissed a long time ago.'

Interview with Mr Puig

That same day Mr Tuset interviewed Mr Puig, chief of the laboratory who was in charge of production planning and control and quality control. Mr Puig was a young man, twenty-eight years old, introverted and reserved. When he entered Mr Tuset's office he seemed a little frightened. Jorge Tuset found out a few days later, that before entering his office, Mr Puig had been warned that he would be interviewed and of the 'dangers' of such an interview. Mr Puig had finished a junior high school and likewise, went through correspondence studies in order to become a commercial expert. Later on he acquired a master's degree in industrial engineering through correspondence which included courses on methods, time study and production planning and control. At the time of the interview Mr Puig was following a course on project design also through correspondence.

The following conversation took place between Mr Tuset and Mr Puig:

Mr Puig:
'I believe that planning could be improved but today it is functioning quite well. My office is also in charge of scheduling orders against available production capacity. We likewise obtain facts about machine and personnel efficiency.'

Mr Tuset:
'Do you have anything to do with the establishment of piece rates for paying wage incentives?'

Mr Puig:
'Not at all. I don't know anything about money matters and I don't want to know anything. A few years ago a readjustment of piece rates was made, but from what I have heard I think it could have been done better.

'The friction between the two foremen creates a poor atmosphere among managers and the workers. What one side says or does, is always considered wrong by the other. Mr Nuguera believes that the laboratory's work constitutes an interference with his duties. He also believes that Mr Feliu has come to take his place. For two years after joining the company I did not speak to Mr Noguera. We talk to each other now but only about the unavoidable. I believe that it was really necessary to have another foreman but everything could have been better arranged. In my opinion Mr Noguera is somewhat more efficient than Mr Feliu, even though he has a worse character.

'The managers are complaining about Mr Boix, but they have no reason for it. This man behaves very well to them, and has the quality of knowing how to resolve the personnel's problems without hurting. Anyway, we must bear in mind that not everyone is of the same opinion.'

Mr Tuset:

'Are Mr Boix's meetings with the managers successful?'

Mr Puig:

'In my opinion they don't express themselves clearly and they talk very little.'

Mr Tuset:

'Why do they speak very little? Don't they dare? Are they afraid?'

(Mr Puig swallowed and after a little while answered)

Mr Puig:

'It may be that sometimes the managers fear to have a contradictory opinion to that of the factory Manager. An argument could follow which might harm him?'

Mr Tuset saw that Mr Puig was expressing himself with suspicion and doubt; he frequently gulped. He perceived him to be careful and not very clear. He subsequently arranged to interview the heads of the three manufacturing sections, Mr X, Mr Y and Mr Z.

Interview with Mr X

Mr X was thirty-five years old and had been with the company for twenty years. He started as a mechanic, then turned to be an installer, before becoming a manager. He had followed a course on spinning in the city. He was previously in charge of the Winding Section. The section progressed under him until six months before the interview when he was transferred to the Twisting Section, without explanation. He considered it a punishment and did not like it. MR X said:

'Without knowing why my salary has been lowered, I now earn less than the others. Mr Boix is characterized by his arbitrariness and preferences. He promotes those whom he likes and blames those whom he doesn't like. I once showed him a defect in a machine and two days later when he was passing through with Mr Puigrodo, he called my attention to it as if he had just seen it. I believe that he wants to have us all frightened and my opinion is that he has succeeded. He has created an atmosphere of panic among us and has taken all authority away from us. We can't decide anything on the basis of our own initiative. We receive orders without any explanation. We are forced to participate in the meetings. Nobody dares to open his mouth there. These meetings are really a farce.

'My opinion is that Mr Boix is a perfect analphabet in the technical area. His system of command is based on cynicism and the whip.

' I believe that Mr Puigrodo has good knowledge of the technical aspects and of spinning. As to his attitude, he used to trust us more before. He seems to have grown further apart. Mr Moret is a very respected person.'

Interview with Mr Y

Mr Y was thirty-five years old. He had studied the theory of spinning and time study. He had been in charge of another company before he was brought to Filfort by Mr Boix two years earlier. Mr Y said:
'The foremen never agree and this results in machine disorganization. There is no coordination. I am in the Winding Section where we often stop because of lack of materials. We lack spare parts. In the warehouse there is nobody who really knows anything. I think that each section should have its own spare parts. The bad atmosphere is caused by the disorganization and because we earn very little. Mr Boix asks for the opinion of others but he doesn't listen, he wants to do everything himself.'

Interview with Mr Z

Mr Z was about forty years old. He used to be an installer. He was now head of the Spinning Section and expressed his opinions with what seemed to Mr Tuset to be great sincerity. He said:
'I realised that many threads were breaking in the old spinning machines because of the entanglement of the thread in the periphery of the rollers. I lowered the boards to reduce contact between the thread and the rollers. This way there was less touch between them, reducing the possibility of an entanglement. The result was that many fewer threads have been broken. When I explained this success to Mr Boix he said, without even expressing his wish to see the machines working: "Put everything back the way it was before!"—As you can imagine, my natural reaction was to think: "Very well, agreed, let him go to . . . Let the threads break! So what? He ordered it".

'You see Mr Tuset, if you come and say rudely to me and without explanation: "You must take this table out through that door, now, because I order it!" my emotional reaction would be to think: "I hope it doesn't pass through" and unconsciously, although I go ahead with the order, I will do it in such a way that it won't be well done. It would be very different if you would say to me: "We shall have to take this table out of here, what do you think, will it pass through that door?" Then I would regard it as part of my own responsibility and would think of the best way of doing it. I would consider myself responsible for its success and furthermore, I would be satisfied because I was consulted.

'There is more comradeship among the young women workers than among the old ones. They tend to form groups. They frequently arrive before the bell rings and organize their meetings in the yard in front of the main entrance. We have dining rooms, but they are very bad and people don't use them. They eat in the yard or at home.'

Having interviewed the heads of the Twisting, Winding and Spinning sections, Mr Tuset arranged for his remaining three interviews.

Interview with Mr Feliu

Mr Feliu, the second foreman, was forty-five years old. He looked calm and strong. He talked slowly and with common sense. After finishing his primary studies in a religious school at the age of fourteen, he entered a nearby factory as a spinner's assistant. He worked as a winder in another factory, where he eventually became a foreman. He was asked by Mr Boix, whom he had known before, to join Filfort as a foreman. After talking about his work which was, according to him, almost always obstructed by Mr Noguera, he said:
'I get along very well with Mr Boix; but I admit that there is great dissatisfaction among the managers. I think that Mr Noguera has never accepted me as a colleague. As you know, we have three shifts in the factory, two during the day and one at night. We, the foremen, don't do any shift work. I work from five in the morning until two in the afternoon. Then I come back at 4.30 p.m. and stay here till 8 or 9 p.m. Mr Noguera gets here at ten in the morning and stays till 4.30 in the afternoon. Then he comes back at 8 p.m. and is in the factory until about midnight.'

Interview with Mr Armengol

Mr Armengol, thirty-four years old, was the head of the Repairs and Maintenance Section. Alter leaving his grammar school he had followed a draughtsmen's course through correspondence. He then took some courses in spinning. He started working in Filfort as an apprentice at the end of 1946. Four years later he was a winding mechanic and was later put in charge of the workshop and the factory repairs. His father had worked in the company before him. He made a healthy and pleasant impression. Mr Tuset was impressed by his straightforward sincerity and his complete lack of fear. He thought that some of the information which Mr Armengol gave him could have been harmful to him, depending on the use which Mr Tuset made of it. Among other things Mr Armengol told him:
'I believe that you must call things by their names. If you have come here to improve the company, I am willing to help you; and I believe that the best way to do it is to tell you what I know and what I think. I am willing to take the risk of what I tell you. I trust that you will make good use of it. I believe that those managing the company don't have the necessary preparation. I also believe that they don't take proper care of their work.

'Mr Puigrodo is competent and a good manager, but he lives outside of what is happening in the factory. He doesn't talk enough with factory's managers. Furthermore he is too much under the influence of Mr Boix. Mr Boix belives himself to be self-sufficient, but he is totally incompetent, also mechanically. I once told him that what he was going to do was a mechanical blunder; but he persisted and, as would have been predicted, it failed because of broken parts. He is an opportunist and insincere. He tries to create a team which will sustain him and over which he can act as a real dictator.

'Mr Moret is very good. Mr Planas is a very good person and a good worker; but a bit troublesome.'

Interview with Mr Coll

Mr Coll was the Sales Manager of Filfort S.A. and was interviewed by Mr Tuset in the company's main office in Barcelona. Mr Coll was forty-eight years old, tall and thin, very talkative and nervous. His father died when he was fourteen years old. In spite of great economic difficulties he managed to finish high school. He then started to work as a salesman in a textile company. He reached the post of sales manager. He moved to Filfort S.A. in 1968, because of personal difficulties with the management of his previous company. The following answer and ensuing conversation took place after Mr Tuset asked Mr Coll to tell him about his feelings about Filfort:

Mr Coll:

'In the company where I used to work I had my own private office. Here, as you can see, all the administrative staff are together in one large room. My opinion is that this is not good for efficiency. On the one hand it encourages small talk about things which are unrelated to work. On the other hand everybody listens to everybody elses conversations, even on working matters. I, particularly, feel confused. Any small talk between two persons may be interpreted by a third one as a comment about himself. You hear, for example, that you work only four hours out of the eight hours you are supposed to work.

'I am the Sales Manager. When I talk on the phone to a client, I must adjust my tone for each client, on one hand I must be either soft or hard, and sometimes it is better to joke with him. Sometimes we must be rude and sometimes kind. To do all this in front of other employees, is very difficult. You know that you are overheard and that you will be the subject of consequent comments. They may even start thinking badly about you. I feel embarrassed. I don't talk freely. Furthermore, facing me, on the other side of the desk sits Mr Ribas, who has been working in the company for a longer period of time than I. He helps me in my job. He is a very good worker and person. The telephone is by his side. When it rings, even if it is for me, he picks it up. He always knows who phones me. Sometimes, when he recognizes the clients, he arranges the matter without passing it to me. Believe me, I sometimes feel like running away from all this. I go out a lot to visit the clients. Nevertheless, when a client comes to see me I can receive him only in the visitor's room.

'We have grown a lot in sales. We now have seventy-five agents, while we had only twenty-five previously.'

Mr Tuset:

'Wouldn't it be better for Filfort to have its own salesmen, rather than sell through agents?'

Mr Coll:

'I believe that at present we need our agents, although we may need to have our own salesmen in the future.

Our clients are very lax in paying, but if I go to the accounts department to find out how things are, I am made to feel an intruder. In my opinion I should always know how every client's account stands. This company has been scared by the mere mention of accumulating inventories and the policy has always been to reduce prices whenever we face such a situation. At present we don't have any inventories, but nevertheless we have outstanding orders for two months production. I enjoy the challenge of not reducing prices and yet keeping the client. I love the battle and I feel like a conqueror when I manage to sustain the price I first had in mind. Nevertheless, the client is grateful and respects you the more. I believe that we should have a warehouse in Barcelona. We are now delivering directly from the factory and it is a mess.'

Other interviews

Mr Tuset subsequently interviewed Mr Ribas, who was Mr Coll's assistant, in Barcelona. He was twenty-six years old, goodlooking, and started working in the company when he was fifteen years old as trainee without a salary. He studied accountancy in a private school. Apart from helping Mr Coll he was also directly involved in selling and in accounting. Mr Tuset thought that his office was noisy and disorganized. Mr Ribas gave Mr Tuset the impression of being a person of goodwill, judgement and good intellectual capacity, in spite of his limited education.

Mr Tuset also interviewed the Chief Accountant and discovered that he considered his work as the most important in the whole company. He was fifty-five years old and had been in the company for a long time. He seemed to Mr Tuset as very sensitive, touchy, a bit stubborn and without an open mind. Mr Tuset did not have the impression that he was very intelligent; but nevertheless, he thought that the Chief Accountant had a deep loyalty to Filfort.

When the interviews were over, Mr Tuset asked himself the following questions:

1. What conclusions could he arrive at, on the basis of the information he received, concerning Filfort's structural problems as well as the problems of motivation, capabilities, objectives, etc. of the persons involved?

2. What could he suggest in order to achieve the integration of the company objectives with those of its employees so as to maintain the company's development, as well as the personal development and satisfaction of its personnel?

3. How could his recommendations be implemented at Filfort?

Exhibit 1. Filfort S.A.—organigramme*

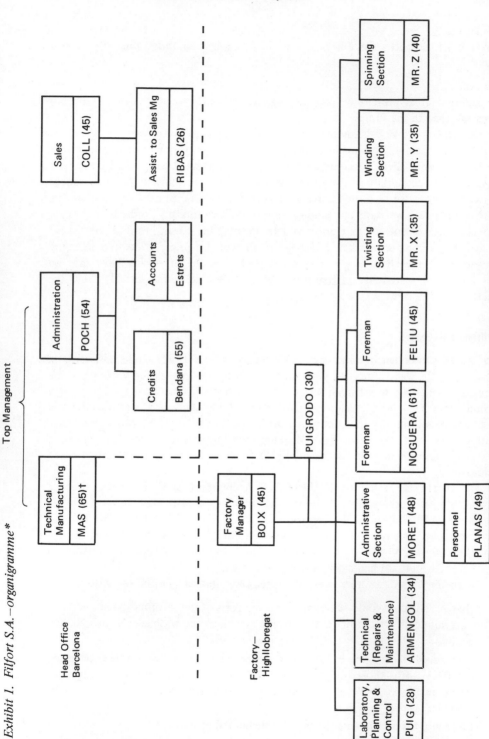

* This 'Organigramme', or Organization Chart, was specially prepared for 'Organizational Problems in European Manufacturing', by its authors. This chart was neither existent at Filfort S.A. nor in the original Spanish Filfort case studies.
† ( ) denote the persons age.

Filfort S.A. (C)

In April 1970 Mr Tuset began a series of interviews with the executives of Filfort S.A. In order to assess the financial position of the company he planned to talk first with Mr Poch who was in charge of the finance and accounting information system. His friend Mr Puigrodo had warned him, however, that it was unlikely that Mr Poch would show confidential financial documents to a stranger. He, Mr Puigrodo, was not allowed to see them since they were regarded as 'top secret'. Consequently only top management had access to them. Before the interview Mr Tuset planned his conversation with Mr Poch, since he considered it essential that his diagnosis should take account of the company's financial situation and its possible effect upon management's attitudes.

He met Mr Poch at the company's head office in Barcelona one Tuesday afternoon. After greetings and a brief discussion of the current situation in the Spanish textile industry, Mr Tuset said:

'Mr Poch, we are in a period when only well-prepared companies are likely to survive in the face of current business difficulties. But this prospect doesn't frighten me since I believe the growth in personal incomes and the desire to buy is an irreversible process. Consumption of all articles, including textiles, will continue to expand. We have only to look at how poorly dressed the people in Spanish villages are to see the potential for increased sales as they expand their wardrobes. Furthermore the enormous increase in foreign contacts will inevitably develop our people's fashion consciousness and their desire for new products. Consumption must increase.

'We can also see a great improvement in manufacturing techniques and labour productivity in the textile industry. Companies which do not keep abreast of these changes or control their operations efficiently will be eliminated by competition. I do not think the total volume of textile products will decrease, but many un-economical companies are bound to perish. We must belong to that group which not only survives but also prospers.'

Mr Poch:

'This is what we want; but believe me we are sometimes afraid. At times I feel as if we were sinking in a sea of unknowns. For many of our articles we do not know whether we are selling at above or below cost. But don't you think we are now entering a period of recession?'

Mr Tuset:

'It is possible. In every growth there are periods of recession. In prosperous times people spend more and demand more goods from industry. Production increases.

But then sales may fail to meet the forecast levels, stocks rise, shops stop ordering, the weaver's demand for yarn falls and the spinners believe they have over-expanded.

'I can see this happening next year. But a sound company, well backed and technically efficient need have no fear. It is a matter of riding out the downturn in the economic cycle; for the long-term trend is a growing need for yarn.

'In respect to costs, I consider it essential that we know the cost of every article we produce and either its profit margin or the contribution it makes to profitability. Then we must focus our sales effort towards the more profitable products without necessarily ceasing manufacture of the less profitable ones when they serve as bait for catching sales of the higher margin articles. Obviously we must be in a position to know what stocks we have and influence the market accordingly.'

Mr Poch:

'Do you think we have a person capable of maintaining good cost control?'

Mr Tuset:

'I think so. Mr Moret is very efficient, although he is at present suffering from a number of circumstances which are affecting his performance. Nevertheless he is intelligent, active, capable of learning, committed to the company and is willing. We must help and support him.

'But in addition to the person we need information. It is important to know the extent of the company's overhead costs, so that we can plan the production of each type of yarn in order to meet the break-even point of the business, provided of course that we know their individual contributions. It is also important to know the company's overall financial situation so that we can assess its ability to survive a downturn in the economic cycle. In addition I would like to know the extent of debts outstanding to the company to see whether they can be reduced so as to improve liquidity.'

Mr Poch:

'You shall see. Mr Bendaña the cashier has very strong views regarding our debt policy. He regards every request for outside funds as a reflection on the company's good name. However, when we expanded we had no alternative but to borrow from the Bank of Industrial Credit. We also have a half-term credit; but it is very small. Also Mr Bendaña will have nothing to do with discounts. He says they have never been used and are not consistent with Filfort's good name. I believe we could move in this direction, but it is difficult for me to oppose Mr Bendaña considering he is fifty-five years old and has been with the company for more than thirty years. He was a very good friend of the previous manager.'

Mr Tuset:

'Does Mr Bendaña manage the accounts?'

Mr Poch:

'No Sir. The accountant is Mr Estret. He is a very good accountant, who is responsible for the accounts of many companies, and only devotes two hours a week to Filfort. He specialises in preparing the accounting reports required for official purposes. These, he bases on information received from the cashier and from other departments. He is assisted by Miss Dolores who works full time for the company.'

Mr Tuset:
'Mr Poch, for my assignment to succeed and also to initiate the industrial accounting system, it would be helpful for me to study the basic accounting documents such as the last balance sheet and annual accounts.'

Mr Poch:
'I understand your wish Mr Tuset, but before agreeing I must consult Mr Mas and the other top managers. Nevertheless I don't believe you will have any difficulty in obtaining what you need.'

A few days later Mr Poch handed Mr Tuset all the documents he had requested, much to the suprise of Mr Puigrodo. From these he came to the following conclusions:

(*a*) During 1969 Filfort's invoices exceeded the volume required for break-even by 20%.
(*b*) The average account collection period was 140 days.
(*c*) The average account payment period was 50 days.
(*d*) Working capital was 100 million pesetas.
(*e*) Current Assets: Current Liabilities = 4·0 : 1.
(*f*) Equity: Debt = 4·5 : 1.
(*g*) Return on sales = 4·2%.
(*h*) Return on equity = 3·3%.

Mr Tuset wrote a report based on the above, in which he emphasised the excess of the company's private funds and the consequent low profitability. He also referred to the convenience of using the bank's discounting facilities and the need to reduce the collection period. He recommended the introduction of a good industrial accounting system which would enable the contributions of each type of yarn to be determined. In addition he recommended a reduction in several types of yarn, combined with an increased sales effort aimed at increasing total sales while at the same time concentrating sales on the most profitable products.

He proposed a change in the balance sheet and income statement to distinguish clearly between the different elements of cost. In the existing documents he had experienced extreme difficulty in determining whether some items were capital or operating expenditures. He prepared a specimen balance sheet and income statement based on a liquidity ratio he considered adequate.

Having presented his report Mr Tuset continued to visit both the factory and the head office. In talks with Mr Puigrodo he discussed the problem of the bad climate in the factory caused by the Boix-Moret relationship and to a lesser degree Noguera-Feliu.

Mr Puigrodo:

'It is clear that we must get rid of Boix, but how do we do it? Furthermore, I cannot carry on unless my job is clearly defined. How are you going to get the "old ones" to realise all this?'

Mr Tuset:

'Look Jaime, they will probably talk to you once they have read my economic report. Take the opportunity to mention that I wish to exchange ideas with all the top management. They won't oppose this, for now they must be much more worried than before. I will then talk to them about the whole situation and perhaps I will give them a general assessment and report. It is evident that the Boix problem must be resolved. Apart from his personal character, I believe that it is no longer appropriate for the head of manufacturing to be an absolute autocrat. Manufacturing functions are different from those of personnel; maintenance, administration etc. We must limit Boix's field of authority and confine him to a specified role. We can make Moret, Planas and Arnangol independent of him. We should also give him firm guidelines, related to our personnel policy, for his authority over the work people—we cannot allow him to play with people as he does. I believe that, given Boix's character, his self-esteem will eventually make him leave if we place these restrictions on him. On the other hand he may reject them giving us grounds for discharging him.'

Mr Puigrodo:

'It's possible. And how will you present my case? I must tell you that I have recently received an offer from SUFASA who, as you know, are one of the largest spinners in Spain.'

Mr Tuset:

'I don't believe in the future of SUFASA. It has survived only because of frequent financial injections from outside. Your future is with Filfort. Your aim should be to become Director-General and I think this is what I shall propose to the top management.'

Mr Puigrodo:

'I wish you could succeed, but I see difficulties. I don't think Mr Mas would mind. I believe he has not proposed it before because of our family relationship. He would not like the others to think he is pushing a relative. For himself, I think he would be happy to shed his responsibilities at Filfort which have become a burden to him. Not so, Mr Poch, for whom Filfort occupies a much larger part of his life. As for the other directors, the company is only one of their interests and because of their professions, age and social position they don't really know what a modern company should be like. They see the company through the eyes of Mr Mas and Mr Poch, but I do know that at least two of them incline more to Mr Poch than to Mr Mas. Nevertheless there exists between them a tacit agreement to avoid any discussion which could lead to friction.

'Have you considered how you would present the papers to make them acceptable?'

Mr Tuset:

'My opinion is that we cannot do anything really constructive for the company until we have changed the attitudes of top management. Their ignorance of human problems and their withdrawal from the problems of their managers provides an inadequate basis for the company's development.

'You live in and with the company and are perfectly able to manage it, if given the authority. Forseeing the departure of Mr Boix, we need worry only about finding a manufacturing director for the factory.

'In view of the limited time the top managers devote to the company I am considering whether to propose the creation of a Management Committee; this will meet frequently and Mr Mas, Mr Poch and yourself would be members. None of them would suffer financially. Mr Poch could be the Chairman of the Committee; I don't think Mr Mas would object. You could then become Director-General, responsible to the Committee, but with formal authority clearly specified and communicated throughout the company. Your dedication to Filfort and your professional success are a good support for my proposal.'

Mr Puigrodo:

'That would be fine, but I see difficulties. If the idea goes ahead I would propose that you should be a member of the Management Committee.'

Mr Tuset:

'I don't deny that I would like to, although I don't have much time. I am becoming attached to the company and would like to cooperate on a permanent, though part-time, basis.'

Mr Puigrodo:

'Jorge. Nobody carries out the function of personnel management as we understand the term today. You would be the right person at the top.'

Mr Tuset:

'The personnel management function may occupy more time than I can spare. However, we have a person who could occupy the post of Personnel Manager at the factory.'

Mr Puigrodo:
'Who?'

Mr Tuset:
'It's Mr Planas.'

Mr Puigrodo:
'Do you really mean it? I have always seen him as a political talker and sneaky.'

Mr Tuset:
'Have you had a lot of contact with him?'

Mr Puigrodo:
'Not really; but I have seen him talking to people in a suspicious manner and I have seen dissatisfied workers go to him on many occasions.'

Mr Tuset:

'Do you know anything bad about him?'

Mr Puigrodo:

'No. The truth of the matter is that my image of him is founded only on these observations and the opinion of Mr Boix upon whom, as you know, I have always depended. It could well be that my opinion of Planas is based upon prejudice.'

Mr Tuset:

'I think so. This political talk you attribute to him may well be an asset in the post of personnel manager if applied judiciously. I can assume the top personnel function, formulating objectives and policies which Mr Planas would develop and apply in the factory.'

Mr Puigrodo:

'That sounds a good plan. Now, turning to another matter, what have you thought of Mr Moret?'

Mr Tuset:

'I think Mr Moret should be in charge of costing for all the company's products. For this he would be more conveniently situated in the head office, rather than have separate offices in Ripollet and High Llobregat.'

(Filfort's main factory was at High Llobregat. Ripollet, near Barcelona, was a small spinning mill employing 100 people which produced a few types of standard thick thread.)

Mr Puigrodo:

'This would create a housing problem in Barcelona. Part of Moret's job in the factory would also be neglected.'

Mr Tuset:

'The housing problem doesn't worry me. So far as the factory is concerned we have enough people to cover all the administrative functions that have to be done there. I also recommend moving the finished products warehouse to Barcelona. Mr Vidosa, Moret's assistant, can be in charge of the raw materials and spare parts store at the factory.'

'Moret would be a different person in Barcelona. Even if Boix left, the psychological effect of his experiences at the factory would stay with him. The mind unconsciously associates events and places. Only a transfer will remove the depression which Moret associates with the factory. The transfer would be good for the company as well as for Moret himself. This does not mean that he cannot make frequent visits to the factory, but by then he will see everything differently.'

Some time later the directors of Filfort called Mr Tuset and Mr Puigrodo to a general meeting. Below are extracts from the report Mr Tuset prepared; a copy was sent to each director a few days before the meeting:

'When studying the company's problems and their possible solutions we must not confine ourselves to good solutions which solve today's problems. I believe that a full man will not be satisfied with achieving stability for only as long as he can influence the organisation, advise it or govern it. We must make every effort we consider necessary to ensure the company's survival not only today when we are here, but also in the future after we have departed. This demands from us, and particularly from me as consultant, a deep sincerity of purpose.

'There is no doubt that the current industrial and commercial position of the company is good and we can look to the future with confidence. After a long period of industrial re-organisation, which is still going on, the textile industry will shortly enter a period of prosperity in which the surviving companies will share. I am confident Filfort S.A. will be one of them.

'Although Filfort S.A. is well placed industrially and financially, the same cannot be said about all aspects of the comapny. The internal structure and organisation reflect attitudes when professional knowledge and business techniques were not so developed as they are today. In these times of intense competition only those organisations attuned to the modern environment will survive.

'The company's organisation structure is not formalised and the responsibilities of existing functions are not clearly defined. In many respects relations between the functions lead to difficulties which result in delays, misunderstandings and inefficiency.

'There are no defined personnel policies. Each case is resolved according to the attitude of the person in charge.

'The factory has traditionally had a manager with authority over all the functions. This type of organisation has created a situation leading to a variety of conflicts, inefficiencies, authoritarianism and injustices because of the difficulty or near impossibility of finding a well balanced manager capable of knowing intimately the different functions and able to exercise real authority over them.

'Many necessary functions are lacking and their need unappreciated.

'The people in charge of the functions do not possess the essential professional and managerial requirements for the jobs.

'There is no adequate communication system between different levels in the hierarchy or between functions. Nor are lines of authority clearly defined. Although there is a person who functions informally as director of manufacturing he has neither the responsibility nor formal authority to act with confidence or effectiveness.

'Although there are two part-time administrators, there is lack of a central unified organ of action with complete responsibility and authority for the company's management . . .'

He then proceeded to propose the establishment of a Management Committee as the top-level organ for executive action. This committee should meet every two weeks and report their progress to the directors every three months. One full time employee of the company should be named Director General.

He continued by referring to the need for changing the organisation structure of the factory. Personnel, administration, maintenance and costing were sufficiently important to be independent of manufacturing management.

By word of mouth he explained the problems caused by Boix's behaviour and of the discontent caused by his handling of bonuses and discipline. He emphasised the necessity of limiting Boix's powers and of easing his possible departure.

In reply to a question from Mr Mas, Mr Tuset said that he could identify nobody with the necessary education to replace Mr Boix as manufacturing manager, although he believed it right to promote from within the company whenever possible. In this case it would be necessary to recruit an outsider.

The report contained an organigramme (organisation structure) covering top management down to the level immediately senior to the heads of manufacturing sections. The diagram omitted names and showed only titles and the principle function of each post. Mr Tuset explained that the lack of detail was because he only wanted to give an approximate idea of the structure of the organisation. The detailed definition of tasks should be related to the personality, knowledge, capability and preference of the people occupying the posts.

The diagram showed clearly:

1. The factory Personnel Manager was responsible to the main Personnel Director,
2. The factory Administrative Secretary was responsible to the main Administrative Director,
3. The Personnel, Administrative, Costs and Commercial Directors and the Purchasing Manager reported to the Director General.
4. The Chief of Manufacture (or Factory Manager) and the factory's Maintenance Manager also reported directly to the Director General.
5. Reporting directly to the Factory Manager were:
   (*a*) the foremen
   (*b*) head of work study
   (*c*) head of quality control
   (*d*) head of production planning and control.

When Mr Tuset was asked for the names of people suitable for the posts under the Director General he suggested Mr Coll for Commercial Director; Mr Ribas for Purchasing Manager; Mr Moret for Costs Director; Mr Planas for factory Personnel Manager; Mr Armengol for Maintenance Manager; Mr Vidosa for the factory Administrative Secretary; and Mr Puig for production planning and control and also for quality control for the time being. He was not in a position to make a recommendation for head of work study.

In reply to a query regarding the need for a main Personnel Director he replied: 'I believe in the need for a person committed to planning the human functioning of the organisation; someone who is able to take care of the company atmosphere, maintaining personnel policies, selection of executives, promotion and development of company personnel. In view of the existence of a factory personnel manager it won't be necessary to appoint a full time personnel director for the time being.'

Mr Puigrodo proposed that Mr Tuset should provisionally undertake this responsibility in view of his expertise in the human aspects of management. All agreed with this suggestion except for Mr Poch whose mind seemed otherwise engaged.

Other recommendations in the report included:

1. The need for a thorough study of the ability, education, feelings, aspirations etc. of everyone concerned with the company's development. The object of the

study would be to obtain information to assist in the aligning of personal and company objectives as well as to enable the improvement of human failings.

2. A study of the main functions and their inter-relationships.
3. Promotion of those prepared for high-level responsibility.
4. Education of those who were capable but unprepared for future higher responsibilities.
5. The establishment of clear personnel policies and the creation of groups of workers with objectives aligned to those of the company.
6. Improving welfare services such as proper dining rooms, and recreation rooms.
7. Job evaluation.
8. Development of a simple and equitable system of worker incentives.
9. A detailed study of the commercial department.
10. The establishment of a centralised costing system at Barcelona.
11. Centralising the finished goods warehousing at Barcelona.

After the report was read most of the directors expressed their approval. In answer to a question, Mr Tuset said that the membership of the Management Committee should be limited to three or four and that it seemed logical that these should be those who had most contact with the company and could devote more time to it. The other directors agreed with a suggestion from Mr Mas that Mr Tuset should be a member of the committee.

Mr Tuset accepted the offer and asked Mr Puigrodo to leave the room. He then suggested that Mr Puigrodo should also be a member of the committee. All the directors, except Mr Mas and Mr Poch expressed their agreement. When one of them asked Mr Mas whether he was opposed to the appointment of Mr Puigrodo he replied that he was reluctant to propose him because of their family ties. Mr Poch also answered that he had no objection.

Another director then proposed Mr Mas and Mr Poch. Both objected saying that some other director should be a member but there was general agreement that this was impossible. It was then proposed that Mr Mas should be the Chairman. He refused and counter-proposed that it should be Mr Poch who signified his acceptance by remaining discreetly silent.

The meeting then considered the post of Director-General. Mr Tuset said that in his opinion it should be a person of acknowledged ability in business management who would commit himself fully to the Company. He proposed Mr Puigrodo. This proposal was accepted.

The meeting was closed after Mr Tuset had been asked to continue with his studies. A certificate would be issued to legalise the agreement reached at the meeting.

A few days later Mr Puigrodo called Mr Tuset requesting an urgent meeting. They met in Barcelona. Jaime explained that he had discovered information in the factory which would allow them to dismiss Mr Boix immediately.

Mr Puigrodo:
'Nevertheless, I am afraid that the departure of Boix without a replacement will cause manufacturing difficulties.'

Mr Tuset:

'Don't worry, I think it convenient that we should take advantage of this incident to dismiss him with proper compensation. The factory managers are competent and Mr Puig can take charge for the time being.

'By the way what progress has been made with formalising the agreement?'

Mr Puigrodo:

'I haven't heard anything more. The only thing I can say is that Mr Poch seems to be very absent minded and almost never says anything. I think you should speak to him again. Maybe he fears that his chairmanship, together with losing his post of sub-manager implies a reduction in his fees.'

Mr Tuset:

'No, this was made clear when you were out. Members of the Management Committee, who previously held a paid post in the company, would continue to receive the same remuneration. I think rather that he believes his nomination as chairman is an excuse to withdraw him from direct action. I believe you are right; I must have a word with him.'

The departure of Mr Boix produced general relief in the factory. Nevertheless, Mr Moret was greatly worried because of the statements he had made. Even though it was made known officially that Boix was leaving the company of his own free will, most people believed this was not so. Mr Tuset had great difficulty in calming Moret.

Several days later Mr Mas received a letter from Mr Noguera:

> *Dear Sir,*
>
> *You know how many years I have devoted myself to the company. You know the former manager had complete confidence in me. I have always done what I could. You know how much Mr Boix made me suffer. Now that he is leaving I beg you to appoint me factory manager.*
>
> *Hoping to be taken care of, I remain*
>
>

Yours sincerely,
Noguera.

Mr Mas discussed the letter with Mr Tuset. During their conversation Mr Mas said that, at a director's meeting the previous day, he had presented his resignation as sub-manager.

Mr Mas:

'You know already that I have been wishing to free myself of the sub-manager's burden owing to my age and other interests. Of course I am still a director and now a member of the Management Committee but I shall give up my total commitment to the company. On the other hand I am glad that formal responsibility and authority has at last been given to Puigrodo, a young man worthy of it.

'Nevertheless I must tell you of a misfortune. After my speech to the directors yesterday, Mr Poch said, "I regard the agreement we made the other day as a result of Mr Tuset's report to be a vote of no confidence in my actions as sub-manager. I have been devoting a half day to the company concerning myself with all administrative and financial matters. If I am no good or a nuisance I prefer to withdraw completely. I present my resignation, not only as sub-manager, but also as a member of the Management Committee and as a director".'

'Mr Poch's words aroused a strong reaction in all the directors who agreed they could not accept his resignation. They praised Mr Poch and told him that if the cause of his resignation was the creation of the post of Director-General and the disappearance of the sub-management, they would revoke the nomination of Director-General and ask Mr Poch to continue acting as Manager. I intervened again saying that I would still resign as sub-manager and suggested that Mr Poch should continue as administrative sub-manager and that Mr Puigrodo should take over my post as technical sub-manager. This proposal was unanimously approved.'

Mr Tuset:
'Was anything said about the Management Committee?'

Mr Mass:
'It was accepted as a fact, that is, you, Mr Poch, Mr Puigrodo and myself form the committee under which there will be two sub-managers—Mr Poch (Administrative Manager) and Mr Puigrodo (Technical Manager).

'The rest of your plan was approved together with the continuation of your work.'

Selected Bibliography

Anthony, R. N. 'Management Accounting: Text and Cases' Fourth Edition Richard D. Irwin Inc. 1970.

Argyris, C. Human Problem with Budgets, *Harvard Business Review*, 1953.

Barnard, C. I. 'The Nature of Leadership', reprinted in Human Factors in Management edited by Schuyler Hoslett, Part College Press 1946.

Batty, J. 'Management Accountancy', Macdonald & Evans 1963.

de Bono, E. 'The Use of Lateral Thinking, Jonathan Cape 1967. 'The Mechanism of Mind', Jonathan Cape 1969.

Bright, J. R. Does Automation Raise Skill Requirements? *Harvard Business Review*, July/August 1958.

Brua, L. A. Directors Compared, *The Director*, November, 1969.

Buffa, E. S. 'Modern Production Management', John Wiley 1961.

Fayol, H. 'General and Industrial Management', Pitman 1949.

Fleishman, E. A. Leadership Climate, Human Relations, Training and Supervisory Behaviour. *Personnel Psychology*, pp. 205-222, 1953.

Gordon, W. J. J. 'Synectics', Harper & Row 1961.

Hartley, W. C. F. 'An Introduction to Business Accounting for Managers', Pergamon Press 1965.

Hertzberg, F., *et al* 'The Motivation to Work', John Wiley 1967.

Jaques, E. 'Equitable Payment', Heineman 1961.

Landsberger, H. A. 'Hawthorne Revisited', Cornell University Press 1958.

Livingston, J. S. Myth of the Well-Educated Manager, *Harvard Business Review*, January/February 1971.

Mayer, R. R. 'Production Management', McGraw Hill 1962.

Roethlisberger, R. and Dickson, W. 'Management and the Worker', Cambridge, Massachusetts, Harvard University Press 1941.

Schein, E. H. Management Development as a Process of Influence, *Industrial Management Review II*, No. 2, May 1961. Reprinted in: 'Readings in Managerial Psychology', edited by Leavitt and Pondy, pp. 331-351, The University of Chicago Press 1964.

Servan-Schrieber, J. J. 'Le Defi Américain', Denoel, Paris 1967. [French].

Shur, Z. 'The Status of the Foreman in the Organizational Structures of an Industrial Enterprise', unpublished thesis, Technicon, Israel 1969. [Hebrew].

Sizer, J. 'An Insight into Management Accounting', Pelican 1970.

Skinner, W. Production Under Pressure, *Harvard Business Review*, November/December 1966.

Smith, R. A. At Saint Gobain, the First 300 years were the Easiest. *Fortune*, Vol. 72, No. 4, October 1965. Reprinted 'Business Strategy', edited by Ansoff, H. I., pp. 313-327. Penguin 1969.

Starr, M. K. Modular Production—A New Concept, *Harvard Business Review*, November/December 1965.

Stettner, N. 'Productivity Bargaining and Industrial Change', Pergamon Press, 1969.

Stopford, J. M. 'Growth and Organizational Change in the Multinational Firm', unpublished doctoral thesis, Harvard University 1968.

Taylor, F. W. 'Scientific Manager', N.Y. Harper 1911.

Timms, H. L. 'The Production Function in Business—Management Decision Systems', Irwin 1966.

Urwick, L. F.   The Manager's Span of Control, *Harvard Business Review,* May/June 1966.

Whyte, W. F.   'Money and Motivation: An Analysis of Incentives in Industry', Harper & Row 1970.

Wold, H. and Jureen, L.   'Demand Analysis', John Wiley & Sons 1953.

Woodward, J.   'Management and Technology', Her Majesty's Stationery Office 1958.

Woodward, J.   'Industrial Organization—Theory and Practice', Oxford University Press 1965.

Index volume II